HOW TO
REPAIR
REUPHOLSTER
AND REFINISH
FURNITURE

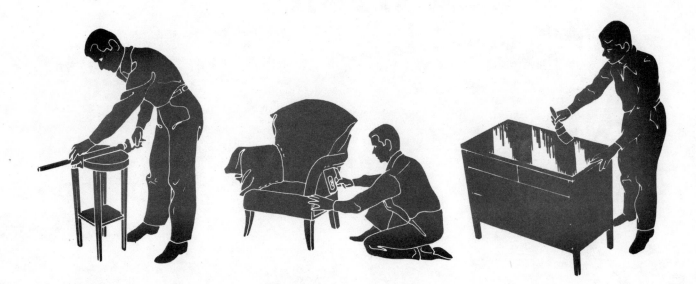

A POPULAR SCIENCE BOOK

HOW TO REPAIR REUPHOLSTER AND REFINISH FURNITURE
Mel Marshall

Photos by Aldine Marshall
Drawings by Eugene Thompson

POPULAR SCIENCE

HARPER & ROW
New York, Evanston, San Francisco, London

Library of Congress Catalog Card Number: 79-4706
ISBN: 0-06-013035-0

Manufactured in the United States of America

Contents

Acknowledgments

For their assistance in providing technical data, product information, tools, materials, and supplies for photographic use, I'm greatly indebted to John Abels of H. Behlen Co., Mrs. Marge Moguin of Black & Decker, Stan Karras of the Borden Company's Adhesives Division, Sage Connors of Brookstone Co., Mrs. Dorothy Docherty of Albert Constantine & Son, Inc., Dennis Johnson of Craftsman Wood Service, David Wehling of Dremel, John Strock of Merit Abrasives Co., Jim Palmer and Mary Ann Miller of Millers Falls Tools, Jack Sheehan of Rockwell International's Power Tool Division, John Webster of Skil Corporation, Bob Campbell of Stanley Tools, Angelo Luongo and Barbara Parris of X-Acto.

For their patience in letting my camera look over their shoulders while they were working, I'm grateful to Charles and Rilene Johnson, Carolyn Hodges, Rita Entrop, Pat Bishop, and other members of Bob Jensen's vocational class in upholstering and to Don Butler for sharing his professional knowledge of this craft.

And for assistance in obtaining photo props that allow this book to show more examples of repair jobs, and examples of furniture styles and construction details than would otherwise have been possible, my thanks to Linda Rowe, Herman Stuller, Bob Knight, Birdie Ooley, Jimmy Hines, and to Lynda and Tommy Lindsey.

M. M.

HOW TO REPAIR REUPHOLSTER AND REFINISH FURNITURE

Introduction

Before starting any kind of repair work on any piece of furniture, there are a pair of key questions you should ask yourself:

1) Is this piece of furniture *worth* repairing?

2) How difficult and costly is the job going to be?

Your answers will be guided by more than worth in terms of cash. The sentimental as well as the intrinsic value of the piece needing fixing will certainly influence your judgment. So will such intangibles as the possibility that while the piece may not have a great deal of value at the time the questions are asked, it may increase in worth with time—perhaps within a short time.

A number of years ago, my wife and I bought a round oak dining table to use in our patio. At the local secondhand shop, it cost the huge sum of $3.50. We gave it a good coat of outside enamel and set it in a vine-covered nook where we liked to have dinner. After several rainy winters the table started to deteriorate. Its glue joints loosened, its top warped. I was always going to fix it, but spending the time on such a cheap piece of furniture never quite seemed justified. Eventually, it went to the dump. A few years passed, and

oak furniture came back into style. A replica of that table today would have buyers lining up willing to pay $350 to $400 for it. It's profitable to look to the future when you think about repairing furniture, although it's difficult to foresee such developments.

As a general rule, the answer to the second question above will take a back seat to the value you place on a piece of furniture because of its current or possible future worth. Your decision to repair an intrinsically valueless piece may be based very largely or entirely on the associations it holds for you.

Let's consider a few quick examples. If you're looking at a genuine antique, a piece of handcrafted furniture made more than a hundred years ago by a skilled worker using what the trade calls "cabinet woods," the answer to the first question would certainly be "yes." And in such a case the second question would almost answer itself, though perhaps with a qualification we'll take note of a bit later on.

You'd probably say "yes" to both questions if the piece is one that might be called "an antique of tomorrow," though this is a somewhat nebulous phrase that we'd better try to define. You might not agree with my definition, but let me state it like this: any carefully and skillfully crafted piece of furniture in which good woods have been used and which reflects conscientious workmanship has an excellent chance of being classed as an antique at some future date. We live in an increasingly plastic world, and the day may arrive when any example of good woodwork will be a collector's item.

ANTIQUES

There are antiques and antiques, of course. The official standard applied by the federal government is that to be classified as antique an object must be at least one hundred years old. What complicates making a judgment is that a lot of furniture—like the table I mentioned—made when mass-production was in its youth is now being accepted as antique, and commanding antique prices. Our table was one of the pieces turned out by the tens of thousands in midwestern furniture factories at the beginning of the twentieth century. As this is being written, such pieces are still appreciating in value, along with good pieces from later years, into the early 1930s. From present indications, this trend is going to continue.

How much? About all that can be done is to look at the amazing appreciation of round oak dining tables, scroll-decorated secretaries, glass-front china cabinets, buffets, desks, and chairs manufactured between 1890 and 1915. These pieces started zooming in price during the 1960s, and are still going up in the late 1970s. The round oak table that zoomed from the $3.50–$8 bracket in the late 1950s to $350–$400 in the late '70s, and the glass-front china cabinets that went from $35–$50 in the '50s to $400–$500 in the late '70s may or may not be good value increase indexes. However, once an in-

creased price level for such items has been established, it seldom drops as fast as it went up.

While this was happening to oak, prices of handcrafted furniture of the period 1800–1850—the latter date marking the time when factory mass-production really began to dominate the furniture field—went up, too. So did furniture made before 1800. Good pieces made during the transition years 1830–1850 went up in price more slowly than pre-1800 handcrafted or shop-made pieces, but just as steadily. Authenticated pieces shot up like skyrockets.

Always, of course, authenticated pieces by master designers and craftsmen have commanded high prices because they combine beauty of design with fine handwork in woods of the finest grade. Such items are exceedingly scarce, and rarely come to market. As this is being written, inflation has added its bite to earlier prices, and pieces of this kind are going at auction sales to bids in the six-figure bracket. Unsigned but "attributable" pieces have risen from the four-figure to the five-figure bracket.

Few of us are likely to own or to encounter these more costly pieces of furniture. In most homes, though, there are usually some pieces made during the 1910–1940 period, which might be called the high-water mark of factory-made furniture. Much, but certainly not all, of the furniture made during this time-span was carefully and meticulously constructed, and a great deal of attention was given to detail. These are the pieces which can be pretty safely tagged as the "antiques of tomorrow," the ones on which you're justified in languishing loving care on repairing for reasons other than sentiment or association.

There has never been a time when a certain amount of what the furniture trade calls "borax" or "schlock" wasn't produced. This was going on in the 1600s, the 1700s, the 1800s, and still goes on today. The two terms, by the way, have come to be interchangeable. They describe pieces made from inferior materials disguised to look like those of good quality, pieces made by using shortcuts, such as joints that were butt-nailed instead of being dovetailed or mortised or dowel-joined, and often the shortcuts used on hidden details crept to the visible exteriors of such furniture. These practices have been employed since the fifteenth century, when furniture made the great transition between carefully handcrafted pieces produced for the rich and primitive homemade pieces used by the poor.

Some of the furniture found in antique shops today is undoubtedly borax, but the respectable age such pieces have attained has given some of them a substantial market value. Because so few examples of it have survived, homemade and farm-made "primitive" furniture has always had relatively high market value. This furniture belongs to no school of design. It is simply, often crudely made, and is strictly utilitarian. Because it was made when hardwood trees still stood on land being cleared for farming, it was quite often fabricated from woods such as maple, walnut, cherry, and ash. It should not be confused with factory-made borax.

To simplify and try to standardize for this book the matter of intrinsic worth, to define basic qualities of pieces you might want to repair, we can rate all furniture in broad general terms on a scale of eight:

(1) Top-quality antique furniture by well-known artisans in the class of Phyfe, Sheraton, Hepplewhite, Chippendale, or one of their contemporary counterparts.

(2) Second-quality antique furniture "attributable" to a famous maker or pro-

duced by one not quite so well known, perhaps one who'd been apprenticed to a master. In this group we can also include the primitive, homemade utilitarian pieces that have survived.

(3) Furniture just entering the official antiques category, often factory-made, but clearly of high quality due to its careful construction and use of good materials.

(4) Schlock or borax antique pieces.

(5) Individually crafted modern furniture of the best quality, regardless of its age.

(6) Factory-made modern furniture of the best quality, regardless of its age.

(7) Second-grade factory furniture of modern vintage.

(8) Modern schlock or borax.

These gradings or categories can't be considered absolute, of course, if only because they represent one individual's opinion rather than the consensus of experts in the field. They don't take into consideration the part that sentiment or association might have in guiding your decision whether to scrap a piece that needs repairing, or to fix it up. It's impossible to be objective about associations or sentiment. You might put greater value on a piece handed down in your family than you would on a certified Chippendale or Sheraton chair. If an item has great sentimental value—the first piece of furniture you bought when setting up housekeeping, or the crib handed down for your family's babies, or the rocking chair used by a parent or grandparent—then you'd certainly have a strong personal reason for repairing it. In such cases the worth of a piece of furniture in terms of cash doesn't apply.

Subjective reasoning would also affect your decision to repair a piece of furniture that's one of your own personal favorites, perhaps a chair that's nondescript when considered strictly as furniture, but one in which you're more comfortable than in any other chair you've ever found. Examples could be multiplied almost indefinitely, but the point's been made. Subjective reasoning will almost always override cash value if a favorite piece can be fixed —and most pieces can be.

Far less likely to meet the test of either intrinsic or sentimental value would be a modern, mass-produced piece which you bought simply because you needed it, and about which you don't really care one way or the other. Where furniture such as this is concerned, your primary interest is to make repairs quickly and at small cost, if indeed you repair it at all. However, you do need to know whether that item's worth repairing in terms of present or future money value. You should be able to tell the difference between a piece of yesterday's or today's schlock and one that you might sell, after it's fixed, to an antique dealer, a secondhand furniture store, or at a garage sale.

HOW TO JUDGE FURNITURE

With this in mind, let's look at the signs that will tell you almost at a glance into which of the eight categories just listed a piece of furniture belongs. We'll skip the first two groups for several reasons. First, this book isn't concerned with restoring or repairing valuable antique pieces, because only an expert specializing in this kind of work can make repairs that won't detract from the intrinsic value of the piece. There's a great deal of difference between restoring an antique and repairing a piece of contemporary furniture, and you're not apt to be called on to handle repairs to a fine antique. If you are, there are a number of books dealing with this specialized type of work, and you should

consult one of them—or, better still, an expert in this field—before you attempt repairs.

Let's get started by looking at category three. The pieces it covers aren't all that rare. They're found in many homes and are also likely to be encountered at estate sales or garage sales as well as in second-hand furniture stores. Incidentally, if you do find such a piece that needs only minor repairs, you'll be getting a better long-term value by purchasing and fixing it than you will if you buy second-grade modern furniture new.

In category three there will be some shop-made pieces, some individually handcrafted pieces, and some early factory pieces. In the years during which category three furniture was made, up to about 1900, even small towns had cabinet-making shops where the well-to-do had furniture made to order. A preponderance of these pieces copied one or another of the styles that were originated by such early masters as Hepplewhite, Chippendale, Sheraton and others. Other pieces simply reproduced the Victorian style that was then still contemporary.

Some of the craftsmen working in these shops were very good indeed; a few were so good that their work now rests in museums and private collections attributed to the masters of an earlier period. It often takes a keen eye to separate the best shop-crafted furniture of the nineteenth century from that made two or three hundred years earlier. The industrial revolution had not yet touched the furniture trade with a heavy hand. The men who produced cabinet-shop furniture used the same fine woods, the same tools, and the same working techniques that had been employed in the past.

You can usually identify a shop-made piece of the pre-1900 period by careful inspection. The clues to look for include the unexposed areas of wood, which in shop-craft tradition was seldom finished except for the application of a wash coat of stain or varnish to prevent splitting or checking. The better pieces will be made of solid wood, for fine hardwoods had not then gotten as scarce as they are today. The lines of decorative details will be deeper, but less sharply incised than on modern pieces, for they were usually hand-cut, and any carving will be of solid wood.

Although veneering was practiced as early as the 1500s, veneers of the period were for the most part straight-sawed to preserve the wood's original graining pattern. There was some butt and crotch veneer produced and used in decorative inlays, in relatively narrow pieces.

The predominant woods at that time were rosewood, satinwood, teak, English walnut, and African mahogany. Later pieces will be of South American mahogany, cherry, hickory, American walnut, maple, and oak.

Furniture made in the early 1800s up to the end of the nineteenth century will tend to be massive and large-scaled. Armchairs will have backs 5 and even 6 feet tall. Cabinet pieces and beds may tower to 7 or even 8 feet. These pieces were scaled to big rooms with high ceilings. Chair upholstery will generally be confined to seats and backs, though roll-arm upholstery will be found on sofas; the square-end style of upholstery and full-upholstered chairs came with a later period.

Interior construction details of good shop-made pieces of an early date will in most cases be superior to pieces manufactured after mechanization of the furniture trade began in the 1850s and became progressively more widespread. In the shop-made pieces of category three furniture, the dovetails on drawers will still be hand-cut, joints mortise-and-tenoned in-

Hand-cut dovetails, narrow and irregularly spaced, are a sure sign the piece of furniture was made before 1830.

stead of dowelled. In all old pieces, though, the glue oozing around corner braces or joints will be a dark brown, almost black, and quite opaque. In later pieces the glue will be light brown and semitransparent. In the older pieces, screws may be handmade.

This brings us to category four. As noted earlier, schlock and borax have always been with us. There are pieces justly classed as antiques which deserve to be placed in the fourth category, for many a proud owner of an antique piece is really showing off an example of early borax.

Schlock or borax antiques will generally have been more carefully finished in their exterior hidden surfaces, such as the insides of chair rails and the undersides of table and cabinet tops, than will the better pieces. This isn't as strange as it may seem. Almost since commercial furniture-making began, schlock-makers learned to imitate costly woods with cheaper ones. Ash, hickory, basswood, and others were stained and grained to resemble walnut or mahogany or one of the other fine hardwoods. The schlock pieces depended for their acceptance on their finish, which had to be uniform in order to carry out the deception.

Internal construction details of category four furniture will be the giveaway. Look for rabbeted and nailed drawer sides and ends, rather than dovetailed. Scarf instead of finger joints will be used to connect butted members. If these joints are strange to you, look at the pictures and learn them, for you'll be encountering them later in repair jobs.

Moving on to categories five and six, you'll sometimes be hard put to tell the difference between shop- or individually-crafted modern furniture of the best grade and that turned out by factories. The chief difference, though in contemporary times it doesn't invariably apply, is that shop and individual craftsmen tend to depend on solid woods while factories favor veneers. In pieces from either source you'll find machine-cut dovetails and other joints, and there will be no substantial difference in the types of finish, though factories switched to lacquer finishes earlier than did individual and small shop craftsmen.

As for categories five and six, good pieces are always worth repairing, whether they come from shop or factory. The work that goes into them follows the best practices of construction. Drawer joints will be dovetailed, frame members mortised or dowelled at joints, glued braces will be used. Drawer interiors and the undersides of tabletops will have been protected against warping or checking with a wash coat of shellac, varnish, or stain. These, as well as integrity of design, are details to look for when evaluating the present and possible future worth of a piece.

Machine-cut dovetails date from the late 1850s. Today, you should expect to find this refinement on all good-quality furniture.

Mortise, dado, and rabbet joints were cut by machine when dovetails were still being cut by hand. Machine-sawed mortises, dados, and rabbets may be found in first-quality pieces dating as early as 1830, but also appear in factory-made pieces from the 1890s.

Second-line furniture of modern manufacture, our seventh category, may or may not be worth repairing. Some second-line pieces have a few of the solid construction details that are always found in first-line furniture, some pieces barely miss being in the borax class. The most common points at which shortcuts are taken to save fabrication cost are the ones hidden under upholstery, the joints in the frame. These may not be glued, merely screwed on. There may be scarf instead of finger joints in butted frame members. On cabinet pieces, pulls may be made from plastic instead of wood or metal.

If we put aside subjective judgments based on sentiment, any repair job contemplated on these pieces must be based on an estimate of how much you'll invest in time and materials as well as on the improvements you'll want to make during the repair job. These may include inserting dowels to reinforce butted joints, gluing corner braces, reinforcing frame members by adding new crosspieces where the members are too widely spaced. Your improvements may very well transform a second-quality piece into a very good one.

As for the eighth of our categories, the wise thing to do when you see that a piece of furniture is schlock or borax is to turn your back quickly and walk quietly away from it. No repair job can cure basically shoddy fabrication. In most borax pieces, nails are used where screws should have been, glued joints are conspicuous by their absence, and inferior wood is used for framing. Always and forever, schlock is schlock and borax is borax, no matter what its origin. It's always overpriced, and will never appreciate in value. Instead of wasting time fixing up a borax piece, you'll be better off to shop the secondhand stores for a used piece of first or second quality and repair it.

FURNITURE STYLES

There will be substantial style changes to guide you in judging furniture in terms of the time it was made, in addition to the details of materials and construction practices already noted.

Most of the pre-1800 furniture had the delicate lines evolved by the famous designers of the preceding two hundred years. In the early 1800s, the trend to massive pieces began, and continued for almost a century. Fine woods—mahogany, walnut, rosewood, cherrywood—predominated until the mid-1800s, when oak became popular. Solid oak began to be replaced by second-grade oak covered with fine oak veneer in the 1870–1880

Rabbeted, nailed drawers identify yesterday's low-end mass-produced furniture and today's schlock. The dresser from which this drawer comes is listed in the 1910 Sears Roebuck catalog for just over $10. In today's antique stores, it costs $250.

Colonial furniture can be identified by its natural, uncluttered lines, lack of excessive ornamentation, as well as by the woods used in it. These were native American woods, with maple predominating.

In early America, walnut was taking its place beside maple, and veneered pieces in mahogany and other imported woods were seen. The lines remained simple and straightforward.

Exterior details will help you to evaluate the quality of old furniture and determine its age. The scrolled leg on this American Empire chest is typical of the pre-1830 period, which featured simplicity of detail.

decade. The popularity of oak began to decline about 1915, and went practically to zero, where it stayed until the 1960s revival. By 1975, oak was in such great demand that many firms began turning out reproductions of old pieces, though often these are made on a slightly smaller scale.

Full upholstery began to become popular in the 1870s, with horsehair, and fully upholstered pieces shared popularity with older styles until the old semiupholstered fashion faded out in the early 1900s. Then, when the United States entered the "bungalow" years of architecture shortly before 1915, furniture styles began to change drastically to accommodate this architectural difference. Bungalow ceilings dropped to a uniform 8 feet, and rooms became smaller. The heavy Victorian styles with 7-foot headboards on beds and bureau or sideboard mirrors soaring 8 feet

Victorian furniture, which dominated the 1800s, can always be spotted by its curves, as well as by its bulk. The Windsor rocker in this room is the only piece which has an unornamented straight line, and it belongs to an earlier period. Notice, too, the elaborate paw-carved legs of the larger pieces.

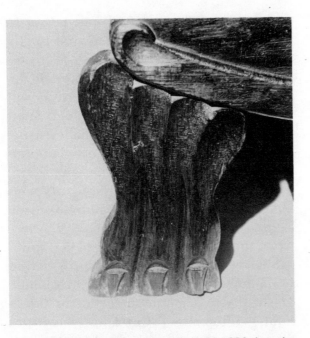

In the later Victorian period, the 1890 decade, carving was done by machine and lacked the fine detail found on earlier furniture.

high had to go; the new small rooms couldn't accommodate them.

Factories began using lacquer-finished softwoods stained to imitate fine woods. In design, the Hepplewhite and Sheraton influences returned. Furniture became thin-scaled, with fluted or turned legs, open or wicker-paneled ends; only the seats and backs of chairs and divans were upholstered. A typical bungalow room might accommodate one "club chair," but seldom was there space for an entire "suite" of full-upholstered furniture.

Toward the end of the 1920s, the ideas of avant-garde European designers began to captivate their counterparts in the United States. Pieces produced abroad during the 1920s and in the U.S. beginning in the 1930s are now called Art Deco furniture.

Straight lines began to be mixed with curves in heavy furniture of the Edwardian period. "Overstuffed" or "club" chairs also gained popularity in this era. However, the Victorian influence still predominated in upholstery styling.

Scaled-down furniture marked the "bungalow" period in the U.S. of the early 1900s. Oak continued to be the chief wood, as it had been in the Victorian and Edwardian periods, and cluttered rooms remained the fashion.

Its characteristics are angularity of line, with backs and corners of arms being squared off on full-upholstered pieces. On pieces lacking upholstered arms and backs, cushions—often freeform—began to appear.

New methods of lamination made possible the production of bentwood pieces. The molded Eames chair is perhaps the most famous example of this type of furniture. Laminates of phenolic resins—the best-known is sold under the registered trademark Formica—moved from countertops in the kitchen to tabletops and cabinet tops in other rooms of the house.

Metal frames supporting leather pads or slings, or having seats of molded plastic, came into transitory style. Ebonized woods, blonde woods, and some of the lumber woods such as pine were used in

exposed members. Some of the Art Deco designers were truly innovative in their work, and the pieces they created are already entering the category of "tomorrow's antiques." There are many more bad copies of these innovators' work than there are well-designed originals, though, and these aren't worth the expenditure of time or money required to repair them. Indeed, because of the materials used and the manner of their design, repairs to some Art Deco furniture require tools and skills that the average home craftsman doesn't have.

In the 1970s, we seem to have entered one of those recurring periods when no single style of furniture predominates. Deep, fully upholstered pieces are seen as often as delicately scaled pieces that show the influence of fifteenth and sixteenth

Angularity finally crowded out the curves and curlicues of earlier periods when the Art Deco days began in the 1930s. Metal and glass came into use, leatherette upholstery that was essentially padding, and blonde woods.

century master designers. We can leave the social philosophers to debate the reason for this. Our interest here is in the unchanging characteristics of furniture construction, which are very much the same today as they were three or four hundred years ago. If the frame of a chair or divan made in 1650 or 1750 or 1850 were to be stood beside the frame of a similar piece made in 1950 or even later, there would be almost total uniformity in their construction details. You would use the same methods to repair one that you'd use in fixing the other.

With a few exceptions, such as raffia, bamboo, and wickerwork, this book tries to cover the methods of repairing all kinds of furniture.

Metal furniture is given only token representation. Repairing cast metal furniture requires welding or brazing equipment, which isn't a big home workshop item. In the home shops equipped to do this kind of work, the owner will generally know what's needed. Tubular metal furniture is another matter and is covered—at least those repairs that can be made with familiar, everyday tools.

Plastic furniture also has limited representation. Often, a piece of plastic furniture can't be repaired at all. Minor patchwork may be possible in some cases where the plastic can be restored with a solvent that causes breaks to flow together, but on a number of plastics even epoxy or "miracle" glues can't make a bond to the material. However, you'll find some suggestions that may help you in experimenting with plastic pieces.

Generally, the book is confined to fixing good wooden and upholstered furniture such as is found in most homes. This kind of furniture is almost always worth your best efforts in keeping it in usable and presentable shape.

When you've finished reading this and the preliminary chapters which discuss tools, materials, and supplies, you'll find chapters that cover almost every type of repair jobs that the average furniture in the average home will require. But honesty compels me to preface those later chapters with a friendly word of caution.

Very little in this book is going to endow you with greater skill in the basics of woodworking than you now have. Skill comes only from practice. Reading about the way a process is carried out doesn't put into your fingers the muscular reactions necessary to guide tools with confidence. On the positive side, any skill can be acquired, learned by practicing it. If you've never sawed a plank, never used a plane or chisel or sandpaper or a paint-

brush, please don't expect to acquire the ability to handle them just by reading about how they're used.

If you're totally inexperienced in woodworking, you're like the beginning pilot who's been checked out in single-engine airplanes and expects to step into the cockpit of a jumbo jet and make perfect landings and take-offs without further instruction. In the course of my years of prowling antique shops and secondhand furniture stores looking for the occasional bargain these places yield, I've seen a lot of inexpert repair work. Usually, it's the kind of thing that can be expected from anybody who's not quite sure which end of a hammer to hold. Inexpert repairs have actually ruined beyond hope of salvaging many otherwise good pieces I've seen. This is why I'm passing along the suggestion that you need to learn to walk before you try to fly.

Practice using tools on scraps of lumber. Develop the "feel" for the tools you'll be working with. Perhaps you can find a piece of category seven furniture that you can practice on, and turn your practice sessions to double profit by selling the re-

Bentwood furniture was a fad of the 1870s, and started coming back into fashion in the 1970s. Original bentwood pieces are relatively scarce, but the furniture is currently being manufactured in large quantities.

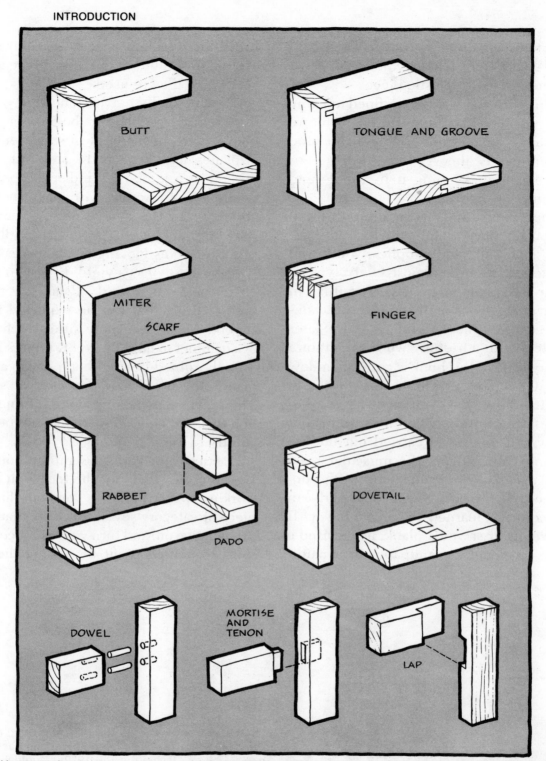

Here are the most common wood joints used in making furniture. Butt joints are found only on the cheapest pieces; they're the weakest of all joints and are commonly glued and nailed. The miter is a framing joint and is found in several variations, usually at corners. It may be reinforced by dowels and is generally glued. The scarf joint is used to join flat boards or moldings and is usually glued. Rabbet and dado joints are usually glued. The dowel joint may appear as part of a butt, miter, rabbet, or tongue-and-groove joint. The addition of dowels to any joint adds almost 100% to its strength and stability. Dovetail joints are exceptionally strong, and are a mark of high-quality workmanship.

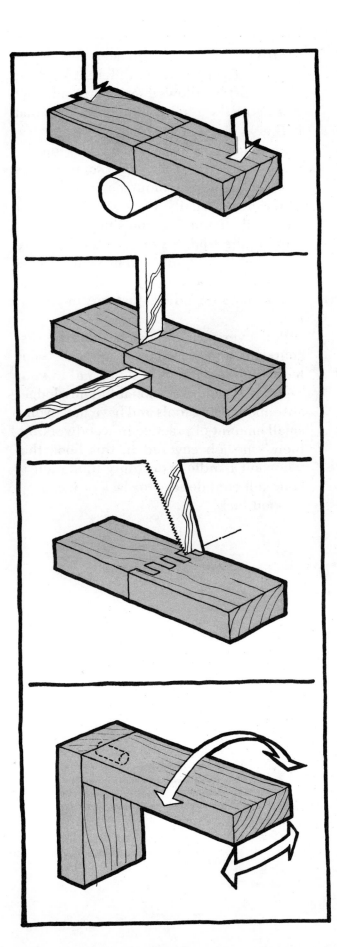

In disassembling a piece of furniture for repair, you will often find it necessary to break a joint or two in order to remove a damaged member.

Butt and scarf joints can be broken by putting a large dowel or woodblock under the joint-line and pressing down on both sides.

Rabbet and tongue-and-groove joints, especially if glued, must usually be parted by tapping a chisel into the joint-lines on each side, then using a woodblock.

Finger and dovetail joints, unless the wood is badly shrunken and the glue has failed, can be parted only by sawing through them. When you do this, be sure to compensate for the kerf of the saw cut with a spacer when you reassemble the piece.

Dowel-reinforced joints can usually be loosened by a combination of twisting and moving one of the joined components from side to side, which will break the glue bond and allow the components to be pulled apart.

paired piece for more than it cost you.

Sometimes, category seven pieces can be transformed from sow's ears into—well, maybe not silk, but at least into rayon purses, by including a bit of alteration in the repair job. Strip off unnecessary ornaments, put on plain metal pulls instead of leaving the cracked ones of plastic. Turn a two-tone finish into one that's uniform. Strangely, a lot of designers of category seven furniture seem to have the illusion that two shades of stain hide cheap wood and slipshod workmanship. It's often possible by altering as you repair to make a mediocre piece look better than it is.

If you're totally inexperienced in woodworking, just remember that nobody's born an expert in any craft. Learn by experimenting what you can and can't expect. Find out how a saw feels when it bites into woodgrain. Look at a wooden surface that's been gone over with different grades of sandpaper, use a magnifying glass to find out the difference in the finish produced by different grades of abrasives. Make and break a few wood joints to learn how long different kinds of glues must be allowed to set up, and what distinguishes a solid joint from one that will give way under stress.

So much for caution. Let's look on the positive side. Yes, there are some repairs you can handle without having had any experience. Usually, these are the simpler jobs, and for some reason simple jobs outnumber the complex ones in the furniture repairing field. Quite often, your success in conquering a simple job will encourage you to take on others that are more difficult.

Whatever your approach, don't be discouraged and don't give up. Grit your teeth and do a job over if you fail in your first try. If you're reasonably knowledgeable about using tools and have had even a small amount of practice in woodworking, there's no job covered in this book that you can't handle. Your only limitation is your self-confidence—or lack of it.

Good luck!

1

Woodworking Tools

If you're already into home repairs as a hobby—or as a household necessity in a period of inflation and a chronic shortage of skilled workmen who'll take on such chores—you've probably got all or most of the basic tools you'll need to do just about any job of repairing furniture.

This doesn't necessarily mean that you'll have each of the tools that will allow you to take the most direct route to finishing a job. Anybody who does any kind of work in any craft knows that there are two kinds of tools. The first are the basic ones required to tackle almost any job, the second are the specialized tools that are designed to do a single job quickly and superbly but have little use outside that one specific chore. The first kind are essential, the second kind are nice to have around because they'll shorten the time required to do a recurring piece of work.

We can divide furniture repair tools into four groups instead of two. Group one will contain the basic tools, group two the ones that are nice to have, groups three and four the specialized tools for such jobs as reupholstering and refinishing. Fortunately, there are very few in these last two groups, and we'll get to them in the chapters devoted to those special crafts.

POWER TOOLS

Unless you're planning to do major reconstruction work, which is really outside the scope of this book, you don't need such bench tools as a lathe, circular saw, bandsaw, or drill press. You'll actually use power tools very little, except when you're making a new frame member, which might involve cutting a mortise-and-tenon or renewing a dowel joint. The three power tools you'll use most often in general repair jobs are a jigsaw or saber saw, a drill, and an orbital sander. If you have a circular saw, it'll see some service. So will a router, if you own one. The first three power tools named will do most of the jobs you'll encounter and will save time and muscle strain.

If you'll be shopping for new power tools to fill gaps in your battery or to replace some tool that's getting worn out, you'll find that the major U.S. manufacturers maintain consistently high quality in their products. I have tools made by all of them, and I'd be hard-pressed to class the products of one manufacturer as being clearly superior to those of another.

There are small differences that might guide your choice, such things as handle

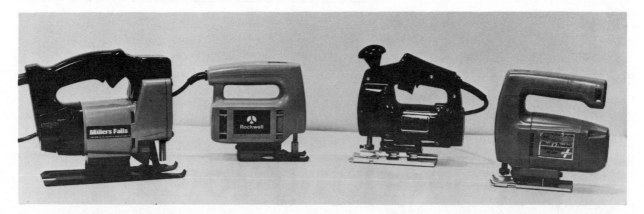

Saber saws by Millers Falls, Rockwell, Skil, Black & Decker have the features that make this the most versatile saw for furniture repair work. All have rip fences, baseplates that swivel either right or left, and variable speed. I've used all of these saws and would be hard-pressed to choose among them.

A circular saw has limited use in furniture repair work, but you'll reach for it to make rip cuts when fashioning a new member to replace a broken one and when cutting joints, veneers, and laminates.

contours and the location of triggers and other controls make different tools feel differently to different hands. This is entirely an individual matter, of course; what suits me best might not suit you.

Leaving personal preference aside, you'll get completely satisfactory performance and service from the power tools made by any of the nation's leading manufacturers: Black & Decker, Millers Falls, Rockwell, and Skil. All of them produce

tools of excellent quality, all keep abreast of technical advances, and all four brands are competitively priced. All the power tools produced by all four accept and operate satisfactorily with the accessories that do so much to reduce handwork and speed up jobs.

Let's take a quick look at accessories while we're on the subject. Drills are the most versatile of all hand power tools in this respect, as you'll see from the pic-

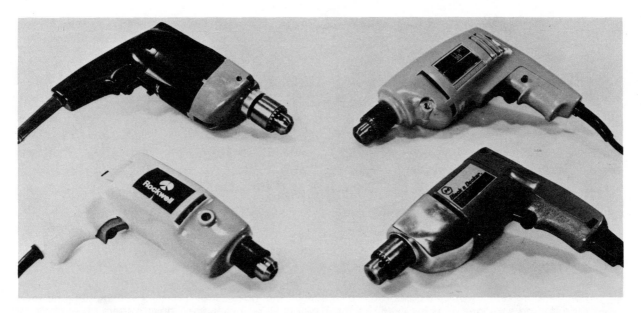

If your selection of power tools was limited to one, this would be your best choice: a $^3/_8$-inch variable-speed drill. At top, Millers Falls and Skil, at bottom, Rockwell and Black & Decker offer their versions of this versatile tool. Common features in addition to variable speed are double insulated cases and the ability to reverse when used as screwdrivers.

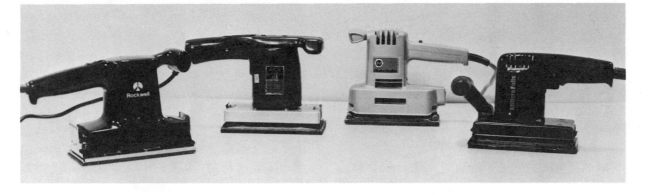

For furniture refinishing, a powered sander is almost an essential tool. These orbital sanders vary slightly in details such as trigger arrangement, weight, and grip contours, but all perform well.

tures. There are drill accessories which aren't necessarily specially designed for use in furniture repairing, but which do perform a lot of functions that make furniture repair jobs go faster. Study the photos and decide for yourself what new tools you'll need—if any—for the jobs you have planned. In the pictures of both tools and accessories you'll find optional choices, devices that will do virtually the same job in slightly different ways, so you've a wide range of choice.

HAND TOOLS

When we begin looking at hand tools you'll find the same kind of optional choices. Remember, there's very little big work involved in repairing and refinishing furniture—except for the sanding in refinishing jobs. Let me repeat what I said earlier about brand choices. Stanley and Millers Falls are the two major U.S. makers of fine-quality hand tools, and while each firm has some individual specialties, both

For furniture repair work, I'd class routers as an optional power tool, unless a substantial amount of reproducing components is involved in a job. Then, they're invaluable. These routers differ chiefly in weight, grip contours, and size. They all did excellent work on the jobs for which I used them when working on the step-by-step photos you'll see in later pages.

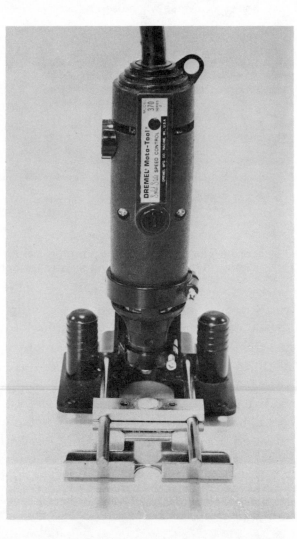

A substantial amount of furniture repair work involves doing offbeat jobs in hard-to-reach places. For these, the Dremel MotoTool is a handy piece of equipment to have around. It saves disassembly time on cabinet pieces when a larger tool can't be used.

Circular sawblades useful in furniture repair jobs are, clockwise from top left: fine-cut, for almost mark-free first cuts which require a minimum of planing or sanding; veneer and laminate blade, designed for shallow cuts with a minimum of splintering; combination, an all-purpose blade; and tungsten carbide tooth, for use on boards where nails or screws might be encountered. Jigsaw blades in the foreground range from rough-cut and metal-cutting blades to the tiny scrolling blade for intricate curved cuts at lower right. The sawing guide by Skil in the background can be used with any saw, hand or powered, to cut precise angles.

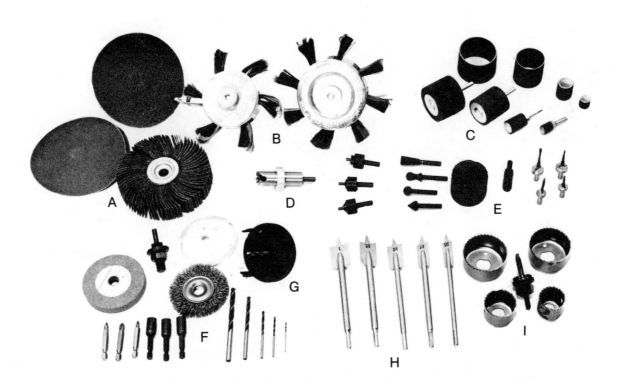

Accessories such as these make your electric drill the most versatile power tool you can own. Shown above are (**A**) rigid sanding discs and lightweight contour sander; (**B**) standard and heavy-duty contour sanders; both groups by Merit Abrasives; (**C**) sanding drums from Craftsman Wood Supply; (**D**) Stanley's Electrochisel, for mortising with drill; (**E**) edgers, rotary files, rotary rasps, and countersinks by Arco; (**F**) Skil's kit-packaged set of drill accessories including grinding and buffing wheels, arbor, screwdrivers and nut drivers for variable-speed drills, and drill bits; (**G**) adjustable hole saw from Skil; (**H**) speed bits from 1 to ¼ inch by Millers Falls; (**I**) keyhole saw set and arbor from Rockwell.

make a full line of basic tools of the best grade.

Saws.   The most useful saw for furniture work is a dovetail saw or a backsaw; these are both designed to make the precise cuts required in forming joints. About the only long cuts you'll make would be cutting a board to insert in a tabletop or the top of a bureau. All the rest of the saw jobs are the precision type encountered in joinery work, and for this kind of sawing you need a fine-toothed saw with a rigid blade.

For special jobs such as veneering, you'll need either a veneer saw or a razor saw. The teeth of both these types of saws are set to make clean-edged cuts in veneers and both will cut at odd angles. If you feel you can afford both—and neither is expensive—by all means get both. Also very handy in veneer work is the mini-key-hole saw shown in one of the photos. It's available from Brookstone, whose address you'll find in the appendix.

A regular keyhole saw, or one of the mini-hacksaws illustrated, will come in very handy. It's sometimes necessary to reach for cuts at arm's length, or to saw apart a stubborn joint or saw between the frame and a glued corner-brace. A saw that takes both wood- and metal-cutting blades is the most versatile keyhole saw to get, and this type of saw generally has a collet which lets you adjust the blade at different angles. This makes it easy to get into odd corners, something you must do now and then when disassembling a piece of furniture. Rusted screws must sometimes be sawed through, which means a hacksaw.

Files.   A selection of good files is a necessity when you're replacing a broken

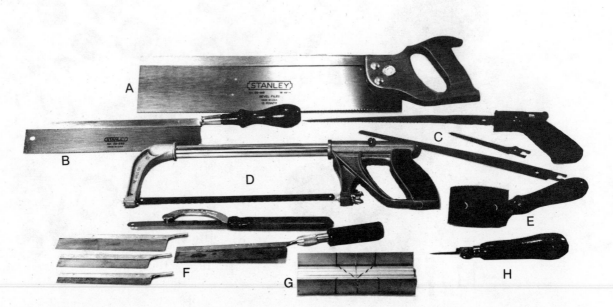

One of the lessons I've learned about handsaws in connection with furniture repairing is that there's no such thing as an all-purpose saw. The backsaw (**A**) and the dovetail saw (**B**) are invaluable for jointing, used with or without a miterbox. The Stanley keyhole saw (**C**) offers a variety of blade choices and is adjustable as to blade angle, which lets you get into hard-to-reach places. The hacksaw and mini-hack by Millers Falls (**D**) are necessary when you must cut through frozen bolts or screws in disassembling. Constantine's veneer saw (**E**) serves well for most veneer cuts, but I wouldn't want to be without a set of the X-Acto razor saws (**F**), for they make virtually kerf-free cuts on even the finest woods, and a miter box (**G**). The little mini-keyhole saw by Brookstone (**H**) makes fine-kerf cuts in difficult places.

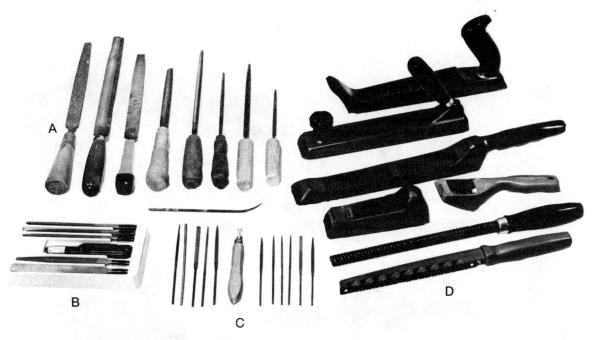

Forming tools (**A**) include coarse wood rasp, half-round mill bastard, smooth-cut, triangular, rattail files, and a riffler; (**B**) mini-rasps from X-Acto and (**C**) X-Acto's mini-files. Surform tools shown (**D**) are the ones I've found most useful.

member that must be worked down to a curve that will match another section of the piece, or when you're splicing in a section of wood to mend a broken frame. In the file category I place Stanley's Surform tools, which come in many different models and function in the gray area between plane and file, or in some cases between spokeshave and file. The Surform tools are unexcelled for roughing-in shapes such as legs and backs. They cut easily, but do leave fairly deep scoremarks on the work, so they're not suitable for finish work.

As for actual files, you'll need a rasp, a half-round mill bastard, a smooth file, and a rattail and triangular file. If you do veneering, you'll find a riffling file very handy for getting into odd corners. It's not designed for coarse work, but for the final touches involved in fitting angled pieces together very precisely.

Knives. Few home craftsmen are without a precision-cutting knife, variously called a skill knife or a razor knife or by a trade name such as X-Acto. All these knives have a common feature: the blades are disposable and, in many cases, you have a choice of several blade shapes to use in the same handle or grip. The odds are overwhelming that you own one or more of these knives and that you have a favorite type or brand. Use the one that you like best, for this is an indispensable aid to doing any kind of precision woodworking. I use mine for marking saw lines when extreme accuracy in cutting is required, in cutting templates, trimming veneers, and doing a hundred and one different jobs.

Planes. About 90% of the planing you'll be called on to do can be handled with a block plane. If I were to be limited to a single plane, this is the one I'd choose. However, in finishing a long piece of stock for edge-gluing, such as you'd need to do in putting a new board in a tabletop or the top of a desk or bureau, a smooth plane or a jackplane would be very handy.

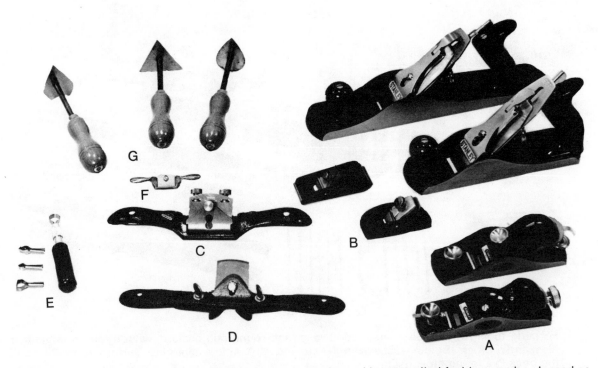

Tools that are designed to remove very small amounts of wood in controlled fashion can be classed as shaving tools. (**A**) Stanley's jackplane, bench plane, and block plane; (**B**) mini-planes by X-Acto and Millers Falls; (**C**) Stanley's standard spokeshave; (**D**) Brookstone's chamfering spokeshave; (**E**) X-Acto's hand routers; (**F**) X-Acto's mini-spokeshave; (**G**) Brookstone's shavehooks.

Another handy but not really essential tool is a spokeshave. Although in a later chapter you'll see how a round table or chair leg can be brought almost to the finished point with a block plane, a spokeshave makes turning square pieces of wood into round ones much easier. A chamfering spokeshave such as the one shown is sheer luxury. It's a fascinating tool, but you'd need to edge a lot of lumber to make owning one an absolute necessity. However, a pair of spokeshaves costs a lot less than a wood lathe.

Chisels. You can get along pretty well with one chisel, but I'll confess that chisels are one of my many weaknesses. There are times when I'll use a $1\frac{1}{2}$- or 2-inch chisel in preference to a plane, perhaps a holdover from gunstock-making, a hobby that I used to enjoy. At one time, I made a set of very narrow chisels from the tang-ends of worn-out rattail files, an easy enough job if you use a light touch on the grinding wheel and don't draw the temper of the steel. Seriously, if this was a two-chisel world, I think I could get along with a $\frac{1}{8}$-inch and a 2-inch chisel and not suffer too greatly for lack of a plane.

Brace and bits. Unless you have some sort of angle guide for your power drill —and such a guide is pictured among the drill accessories—you'll find that boring for a chair leg or a stretcher or splat at the exact angle required will be easier with a hand brace. This is especially true when you get into the larger diameter bits; with any bit bigger than about $\frac{1}{2}$ inch, a hand brace does more precise work.

Hammers. These come far down the list of tools used in furniture repair jobs. A standard carpenter's hammer, claw or rip type, is satisfactory for everything but upholstery work, and we'll get around to that in a later chapter. I do like a little 6-pound hammer, though, when driving in locking wedges and other jobs that call for just a series of light tap-tap-taps. A little ball pien hammer is something you'll also reach for occasionally, if you have one handy, and need to land a solid rap on a metal punch or something like a screw head that would mar the face of a carpenter's hammer.

A mallet is another upholstering tool that we'll meet again later on, but when you're disassembling a chair, prying stretchers from legs and legs from seats or rails where they've been set with glue, a mallet has authority that a hammer lacks. A rubber or soft-faced mallet will be a lot kinder to a finished wooden surface than even a padded hammer head will.

Clamps. A huge assortment of regular cabinetmaker's clamps isn't called for. C-clamps are useful; so is a pipe clamp that will span the width of a desktop or table-top or the frame of a chair or sofa. In the photos you'll see web clamps that are used for holding the legs of chairs and tables in place while glue sets up (and for assembling picture frames as well), but for wide-span clamping on jobs that are too big for C-clamps you'll find in later chapters ways of using wedges and rope windlasses that make most special cabinetmaker's clamps unnecessary.

Vise. For some jobs you can use a big C-clamp to hold work on a bench instead of a vise, but a vise is worth much more than its weight in gold when you really need one. And count on needing one, unless you have the Black & Decker Workmate,

Just how far you need go in miscellaneous tools will depend on how many power-drill accessories you own. You can pass up a hand brace and bits and the Yankee (Stanley) push-drill, center, if your set of power drill bits is adequate. Brookstone's impact tool at bottom center is handy, as it removes frozen screws quickly and easily without marring surrounding surface areas, but it's not an essential. The rest of the tools shown fall into the necessary category: screwdrivers, chisels, pliers and wrenches.

You'll use mallets more than hammers in most furniture repair jobs; there's something about a tap from a nonmarring wooden mallet that makes wood behave. From left are mallets by Brookstone and Constantine, above them, rubber and vinyl-faced mallets from Millers Falls and Stanley respectively; in the right foreground, Millers Falls curved claw, tack and rip claw hammers; at upper right are a small ball pien, a small curved claw, and an upholstering tack-hammer.

which serves as an all-purpose vise as well as a workbench, upholstering platform, and a number of other functions. The longer you use one of these, the more uses you'll find for it.

Measuring tools. A steel tape, a try-square or combination square, and a framing square are essentials. I'd put a traditional folding carpenter's rule with a brass depth gauge insert very high on the list of handy-to-have extras. You do need a depth gauge of some kind, and the little pocket job in one of the pictures is an inexpensive, accurate, and handy one. Let me urge you right here to avoid the sleazy measuring instruments you'll find on the market today. Whether you're measuring in inches or centimeters, accurately scribed measuring tools are vital when

you're jointing—and furniture repair work is 95% jointing. Get steel rules and squares with etched markings for long-lasting accuracy. Omar, the poet tent maker, wrote many years ago, "A hair perhaps divides the false from true," and this is as accurate a statement today as it was eight centuries ago. When you're edge-gluing a board, or fitting a chair rung, or patching veneer, or splicing a sofa frame, the difference of a hair can make the finished job excellent or mediocre.

Some strange quirk in my mental processes causes me to class precision sawing aids such as miter boxes with measuring tools. Even professional woodworkers, who know the craft much better than we amateurs will ever learn it, depend on this kind of help in sawing accurate angles. Anything that reduces the job of producing precise angles with a saw must be classed pretty high on the list of handy-to-have tools, if not among the basic ones.

A final thought now about tools. In this chapter and the pictures that are part of it, many dozens of tools have been discussed and illustrated. You may by now be wondering if you really need all or most of them to do a good job of repairing furniture. The answer is a qualified "no." You certainly don't need every tool pictured, because in most cases the illustrations show one or more alternate choices, perhaps a different model of the same tool by

different manufacturers. If you have the basic tools that are identified as such in the text, and are reasonably familiar with them, you can probably figure out a way to adapt one of them to special jobs that some of the optional or handy tools are designed to do. That's one good thing about those essential tools. Given enough time and thought, they can serve much more than one function.

A highly specialized tool is worth its keep only if it's used often enough to repay its price. From the practical and economical standpoint, you can save

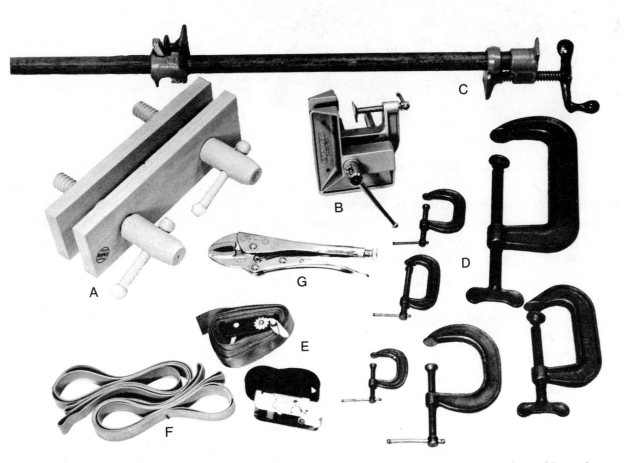

In furniture repair work, you constantly find yourself wishing for another pair of hands, and here they are: (A) Brookstone's woodworker's vise has wooden jaws that won't mar what's clamped in them. (B) Stanley portable vise can be fitted with fiberboard inserts for woodworking and attached to the end of a sawhorse. (C) Pipe clamp is helpful in gluing up a complete chair or tabletop. (D) C-clamps in several sizes are essential. (E) Web clamps from Stanley and Constantine or the very inexpensive rubber clamps (F) from Brookstone are necessary in chair repair jobs when you've got to hold four legs or a back steady. (G) Locking jaw pliers from Millers Falls have a wide span—big enough for almost anything you want to get a firm grip on.

Most of your clamping problems can be solved with Black & Decker's Workmate. It's extremely versatile and takes a lot of the toil, sweat, and tears out of the problem of holding an unwieldy piece of furniture at the angle needed for you to work on it.

money by spending time figuring out how a basic tool can do the work of one of the specialized variety. After all, you're not going to make a business out of repairing furniture, you're going to do the occasional jobs that are needed to keep your household functioning. This puts you in a different situation than that faced by professional cabinetmakers, to whom tools represent a tax-deductible business or operating expense, and to whom time *is* money.

Use the guideline that the professionals have used for many years. Highly specialized, one-purpose tools are fine to have, *if* you do a volume of specialized work that calls for their use *regularly*, not just once every two or three months. Tools that do nothing but gather dust on your workshop wall and take up space in cabinets and drawers are a dead investment. I've shown and discussed a number of such

tools in this chapter simply to show you the easiest, fastest way to do a given job—if you want to take that route. If you want to go the other road, it's wide open.

Playing the devil's advocate, let me now argue on the other side. When you get into some of the jobs called for in repairing furniture, especially the associated crafts of refinishing and reupholstering, you'll find a number of highly specialized tools developed for specific purposes. Yes, you can usually improvise, as I've just pointed out, but improvising takes time and extra effort. Cutting a rabbet with a circular saw takes two to three times as long as cutting one with a router, but the job's just as satisfactory. Rabbets were cut with saw and chisel long before routers were invented, long before their price dropped to the level where they were an affordable tool for the home workshop.

Ask yourself a question: How many

Because furniture repairing demands a certain amount of precision in matching joints, angles and sizes of components, you need reliable tools with which to measure, and to help you cut the kind of joints produced by machines. A miter box, like those by Millers Falls and Stanley, at top left and right; a drill guide (Brookstone's) that allows you to drill at any angle, or at least a saw guide like the Stanley product just below that firm's miter box. For measuring, a carpenter's folding rule, fixed-angle and bevel squares, also from Stanley, a contour gauge and center-finder from Brookstone, and a high-precision depth and thickness gauge from Craftsman are all useful.

pieces of furniture am I going to repair? Reupholster? Refinish? If you've got a long list of work waiting for you, buying special-purpose tools may turn out to be a very wise investment indeed. But you should also consider alternatives. Renting is one of them. Finding another hobbyist with whom you can split the cost of specialized tools on a share-the-use basis is another.

Of course, if you're a tool buff, you're going to toss reason out the window and buy special tools for the sheer pleasure of owing—and occasionally using—them. I know, because I'm a tool buff myself. If I were able to, I'd even buy a left-hand distelfinker—a legendary tool that sets dowels in solid wood without the need to drill holes—just for the pleasure of having it.

Seriously, though, get the best quality basic tools you feel you can afford, and take care of them. You'll use just about every tool required in furniture repairing on other jobs as well. Good all-purpose tools are truly a wise investment for every craftsman.

2

Materials and Supplies

WOOD

When you think about repairing a piece of furniture, quite likely the first thought in your mind is that you'll need pieces of hardwood. This isn't always true, of course. Relatively few repairs require any sizable quantity of wood. Unless you're making a new sidepiece for a bed, inserting a new board in the top of a table, making a new drawer for a bureau or dresser, or a new table leg, you won't be shopping for hardwoods. It's just as well, because aside from specialty houses and a few lumberyards in large cities, sources of supply for cabinet woods aren't all that common.

You'll need framing lumber of pine or ash or straight-grained maple much more often than you will oak, mahogany, walnut, birch, or one of the more exotic hardwoods. Framing lumber can be found in almost all lumber yards, but for hardwoods your best bet is one of the specialty suppliers. The major firms in this field are Constantine in New York and Los Angeles and Craftsman Wood Supply in Chicago. Their addresses are in the appendix. For hardwoods used in table legs, your best source is Herter's, in Waseca, Minnesota;

this firm specializes in gunstock blanks, which are long enough and thick enough to make table legs. All three firms have catalogs and specialize in filling mail orders. Constantine and Craftsman Wood Supply also stock veneers in an almost limitless variety, as well as adhesives, finishing supplies, and woodworking tools. Their emphasis in tools is on the special-purpose as well as the basic tools you'll need for furniture repair work.

Five hardwoods will serve about 90% of your needs in fixing furniture: mahogany, walnut, oak, cherry, and maple. Both Constantine and Craftsman stock these and some other hardwoods in boards ranging from $7^1/_2$ inches wide and 24 inches long on up to $9^1/_2$ inches wide and 6 feet long. The more exotic woods such as rosewood, satinwood, teak, bubinga, and others are generally smaller-sized boards, 3 to 5 inches wide and in lengths from 24 to 48 inches.

VENEERS

In both the Constantine and Craftsman catalog you can choose from fifty or more varieties of wood veneers, ranging from amarath to zebrawood. Veneers are available in 8-inch squares and in sheets from 3 to 16 inches wide and up to 6 feet long. Most of the veneering material is available in standard thicknesses of $\frac{1}{20}$, $\frac{1}{28}$, and $\frac{1}{40}$ inch. These firms can also supply you with hardwood-faced furniture plywood in various dimensions and in the cross-banding core materials from which you can make up your own hardwood-faced plywoods. In ordering veneers, be sure to get a larger piece than you'll need for the repair job, in order to make it easier to match graining.

Don't overlook the fact that you can use veneer for most surface repairs to solid wood furniture. However, most of today's furniture is veneered, so your chief problem in carrying out repairs will be to select the veneering wood required, match its grain as closely as possible to that already in place, and fit an insert into place after removing the veneer from the marred area. In Chapter 4 you'll find the procedure for doing this common job.

DOWELS AND SCRAPS

Aside from the hardwoods or veneers used in repairs to visible sections of a piece of furniture, and straight-grained lumber for framing, the rest of the supply list is very short indeed. You'll need a few short pieces of 2 x 4 lumber for gluing blocks and reinforcements, some scraps of plywood or hardboard to use as mending plates—though metal mending plates for special applications will also come in handy on occasion—and, finally, the most important item on your materials list: dowels. These are so important in so many repair jobs that we might as well begin with them.

While most lumberyards as well as mail-order suppliers such as Brookstone, Craftsman, and Constantine sell short precut dowels, already pregrooved, you should also keep on hand an assortment of long dowels. The most useful diameters are $\frac{1}{8}$, $\frac{1}{4}$, $\frac{1}{2}$, $\frac{7}{8}$ and 1 inch. The tiny diameter dowels are very handy for reinforcing delicate splices that might splinter if a large-diameter dowel is used; the bigger ones provide the raw material for chair stretchers and splats. Remember, you can always cut a long dowel to any required length, but you can't stretch one that's too short.

Actually, repair materials such as cabinet woods and veneers can't very well be kept on hand in any sizable quantities because until you actually begin a repair job you're not always certain just what you'll need. Most people who work with veneers soon learn the value of a scrap box, though. I keep an old shoebox into

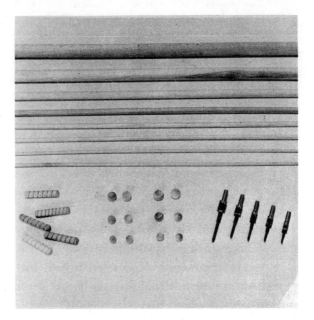

Dowel joints and plugged screwholes are commonplace in furniture assembly. Precut spiral-grooved dowels from Craftsman will meet most needs; your local lumber dealer has 36-inch dowels in all the sizes shown, from $\frac{3}{16}$ to 1 inch; and Brookstone's plugs and buttons can be set in properly sized holes drilled by the Stanley countersinking bits at lower right.

Though I'm not enthused about mending plates or angle-reinforcing plates, they do have a place. So do angle braces. Commonplace furniture hardware you may need to replace, such as the table hanger-plates and bolts and the tabletop hanger at lower left, can be ordered from Craftsman and other specialty houses listed in the appendix.

which I toss any scraps of hardwood veneer longer than 3 inches and wider than 1 inch, because these scraps will sooner or later be used to make a small plug patch, or to test the shade of a stain. A veneer scrapbox doesn't really take up a lot of room.

As for metal mending plates and braces, you'll probably find it a good idea to keep a few around. The number of shapes and sizes these come in is very limited, and usually one medium-sized plate or angle will fit in just about anywhere you need to use one. I'm not enthusiastic about flat mending plates. Usually, a scrap of hardboard or 1/4-inch plywood can be used in place of a metal plate, and this kind of mend costs nothing but the time spent in trimming a scrap to size and drilling a few holes in it. This kind of hardware is "hid-

den" hardware; the other kind is visible hardware, which means drawer and door pulls, ornamental hinges—or even concealed hinges, for that matter.

ADHESIVES

Going on to supplies, glue heads the list. If you're coming with little previous experience to the craft of repairing furniture, you'll discover quickly that nails are seldom used, screws are used sparingly, and bolts are relatively rare. You'll need a few screws around, in the bigger sizes and longer lengths, but your chief use for them will be in hidden places. This is also true of bolts; they are usually found only in special applications.

In most repair jobs, a pair of screws might be used to hold a glued joint firmly in place while the glue sets, but the strength of the joint lies in the glue, not the screws. It's common practice, though, to leave screws in place after the glue is dry. Any exposed screwhead or bolthead should be hidden with a plug. There are two types, button plugs and surface plugs, and Stanley makes a special bit that drills the pilot hole for the screw, countersinks it, and then forms the recess into which the plug is fitted.

Now, getting back to glues, there are so many good, new adhesives available today that your problem isn't finding the right kind to handle the job you're doing, but rather one of selecting from several choices the glue you prefer or the one that best fits whatever special use you've encountered.

Let's dispose of the no-nos first. Epoxy adhesives don't work well with wood. Epoxy is designed to cling and bond to smooth surfaces rather than penetrating porous ones, as do wood glues. When applied to wood, an epoxy must be put on in a very thick coat to be effective, and this pretty much precludes its use in tightly fitted joints such as are required in furniture. Used on the slick, impermeable surfaces for which they're intended, epoxies are very good indeed, but they're best avoided in all woodworking applications except that of joining wood to metal. Then, the wood must be varnished or given a very thin preliminary epoxy coating in order to get a good bond.

Rule out the so-called "miracle" adhesives for woodwork, too. These cyanoacrylate monomer glues are, like epoxy, designed for use on impermeable surfaces such as glass, metal, and some plastics. Their very penetrating qualities rule them out in woodworking, though they will bond two painted or enameled surfaces. And if you do use these "miracle" glues, handle them very carefully indeed. They are now being used in some surgical cases instead of stitches, because they will bond flesh to flesh. Cases have been reported of youngsters touching their glue-moist

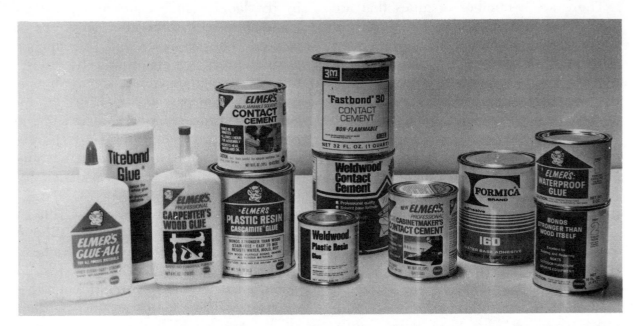

Furniture repairing is a craft that calls for the proper adhesive in the proper place. As the text explains, you should be prepared with a minimum of three kinds: regular carpenter's glue, a waterproof glue, and contact cement. Most adhesive-makers produce more than one type. See the chart for details.

fingers together, or to an eyelid or nose, and requiring surgery to part the instant bonding of skin to skin that followed.

Gloves don't always offer adequate protection when you work with these "miracle" glues. On one occasion when I was using a cyanoacrylate monomer glue, I took the precaution of putting on a pair of thin surgical gloves, because the small scale of the parts I was joining was an almost certain guarantee that I'd get some of the adhesive on my fingers. I did, and without really thinking, I touched my gloved thumb and forefinger together. The result was a bright spark, a puff of smoke, and the glue-covered areas on the glove disappeared. The reaction didn't harm me, but it was startling enough so that I don't want to repeat it. According to a chemist friend who specializes in synthetics, the gloves and the glue combined to create a spontaneous chain reaction. Now, when I must use one of these "miracle" adhesives, I use the kind of extra caution that I recommend you employ when you handle them.

There are a number of glues that are used for different purposes in furniture repair, but only three of them are needed in your supply cabinet. These are the polyvinyl resin or aliphatic polymer types, the urea or resorcinol resin types, and the contact types. These synthetic-based adhesives have very largely replaced the traditional animal-based glues of the past. The best-known of several national brands is Borden's Elmer's trademark; others are the 3M and Weldwood glues.

Polyvinyl resin and aliphatic polymer glues are white or cream-colored, and are used on furniture that will stay indoors. They are the basic glues of carpentry and joinery. Both can be cleaned up with water before they set hard. Both require pressure to make a good bond. Aliphatic polymer glues set up faster and require less bonding pressure than the polyvinyl resins. Basically, they serve the same purpose and have similar characteristics. Both are used as they come from the container and require no mixing or other advance preparation, and both give very dependable bonds.

Urea resin and resorcinol resin glues are used in furniture that will see use on a porch or patio and will be exposed to rain or other kinds of moisture. Urea resin glues come in powder form and must be mixed with water. Resorcinol resin types come in two liquid solutions, a base and a catalyst, which are mixed before using in the desired quantities. Both these glues are dark in color.

Contact cements are special-purpose adhesives used chiefly in veneering, though they are used in a small way in upholstery, usually to apply a trim strip of cloth or braid to an upholstery fabric's edge to hide tacks or staples. Contact cements are of two types: one is an acrylic latex-based material, the other is elastomer-based. The difference can be told by the label, which cautions against the flammable nature of the acrylic-based cement. The acrylic-based type changes color as it dries, signaling the time when the surfaces can be joined, and as much as two hours can pass between drying and contact. Elastomer-based contact cements don't allow this much time lapse; joining of surfaces coated with it must be done within a few minutes of the cement's drying.

If you're a sturdy traditionalist, you can still get the old-style hide- or fishbone-based carpenter's glues. These come in flake form, and must be dissolved in hot water, and give the best bond when they are used warm. Clamps or other methods of applying pressure must be used to get a good bond with these glues.

To help you make your selection, the

chart included in this chapter summarizes the properties, appearance, and general uses of the glues you'll find useful in furniture repairs, as well as of those you might be tempted to use but shouldn't.

Masking tape is the only other adhesive you'll need, though recently I've been using duct tape, the silvery kind that sheetmetal workers wrap around joints, on jobs that require a sustained tight pressure. Duct tape has several features that masking tape lacks. It's a lot sturdier, and adheres much better to the kind of smooth surfaces common to furniture. It strips as cleanly as masking tape, unless it's allowed to stay in place for several months. Masking tape, though, gets brittle faster than duct tape. However, masking tape has an advantage of its own. It's translucent, which makes it possible for you to see pencil marks through it. This is very desirable when you're using it on a sawline to keep brittle plastic laminates or veneered surfaces from splitting.

ABRASIVES

Next on the list of expendable supplies comes abrasives. Your greatest use for these will be in refinishing, but refinishing is part of the repair job when you're working on any visible surface, so we'd better handle abrasives here instead of in Chapter 12.

You'll need graduated grades of sandpaper, ranging from the very coarse to the ultra-fine silicon carbide paper originated for use in auto body finishing. When used wet, the finest grades of these papers give you a glass-smooth surface over which to apply varnish or enamel, and the very finest grade can be used to buff varnish for a satin finish. If you must choose between variety and quantity, go the variety route. Often the difference in one grade of sandpaper is the difference be-

tween an eggshell-smooth surface and one that's less than perfect. You should have a selection that begins with about #50 and goes all the way up to the #420 and #600 wet-or-dry finishing paper. A couple of sheets of alternate grades of the coarser papers will be adequate, but you'll want a sheet or two of each grade of the finer papers, from about #220 up to #600.

In addition to grades of sandpaper there are also several types, using different kinds of grits: flint, garnet, aluminum oxide, silicon carbide. Coarser grades also come in two kinds of coated surfaces, production and open coat. The former has a larger number of grit granules per square inch, and is used on raw wood, while the open coat papers are better suited for use in stripping and in between-coat sanding, as they have less tendency to clog.

My own preference in sandpaper is the garnet type for rough work, the aluminum oxide for intermediate jobs, and the silicon carbide surfaces for fine finishing work. The 3M Company makes an incredi-

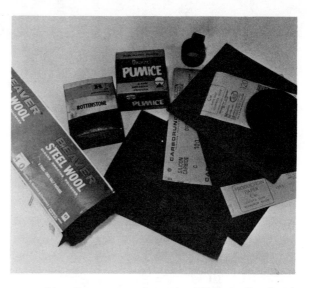

Abrasives are an important item in the furniture repairer's materials stock. Abrasive wheels and discs perform a lot of shaping jobs faster than they can be done otherwise; refinishing calls for a wide range of abrasives such as those pictured.

GLUES USED IN WOODWORKING

TYPE	APPEARANCE	PREPARATION	APPLICATION	CHIEF USE	DRIES	DRYING TIME
Polyvinyl alkyd	White liquid	Ready to use	Spread on both surfaces	Interior	Clear	18 hours
Aliphatic resin	Yellow liquid	Ready to use	Spread on both surfaces	Interior	Translucent	10–12 hours
Polyvinyl resin	Cream powder	Mix with cold water	Spread on both surfaces	Interior	Clear	18 hours
Casein	White or cream powder	Mix with cold water	Spread on both surfaces	Interior	Amber	24 hours
Urea-formaldehyde resin	Cream powder	Mix with cold water	Spread on both surfaces	Exterior, Interior	Clear	6–10 hours
Resorcinol resin	Brown powder + purple liquid catalyst	Combine powder with catalyst	Spread on both surfaces	Exterior, Interior	Dark brown	12–16 hours
Resorcinol resin-urea	Brown powder + cream powder catalyst	Combine powders in cold water	Spread on both surfaces	Exterior, Interior	Amber to brown	10–12 hours
Hide	Brown or amber flakes	Mix flakes with hot water, keep warm	Spread warm on both surfaces	Exterior, Interior	Amber to brown	24 hours
Contact cement, acrylic latex	Milky-white liquid	Ready to use	Spread on both surfaces, join within 2 hours of spreading	Bonding laminates to wood	Clear	Bonds instantly on contact
Contact cement, latex	Light amber liquid	Ready to use	Spread on both surfaces, join within 30 minutes of spreading	Bonding laminates to wood	Clear	Bonds instantly on contact
Epoxy*	White gel + amber gel	Mix gels in equal parts	Spread on one surface	Not recommended for wood joints	Clear to amber	5 to 45 minutes
Cyanoacrylate monomer	Clear thin liquid	Ready to use	NOT RECOMMENDED FOR WOODWORKING**			Instantly

*Epoxy does not hold well in wood-to-wood joints; use for bonding metal or plastic parts to wood.
**Cyanoacrylate monomers are the so-called "miracle" glues that come in tiny tubes. They do not bond well when used on porous material such as wood. If used at all, handle with great care. They adhere to skin, and will glue fingers together.
Types of glues vary between brands in color, mixing quantities, and drying times. Always follow label directions. Drying times change with humidity and temperature. All glue joints made with the first eight types of glue listed above must be clamped or weighted to assure best adhesion.

bly diversified line of abrasive papers, and is the brand most widely distributed. Carborundum Company papers are also very diverse and very good. For medium-coarse work I especially like the Carborundum Alcoat aluminum oxide paper. Merit produces a very good and innovative selection of abrasives.

For help in choosing abrasive papers, consult the chart. It covers the entire field, including items such as steel wool, pumice, and rottenstone, which are primarily used in refinishing work. If you have a power sander, you'll find self-adhesive sheets in the 3M line; these will generally give longer use than the sheets which are held on the sander's platen by clips, and tend to tear at the front and back corners. Merit has a new sanding disc that snaps into a special arbor for use in power drills, and does away with the center hole that causes papers held by a bolt and washer arrangement to wrinkle and tear. Sanding discs are chiefly used in rough work, for reducing stock. They aren't designed or intended to produce a surface suitable for varnish or enamel.

Other abrasives are covered more thoroughly in the chapter on refinishing. You'll seldom use them in direct connection with repair jobs, except in preparing small surface areas.

WOOD FILLERS

Add wood fillers to your list of expendable supplies. These include wood pastes, which consist of fine-ground sawdust or fuller's earth mixed in an adhesive base, and are used for surface repairs. Also add stick shellac and stick waxes, which are other surface repair items that are useful in avoiding a complete refinishing job when only a minor blemish is being repaired. These items are covered in de-

tail in Chapter 4, so our look at them here will be cursory.

Wood pastes are of two types. One incorporates a stain in its base, and will not accept stain when dry. The other is a neutral tan which accepts stains. If you're using the first kind in a visible area of a piece of furniture, test it for its dry shade by putting a dab on a chip of wood and comparing it with the tone and hue of the finish on the piece being repaired. Test the second type the same way to make sure the same stain that is used on the wood around the repaired spot will match that covered by the filler. You can mix stain with most of the fillers that do not have stain in their base, and your blending should also be tested this way.

Chief brand names of the wood pastes are Plastic Wood, Duratite, F.I.X., and Borden. Constantine has its own house brand of fillers; the Behlen Company has quite a complete line which as this is written is just getting into national distrubution. Craftsman also has its own brand of paste filler.

Stick shellac and stick wax are both used in repairing minor surface blemishes, such as dents, gouges, and cigarette burns. These are dealt with in detail in Chapter 4.

FASTENERS

Your expendable supplies list might very well include a few pinch dogs and/or corrugated fasteners. These are the repairer's Band-Aids, fast to use, but not necessarily intended for permanency when used alone. Pinch dogs are squared U-shaped fasteners that are driven in at right angles across a crack or joint, and because of the angle at which their twin prongs is formed, tend to pull the edges together. They're commonly used in place of a mend-

ABRASIVES USED IN WOODWORKING

COATING	GRADES*	BACKING	USE
Flint	12–180	Paper	Stripping, preliminary surfacing. Lowest priced paper-backed abrasive, but clogs quickly and has relatively short life. Grades most useful, 40–180.
Garnet	40–220	Paper	In coarse grades, for stripping, shaping, preliminary surfacing. More costly than flint paper, but has longer life, and finer grades produce smoother surface. Finer grades most useful. Cuts very well on end-grain. Use cloth-backed type in power sanders.
Aluminum oxide	60–320	Paper & Cloth	
Silicon carbide	40–600	Paper & Cloth	In coarse grades, for preliminary finishing, shaping. Can be used wet with water or thinners in hand-sanding for longest life, as liquid flushes the grits clean. In grades from 220–320, use wet for smooth surface finish; in grades from 360–600, use for polishing varnish and lacquer between coats. Use cloth-backed type in power sanders.
Emery	20–180	Cloth	In coarse grades, for stripping, preliminary shaping. In fine grades, for cleaning hardware, cross-grain sanding of hardwoods. Not available in grades fine enough for finishing wood surfaces.

			OTHER
Steel wool	3–000000		Avoid grades 2 and 3, they will gouge furrows in wood. Use Grade 1 for paint removal, stripping, especially with liquid removers. Grades 0 and 00 are useful in final paint removal and surface cleanup; grade 00 in preliminary finishing and removal of excess linseed oil or paint remover neutralizers. Grades 3/0 to 6/0 used after final sanding and to polish varnish and lacquer finishes between coats. Grades 5/0 and 6/0 are commonly called "steel fur" and are hard to find; useful for pre-varnish polishing of hardwoods and for between-coats polishing of varnish and lacquer.
Pumice	C, F, FF		Mix with water or thinners to polish wood surfaces after final sanding and between coats to polish varnish and lacquer finishes. Use in spot refinishing to remove finish from small areas.
Rottenstone	F, FF, FFF		Same uses as pumice. Rottenstone in coarsest grade is finer than finest grade of pumice. Use in spot refinishing, between-coat and final polishing of varnish and lacquer finishes.

*Paper and cloth-backed abrasives are graded in two ways, by grits size ranging from 12–600 and by "0" symbols ranging from 4½ to 10/0. The use of numbers or "0" symbols varies between manufacturers, some brands carry both designations of grade. Equivalents are:
Grits #12=4½; #16=4; #20=3½; #24=3; #30=2½; #36=2; #40=1½; #50=1; #60=½; #80=0; #100=00; #120=3/0; #150=4/0; #180=5/0; #220=6/0; #240=7/0; #280=8/0; #320=9/0; #400=10/0.
There are no "0" symbol equivalents for #360, #500 and #600.

ing-plate but should be driven in only after the joint or crack has been pulled tight with clamps. Corrugated fasteners serve the same purpose. These are short corrugated strips of metal with one sharp edge that are driven into the wood across joints or cracks. There is a third type, called "skotch nails," which perform the same function, but don't have the pulling tendencies common to the two just de-scribed. All these come in assorted sizes, and none of them should be used on any surface that will be visible.

You'll need a modest assortment of screws; most of the screws used in furniture repair jobs are flathead wood screws that can be countersunk. Old pieces may have round-head screws left with their heads exposed. Flathead, countersunk screws are usually masked with a button

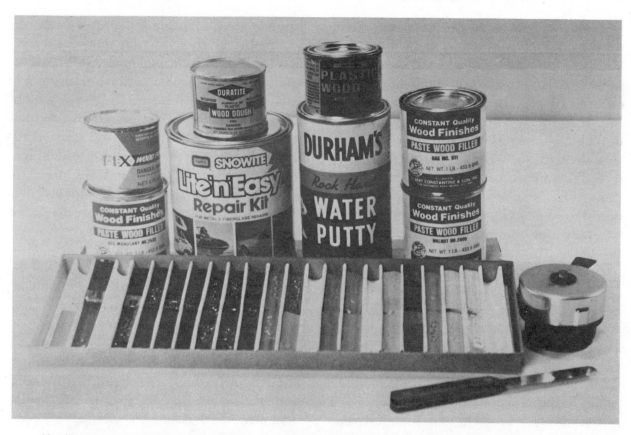

You'll use most of these wood fillers at one time or another if you do a great deal of furniture repair work. The array includes paste, powdered, and stick fillers.

These fasteners can be used to make temporary repairs until you can get around to doing a more lasting job. The most useful are pinch dogs, upper left; corrugated fasteners, lower left; and Skotch nails, lower right. The inner-outer threaded fastener at upper right comes closest to being suitable for permanent repair jobs; it's available from Constantine.

or plug, as mentioned earlier in the section in which dowels were discussed. You'll find the larger diameter and longer screws to be the kind you'll use most often. Nails, as already noted, are useless in furniture repair work. They simply don't have the holding ability to withstand the stresses to which furniture is subjected. Primitive cabinet pieces may have their tops attached with nails, and rabbeted drawer joints are commonly nailed together on borax pieces. Generally, though, nails should be shunned in making repairs.

SURFACE HARDWARE

There's very little point in trying to keep on hand any kinds of surface hardware, because every job you encounter will call for pulls, hinges, latches, and so on of a different type or style. In many cases, where this hardware is one of the standard patterns, missing or broken items can be matched exactly at a hardware or building supply store. Hinges are the easiest bits of surface hardware to match, but whether you're trying to find a replacement for a hinge, pull, or latch, take what's left of the old one—or one that's still intact—along with you when you begin searching. Many times someone in one of the places you visit will recognize the source of the item and know where you can find or order an exact replacement.

Often, you'll need to replace all the hardware on a piece if matching pieces aren't available. Furniture manufacturers bringing out a "line" generally design or have a fabricator of hardware design for them a special style of pulls and hinges for the "line." This style will become the exclusive property of the furniture maker, and he will order only enough sets to fit the number of pieces in his production run. Once the run's completed, the style is discontinued. The manufacturer or hardware fabricator may or may not keep a few sets in reserve for replacements. Pulls that are all-plastic or have plastic insets go fairly quickly, and if the "line" for which they were made is no longer in production, bow to the inevitable and replace all of them. Five to six years is the average life of a furniture "line," so if the piece to which you're fitting new hardware is older than that, replace all the hardware, and save time.

If you're working on a piece that's valuable to you either intrinsically or sentimentally, Period Furniture Hardware Co., whose address you'll find in the appendix, will duplicate both antique and modern metal pulls and hinges, if you can provide an intact piece of the originals. Sometimes diligent scouring of secondhand stores will turn up a piece of furniture with matching hardware.

Often, a mismatched pull that resembles the originals will go virtually unnoticed on a piece such as this antique commode.

To repeat, though, always take an intact piece with you on your search. You might find a duplicate, or a set of near-duplicates, but these may not cover and conceal the areas the old piece covered. When a piece of furniture has been used over a period of years, waxed and polished at intervals, or simply wiped and dusted, an accumulation of dust and polish builds up around the rims of its pulls and other hardware. This is inevitable. The only way to keep it from happening is to go around the rim of each piece of surface-mounted hardware with a toothpick, and not even the most meticulous house-keeper is going to do this. Sometimes, too, a piece will have been varnished without the surface hardware having been removed, and a ridge is left that's impossible to remove.

When you can't find a new piece of hardware that will cover the area hidden by the old, the wood around each piece of the new hardware should be refinished before installation. The method of doing this is given in Chapter 12, but if you can foreseee the problem when buying new hardware, you'll have saved a lot of work.

Of course, next week or next month, you'll find a piece that's the exact duplicate you were looking for, and will kick yourself mentally for having been in such a hurry to put on new hardware. That's just one of the furniture repairer's little hardships that you'll get used to.

Now it's time to get to the jobs themselves. Any items missed or omitted from this chapter are special things that will be covered in detail in the appropriate places.

3
Repairing Solid Wood Surfaces

Most surface repairs to solid wood furniture are cosmetic in nature. They take little time, require a minimum of materials, and can almost always be carried out without disassembling the piece. This applies equally to chairs, sofas, tables, and cabinet pieces like desks and bureaus. Generally the piece won't have to be moved from its regular position in the house.

There aren't any set rules that can be applied to the repairs, because no two jobs are exactly alike. They can be separated into two categories, though: those that are very simple and those that are fairly complex and require a bit of extra time and effort.

In the simple category we can put such problems as the minor scratches, scrapes, and gouges that at one time or another are inflicted on any piece of furniture in everyday use. Edges of tables and desks get chipped, heavy objects with sharp corners fall on tabletops, cigarettes or cigars left unattended on the rim of an ashtray inflict blisters and burns. Glasses containing cold liquids are set down on varnished surfaces and leave white rings. Fingernail polish and remover are splattered or spilled. Curing these problems seldom requires moving the piece to work on it.

In the middle area falls the restoration of more extensive damages, large areas that have gotten alligatored by being too near a stove, or simply by aging of the varnish, or such jobs as replacing the corner broken off a tabletop or bureau. For some reason, the corners of furniture seem to be accident-prone. While these middling difficult jobs can be done with the piece in place, it's usually easier and more satisfactory to move it to your workshop.

Major, or what might be called second- and third-degree repairs, are another matter entirely. These almost always require a certain amount of disassembly, or involve a large area that must be refinished. Or, you might get into jobs that take time because they require fitting a patch and, after the patch has been fitted, allowing the glue sufficient time to dry. I'd class as a major repair a job such as straightening a warped tabletop or bureau top, repairing a wide split, or replacing a broken corner. Certainly fixing an oversized dent would fall into this category, as would regluing edge-glued boards that have separated, or going over a large area that's been alligatored. Any job as big as these belongs in a work area that's out of the way of household traffic.

Nobody's judgment is infallible, of

course. Many times, a job that looks complicated will turn out to be one that can be done in ten minutes with the simplest tools. Usually, if you're not positive that a repair of the instant type will be successful, you can safely experiment with it. All you'll lose is a bit of time, and if the instant repair approach fails, you'll know a lot better exactly what you'll have to do to carry out the job satisfactorily.

Let's look at common surface repair jobs in the order of their frequency and the ease with which they can be handled.

MINOR SURFACE DAMAGE

Very thin gouges in a polished surface are the most common of all jobs and the easiest to fix. The exception is when a pointed metal object has gouged deeply enough and with force enough to tear the wood fibers and splinter them. Mars that only go through the finish, or just a bit below it, can be dealt with at once. Use one of the several kinds of liquid preparations that combine a solvent or an amalgamating agent with a stain that matches the surface being worked on. The solvent softens the finish around the scratch, the stain covers the wood that has been laid bare. A brush stroke or two will do the job.

You can get these surface-mending amalgamator-stainers at most building supply, paint, and housewares stores. There are several brand names. One is Scratch Magic; another, which comes in a tube rather than a bottle, is part of a two-product Fix Kit made by Behlen. If you can't find these locally, you can order similar preparations from Constantine and Craftsman. Shades that match just about any finish are available.

If the scratch has jagged edges, and the finish on the piece is rather thick, it's a good idea to soften the edge lines. Use a tiny strand of #4/0 steel wool on your fingertip and rub along the edges of the scratch to reduce their sharp lines. Wipe the area clean, and flow the mending fluid on evenly. All the preparations of this kind I've seen or used tend to be thick, and will actually fill in a very shallow scratch. Remember that you must work fast with even brush strokes, for these amalgamating-staining liquids set almost instantly. They don't dry for ten or fifteen minutes as a rule, so give the mended area a bit of time before polishing.

Shallow dents and gouges that don't break the fibers of the wood can often be raised by steaming. However, be prepared to refinish a fairly large area around the repair itself when you use this kind of mending technique. Inevitably, the

Rubbed spots as large as the one shown here can almost always be cured with one of the liquids that combines a stain with an amalgamating agent. The latter softens the finish of the area around the stain and allows the two to blend imperceptibly. However, you must be sure that the liquid you're using matches the existing finish. Make a test in an inconspicuous spot by applying a drop or two of the liquid. If it matches the existing finish, then brush the filler on the scratch or rubbed place, allow it to dry for three or four minutes, and polish.

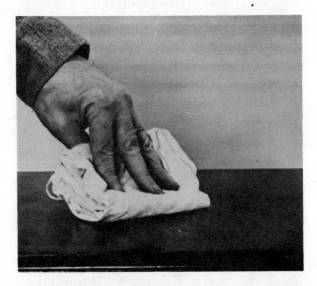

Using solvent alone, or a mixture of solvent and stain that you've blended to match the surrounding finish, wipe the scraped area with a lintless cloth moistened with the blend you've found to be the best match. Work with a light touch from the center of the bared wood, and feather in the fresh stain to the edges. A cloth pad is superior to a brush in this kind of work.

When raising wood grain that has suffered a dent, the finish over the dented area must first be removed. Use very fine abrasive paper such as #400 wet-or-dry silicon-carbide paper used wet, and try to avoid removing any of the finish around the dent. Then, cover the dent with a pad of wet cloth and make repeated passes over the cloth with a hot iron. The treatment may have to be repeated—without further sanding—two or three times before the surface grain comes up to the level surrounding the dent. The raised area can then be refinished to match the rest of the surface.

steaming process is going to whiten the edges of the depression.

Begin by scraping the surface free of varnish or other protective coating. Don't dig into the wood; use a very light touch. Wet several thicknesses of cloth and lay over the dent. Apply heat with a flatiron or a soldering iron with a smoothing tip. Two or three applications of heat, wetting the cloth pad between each one, should do the job. You may raise the area around the depression. If this happens, it must be sanded smooth after the work has been allowed to dry thoroughly. Don't try to sand before the area surrounding the raised portion dries and settles back.

For small, deep dents apply steam with a small piece of cloth, just a bit bigger than a pop-bottle cap will cover. Moisten the pad, which should be only two or three thicknesses of cloth, lay the bottle cap on it, and touch the cap with a hot soldering iron. Again, you may have to repeat the application of heat several times to raise the grain in the dent.

Small dents can often be spot-raised by putting a tiny pad of wet cloth over the dent, and putting a metal bottle cap on the pad. Then, hold a hot soldering iron to the cap. The steam generated by the pad's moisture will work only on the surface it covers. Again, more than one application of heat may be required to raise the wood.

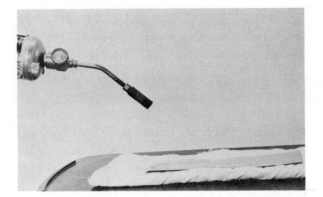

Large, deep dents may call for heroic measures. Take the piece outdoors. After sanding the finish from the area to be raised, cover it with a pad of wet cloth, and put a piece of sheet aluminum over the dented spot. Apply heat with a propane torch to the aluminum. Keep the torch in constant motion, don't concentrate it on one spot. It may take two or three or even more heat applications to bring up the dented area.

Conversely, treat large areas by using a plate of sheet aluminum—a cookie sheet, for example, if you can find one without a Teflon or other nonstick surface. Make a large cloth pad to cover the area of the depression, wet the cloth, put the aluminum sheet on the cloth, and pass a lighted blowtorch—or, better still, the flame of a propane torch—over the area several times. Repeat as needed until the grain is brought up.

EXTENSIVE SURFACE SCRATCHES

I don't recommend instant-repair liquids for covering a large area of scratches. If you're faced with any spot that's ¹/₄ inch or more in width, you'll get a better job if you blend your own cover-up liquid. Usually, there'll have been some damage to the wood itself if a large spot has been scraped. Smooth the scraped area with #4/0 steel wool or, in the case of deep scratches, with #600 aluminum-oxide finishing paper, using an absolute minimum of pressure. Don't use a wood or metal sanding block, but make a pad of cloth or

cotton to back up the paper and stroke gently until the damaged grain has been smoothed. Feather the edges into the old finish.

Your next job is to find out the kind of finish you're working on. There are three major types of wood finish used in furniture-making: varnish, which is the most common; lacquer, running a close second to varnish; and shellac, which is commonly found only on older pieces, but is still used in some of the smaller plants.

To determine the kind of finish you'll be mending, you will need a thimbleful each of denatured alcohol, lacquer thinner, and mineral spirits, usually called thinners. Your exploratory work is based on the fact that denatured alcohol will dissolve only shellac, lacquer thinner will dissolve both shellac and lacquer, mineral spirits will dissolve only varnish. You'll also need some small cotton swabs, or the materials with which to make your own, toothpicks, and a thumb-sized chunk of cotton.

First, wipe clean the surface you're going to be working on; be sure there's no lint or grit on it. Dip a clean swab in denatured alcohol and rub it over a small surface area. If the finish is shellac, it will soften and start to flow. If nothing happens, dip a second swab in lacquer thinner and rub. If the surface flows and almost instantly dries to a fresh film, it's lacquer. There's not much point in making a third test, but do it anyhow to learn the drying speed of the varnish used in the finish. Dab on a bit of mineral spirits with a fresh swab; mineral spirits won't affect shellac or lacquer, but will soften varnish.

Now that you know what kind of surface you're working on, use only the solvent that matches the finish: denatured alcohol for shellac, lacquer thinner for lacquer, mineral spirits for varnish. Fold a piece of cheesecloth into a pad about 2 inches square and saturate it with the correct solvent. Wipe it gently over the marred area in line with the scratches, beginning about ¹/₂ to 1 inch away, to flow a bit of the old finish over the blemish. Use very little pressure, especially at the beginning of the strokes, to avoid a sharp line that will indicate the old finish has been disturbed. You may have to refold the pad and rewet it several times.

Keep stroking until you've flowed enough of the old finish over the mar to blend it in with the area around it. Be careful not to take off too much of the old finish and create a light spot. Don't overdo. As soon as the marred area has been covered, stop. Let the blended area dry overnight. Don't try to speed up the drying with heat or with a fan.

When the patched place is totally dry, flow on a very thin coat of white shellac thinned with denatured alcohol. Use a mix of about half shellac, half alcohol. This will dry at once. If the area you've worked over is lighter in tone than the rest of the piece, make up a new batch of cotton swabs. Add penetrating stain of the correct color to your thinned shellac; add the stain a single drop at a time and test it with a tiny dab on the mended spot. When you've got the new mixture matching the old finish to perfection, take a fresh cotton pad and use it to wipe on a thin coat of the mixture over the light area. Finally, brush on a thin coat of the appropriate finish: shellac, lacquer, or varnish. Feather this clear topcoat into the area around the mend. As a last step, after the surface is dry, wax and polish.

If all this sounds like a lot of work, remind yourself that it beats stripping and refinishing the entire piece of furniture.

DAMAGED WOOD

Deep gouges, chipped spots, small cracks, and other mars that have damaged the wood itself can't be cured just by treating the finish. Nor can burned spots if they're more than finish-deep. You're going to have to fill areas of this kind. There are three ways of doing this, and you're the best judge of the one to use. Thin scratches, such as those made by the skidding claws of the family cat, can usually be fixed with stick wax. Deeper, wider gouges will have to be mended with stick shellac. Very extensive dents or deep creases will probably require the use of a wood paste filler. The size, and especially the depth of the scratch, will have a great deal to do in guiding you to a choice.

Stick wax is very easy to use in mending intermediate-sized gouges, anything up to about ¹/₁₆-inch wide. This is a crayon-type material, combining a wood stain with a wax base into a crayon very much like those children use in school. The difference is that the ordinary school crayon is made in a base of paraffin wax, which is

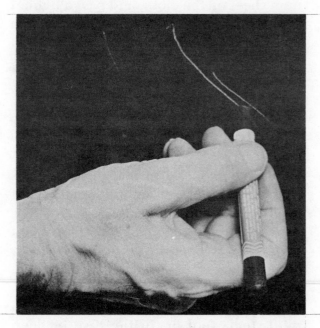

Repairing a scratch with a wax stick requires vigorous rubbing on of the wax so that it will fill the marred area. Rubbing also creates a bit of heat from friction which helps the wax to penetrate the scratched wood. You can heat the wax stick slightly to soften it.

soft and won't take on a good polish, while furniture stick wax is blended in a base of beeswax, which is hard and can be buffed to a high sheen. Wax sticks—or stick wax, it just depends on which is easiest for you to say—come in shades to match virtually all stained finishes and many painted ones. The sticks can also be blended by melting tiny blobs together and stirring.

Repair narrow, shallow scratches or gouges by rubbing the wax stick across the mar and when it's filled, wiping off the excess with a soft cloth. A fairly deep pit can be filled by melting the wax with the tip of a heated spatula or knife, dribbling it into the gouge while soft, and then leveling it with the spatula blade or by rubbing. Remember, this material isn't the best one to use on a wide scratch or gouge. The surface of a wax repair will always be a bit softer than the varnished area around it, and if very wide the mend will eventually

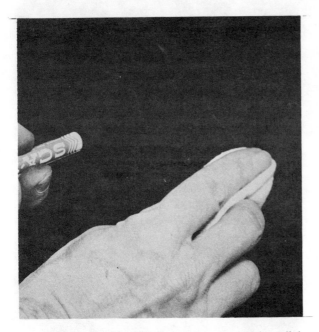

When the scratch has been covered, polish the mended area vigorously with a soft cloth. This will remove the excess wax that has been rubbed on along the path of the scratch and polish the surface of the wax filling the scratch. No other refinishing should be needed. Don't apply varnish or lacquer.

become a shallow valley as the piece is wiped and rubbed while polishing.

For wider, deeper gouges or dents or for spots caused by burns, you'll want to use stick shellac. This material is exactly what it is named, shellac that's been tinted and allowed to harden in stick form. Like stick wax, stick shellac is available in a comprehensive range of wood tones, from clear through very light to very dark, in furniture finish terms from maple or birch to ebony. It can also be blended to produce any exact shade not offered by its makers. Your local lumber or paint dealer may not carry stick shellac in stock, but you can order by mail from Constantine or Craftsman or from other mail-order specialty houses.

Stick shellac is more durable than stick wax. It hardens to a firm, glossy finish that needs no buffing or other attention, and because of its hardness when dry, it can be used to fill larger gouges. On wood surfaces that have a pronounced grain pattern, you can carry the pattern through a stick shellac mend by using the Behlen Graining Tool. This is in effect a hard-felt tipped pen using furniture stain instead of ink.

You must melt stick shellac in a sootless flame to apply it, so don't reach for the candlestick on the mantel, or begin digging into last year's Christmas decorations. If you have a chafing dish, the canned heat or alcohol burner used under it are both ideal. So is the little butane burner called the Ronson Cookette which I discovered years ago to be easier to handle and control than either canned alcohol gel such as Sterno, or an alcohol burner. You can, of course, use a canned alcohol gel right in its can; just sit the can on a slab of wood or other insulating material.

Working with stick shellac requires a certain amount of speed, for it sets up al-

HOW TO USE STICK SHELLAC

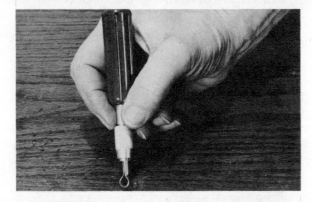

In making a mend with stick shellac, first thoroughly clean the area where the shellac is to be applied. A good tool for the purpose is the X-Acto hand router shown here.

Another tool you might use for cleaning out a deep mar is the blade of an X-Acto knife. Choose the blade size and shape that conforms best to the contour of the marred spot.

A third option, the Dremel MotoTool, will do a very fast and efficient job of clearing a charred spot to expose fresh wood. Use the tool's burr with a light touch to avoid unnecessarily deepening or enlarging the flaw.

Heat both the spatula you will use and one end of the shellac stick in a sootless flame. An alcohol lamp or butane chafing-dish heater such as the one shown are equally efficient. Don't use a candle, match, or any other flame source derived from oil or wax.

Stick shellac sets very quickly. When the spatula and stick are both heated, move both to the mar and scrape enough of the shellac off the stick to fill the blemished spot.

On surfaces that have a pronounced grain, use Behlen's graining pencil on top of the shellac after its final polish to blend the mend in with its surroundings.

most instantly. The job of making a stick shellac mend is pictured from the beginning, which is cleaning the crack or burn to solid wood. For this, the tiny gouges made by X-Acto, or even the narrow blade of an X-Acto knife, are ideal. If you want to motorize the work, use the Dremel Moto-Tool, which can get into small crevices with its little cutters. Be sure the area to be filled is completely free of sawdust or chaff. To get a lasting mend, you may have to deepen a shallow dent, for stick shellac should be at least $1/32$-inch thick in order to hold well.

If you do a good job of cleaning, you'll never have to worry about a stick shellac mend giving way. I've used it to fill minor flaws in gunstocks and have never had a mend jarred loose by repeated firing of the weapon.

After the surface of the gouged area is cleaned, and deepened if necessary, heat the tip of the spatula. Not red-hot. It should be too hot to touch, but certainly not glowing red. Then pass the tip of the shellac stick through your sootless flame. Scrape off a bit of the melted shellac with the spatula and without losing an instant, apply it to the gouge. A little shellac fills a lot of dent. If you've under-filled, take off more shellac and press it on top of what's already in the gouged area. It will bond if it's the right temperature. Continue adding until the gouge is full.

Don't worry if you've over-filled. Heat the spatula and scrape its edge along the mend to form a smooth, unbroken surface. No sealing with a varnish coat should be needed, but go ahead and put one on, if it makes you feel more secure. The practical area limit of a stick shellac mend of this kind is about $1/2$ to $5/8$ inch, but you can make the repair more unobtrusive by using the graining device already mentioned to carry the grain pattern through the surface of the repair.

To blend stick shellac, use an old spoon or a piece of clean, thin tin or aluminum bent to form a small depression in its center. Mix two pea-sized bits of dark and light shellac while they're hot and liquid. The reason for beginning with equal parts is that you can readily tell whether your mixture is too light or too dark, and add rice-grain sized bits of the required color until you reach perfection. Remember, in order to judge the precise shade of your blend, the shellac must be allowed to harden.

Dents and gouges in a solid wood piece that are too big for either stick wax or stick shellac repairs can be filled with a wood paste. There are many of these preparations on the market; the best-known is sold under the trade name of Plastic Wood, and you'll find it in most lumberyards and paint stores. Others are mentioned in an earlier chapter. Like a lot of materials used by craftsmen, the brand you select is the one you find easiest to use. Just be sure, if you're using one of the types of filler that's impervious to stain, to select one factory-tinted to the correct shade. Most of the neutral-colored fillers or pastes can be stained. So can Durham's Wood Putty, which is mixed with water, and is excellent for filling very tiny flaws. You use these like putty, but I prefer a flexible spatula rather than a putty knife in applying them. X-Acto makes very narrow sanding blocks that are ideal for smoothing the surface of mends made with wood pastes. After the paste sets hard, stain and varnish it to match the surrounding area.

PATCHING WITH VENEER

In drastic cases you might find it necessary to restore a marred surface by inserting a patch made from veneer or from the same wood of which the piece of furniture

Wood putty, or paste, is the preferred material with which to fill deep scratches or cracks. Be sure that you choose a putty which will accept wood stain. Not all of them do. Spread the putty with a flexible spatula along the crack until it is level with the wood, and wipe away any excess with a moist cloth.

When the wood putty has set, touch up the filled line with a stain that matches the finish around it. The Behlen graining pencil will allow you to carry the grain lines across the filled area to make the patch almost invisible.

is made. You can make the "grave," which is what professional cabinetmakers call the shallow area into which the plug is inserted, by using hand tools, but it's much easier to do if you have a router. For very small patches, the Dremel MotoTool used with its router accessory is ideal.

Cut the grave in an irregular shape, a diamond or a triangle, or a rectangle with serrated ends. The bottom, needless to say, must be very smooth, and the depth of the grave should be just a hairbreadth shallower than the thickness of the veneer you plan to use as your patch.

When the grave has been cut, lay a piece of carbon paper on it, surface up, and a sheet of white paper over the carbon. Rub the edges of the grave with your fingertip to transfer the outline of the grave to the paper, and cut a pattern to guide you in making the patch. A veneer saw or razor saw will cut the patch; it

should be just a tiny smidgen oversized. Sand the edges until they fit the grave without a crack showing around the sides of the join. Glue the patch in place and weight it with books or magazines or a brick until the glue sets up. Then, sand the area to bring the patch down to the level of the rest of the top. For refinishing methods, see Chapter 12.

EDGE REPAIRS

So far, we've dealt only with flat surfaces. But, as already noted, edges and corners of furniture take the greatest beating of any part of a piece. You can usually repair an edge with one of the surface techniques already covered, but unless the dent is very small, no more than a surface scratch, use stick shellac rather than stick wax. Large dents can be filled with wood paste, but in such critical, wear-prone areas as

PATCHING WITH VENEER

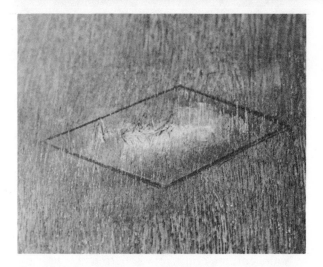

1   Serious surface damage like this deep gouge can be cured only one way—with a plug of veneer of the same wood. If the veneer has a grain that roughly approaches that of the marred piece, count it as a bonus.

3   Mark the section that the plug will fill. Avoid a square shape if possible. Cut out a diamond or triangle, and the mend will be much less likely to draw attention. Route the outline of the area marked. The Dremel MotoTool is ideal for such small jobs; guide its routing fence with a straightedge.

2   Match the grain of a section of the veneer as closely as possible to the spot it will be filling, then sand the veneer and make it ready for finishing. Set the bit of the router to the exact depth of cut that will match the width of the sanded veneer. Do this by making trial cuts on a scrap of waste lumber and fitting an edge of the veneer into the cut until your fingers tell you the depth is correct.

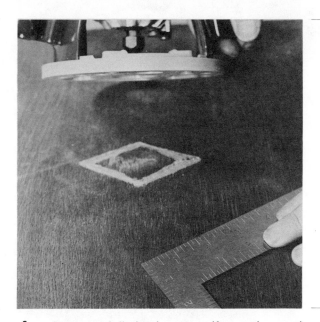

4   Guide a full-sized router, if one is used, with a straightedge against which its base-plate can run. After the outline of the mend has been established, clean out the center of the area to be plugged, called the "grave."

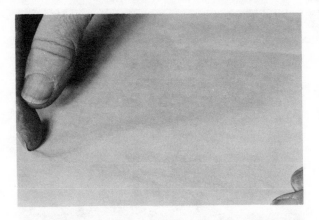

5   Put a piece of carbon paper, carbon side up, over the routed area. Place a sheet of white paper on the carbon and trace the outline of the grave with a fingernail, to give you the shape the patch must be cut.

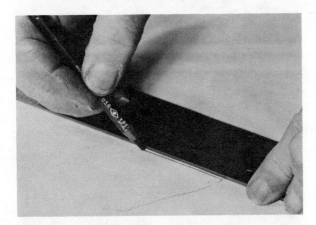

6   Transfer the pattern from paper to the spot you've chosen for the plug on the veneer. Use a straightedge to insure that you're getting straight lines.

7   With a veneer saw or razor saw, cut the plug from the veneer. Again, guide the saw with a straightedge, and cut the plug just a hairsbreadth bigger than the outline.

8   Clean the corners of the grave. Veneer saws don't make nice, sharp-angled corners. Use a razor saw, then a riffler. Lacking either riffler or razor saw, use a fresh blade in an X-Acto knife and work very carefully to get the corners of the grave sharp and true.

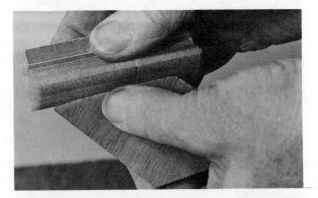

9   Sand the edges of the patch until it fits exactly into the grave.

10   When the edges of the patch fit properly, stain the patch and glue it in place. Weight it with books or a stack of magazines until the glue sets, but put a sheet of waxed paper between the patch and the weights to keep any oozing glue from bonding the weight to the surface of the table.

edges and corners, a paste mend should be reinforced.

There are two ways of doing this. One is to drill a few tiny holes around the bottom of the dent and force the paste into these holes. When it sets up, the holes will help to anchor the filler in place and keep it from popping out. It'll help if you drill the holes at odd angles. The second way to reinforce an edge repair when using paste filler is to insert two or three short lengths of smaller-diameter dowel into holes drilled in the bottom of the dent. The dowels should be cut short enough so they won't protrude above the surface of the paste filler after it's dry and has been sanded into shape. Either type of reinforcement will give you a much more permanent repair.

When mending an edge, you can improve the durability of wood putty in two ways. The first is simply to drill a couple of small holes into the bottom of the dent and force the filler into them with a putty knife or spatula. The putty in the holes will anchor the rest.

For a large edge repair, drill holes large enough to accept small dowels or cocktail picks. Smear the dowels with glue, tap them into the holes, and cut them off below the surface of the wood.

With putty knife or spatula, fill the dent, pressing the wood putty to the dowels firmly. Overfill just a bit, and when the putty dries, sand the mend to contour. The sanding will level off the tips of the dowels, if you failed to cut them short enough. Follow either mend by refinishing with stain and varnish.

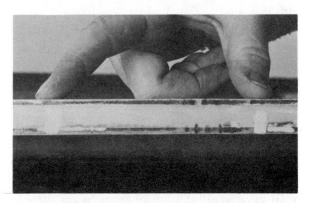

Even before staining, these mends are inconspicuous. When stained, they should disappear completely.

REPLACING A CHIPPED CORNER

1 Start the replacement of a chipped-off corner by sawing at an oblique angle to the chip to remove all broken wood.

2 Carry the slanting cut to the end of the chipped spot, where you can make a right-angled cut to remove all the broken wood.

SMASHED CORNERS

Corners and edges are perennial problems on furniture that is moved often, or is located in traffic lanes where hard objects bump its corners with any frequency. Stick shellac and wood paste repair jobs don't hold well on corners; they tend to crumble when bumped. The most satisfactory way to curve a smashed or chipped corner is to perform a wood transplant. I mean that quite literally, because often the only way to get a scrap of wood matching the kind from which the piece is made is to take it off the inside of a skirt, or from a glue block. Some furniture makers still follow the old custom of using scrap pieces of the same wood used in a piece to make glue blocks for it.

Most corner-chipping is along the grain of the wood, which makes a transplant easy. Trim out the chipped area with a razor saw to give you a flat surface to which the patch can be glued. The picture will give you an idea of how to do this. If possible, cut the transplant a bit over-sized. Glue the patch in place, and hold it

with a clamp; you may have to use a web clamp or windlass (see Chapter 6 for details of these) to get pressure at the right point.

Reinforce the transplant with a dowel or two made from the midsection of a cocktail pick; these picks make excellent small-diameter dowels for this kind of repair job. The final step is filing and sanding the transplant to match the contour of the corner, and then staining and finishing it so it becomes invisible.

You'll find a lot of furniture repair jobs that have a sort of kissing cousin relationship to those detailed in this chapter. That's really what makes furniture repair work easy—so many times the same methods are used when carrying out different kinds of jobs on different pieces. You might find it necessary to vary the basic procedure a little bit when going from one repair job to the next, but you'll find the same tools and techniques usable in an amazing variety of applications. Furniture repair work is like any other acquired skill: the more of it you do, the easier and simpler all of it becomes.

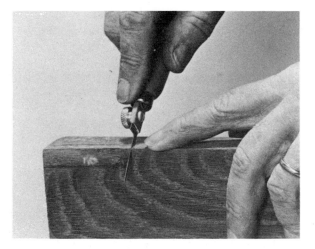

3 From wood that matches the grain of the furniture, cut a piece slightly larger than the one you removed.

4 With a file, true up the surface of the wood so the new piece will fit.

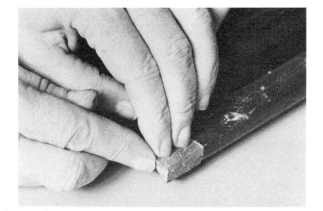

5 Fit the new wood into the gap left by removing the chip. Glue the replacement piece in place, hold with a web clamp.

6 When the glue has set, drill through the replacement piece for dowels.

7 Cut a cocktail pick in half to make small dowels and glue them in place.

8 When the glue holding the dowels has set, saw the protruding ends off flush.

9 File the new wood to match the contour of the intact corners, and sand smooth (*continued*).

10 Your job should look like this when the filing and sanding are completed; an absolute merger of the old wood and new.

11 Final step is staining the new wood to match the old.

4
Repairing Veneered and Laminated Surfaces

More of today's furniture is made with veneered surfaces than with tops of solid wood. A substantial number of modern pieces also have veneered side and drawer facings. The veneer might be wood or a sheet of laminate such as the formaldehyde/urea or polyester types of rigid material. Very low-cost pieces might even be finished with what can best be classified as an "almost-veneer" made of a paper-thin plastic sheet imprinted with a woodgrain pattern on one side and coated with adhesive on the other. On better-grade pieces, the material below the veneer will be either solid wood or the conventional multiple cores of plywood. On low-end furniture, the substance under the veneer may well be particleboard

In this chapter we'll take a look at the techniques involved in repairing all these kinds of veneered surfaces, including the major job of applying an entirely new surface to a veneered piece that's been so badly damaged that spot repairs aren't possible. The technique here is the same as covering an extensively damaged solid wood surface with veneer as an alternative to junking what is otherwise a useful piece of furniture.

WOOD VENEERS

Let's begin with wood veneers, which are in almost all respects a bit easier to work with than laminates. And, before going into working techniques, it might be helpful if we examine wood veneers, how they're made and what their capabilities are.

Veneer is usually the term applied to the outer surfaces or face of common woods, including the cores of plywoods. The veneer is made either by sawing thin strips of wood with the grain of a tree trunk, or by revolving a tree trunk in a giant lathe while a razor-sharp knife peels off a thin layer of wood. Sawn veneers may be sliced or flat-cut, that is, one sheet after another cut the full length of the log to produce strips that vary in width from the outer diameter to the center and then to the opposite side's outer diameter. Or, the veneer may be quarter-sawed, cut at right angles to the growth rings; or rift-sawn, cut at about a 35° angle to the growth rings. The manner in which the tree trunk was cut produces different grain patterns in the veneer, so in patching or replacing it's important to be able to recognize the manner in which the veneer was cut so that you can get pieces cut in the same way to match the grain pattern.

After having been rough-cut from the tree trunks, the veneer strips are sanded to one of several standard thicknesses: $1/20$, $1/28$, $1/42$ or $1/49$ inch. Here again, it's important to know the thickness of the veneer you're going to patch, so that you can match it with the patching veneer you buy. After sanding, most veneer strips are cut into 8-foot lengths; their width will vary from about 6 to 12 inches or more, depending on the arc of the tree trunk at the point they were cut.

A good rule of thumb in ordering veneer for a patching job is to specify the thickest, $1/20$ inch. You'll find that on older pieces of furniture the veneer will be thicker than on modern pieces. The technology involved in cutting veneers thinner than $1/28$ inch is relatively new. It's very difficult to gauge the thickness of veneer already in place around an area to be patched unless you have a micrometer depth-gauge. However, it's a very easy job to sand a few square inches of $1/20$-inch veneer down to $1/28$ inch or even to $1/49$ inch; the job requires only a moment or two. And by sanding the veneer down yourself you can

Veneer can be bought in several forms. Long strips or sheets (foreground) are priced by the square inch or square foot, depending on the rarity of the wood in the veneer. Squared veneer is sold by the piece or by the bundle of ten or twelve pieces. It can be all one kind of wood, or assorted. The newest veneer is an ultrathin type, edge-glued and laminated to a backing that will accept glue. This veneer can be worked with a skill knife or scissors, but a razor saw will do a better job. Priced by the roll, it's available in 8-foot rolls either 18, 24 or 36 inches wide. Roll veneer isn't well-suited to repairs; it's designed to reveneer an entire piece.

get a very precise matching thickness.

Your chief interest is in the hardwood veneers that are used to finish furniture. There are dozens of different kinds of these veneers; the Constantine catalog lists more than a hundred, as does that of Craftsman Wood Supply. It's a pretty good bet that no matter what kind of veneer you're trying to match in a piece of furniture you're repairing, you can find what you're looking for from one of these two supply sources. Hardwood veneers are priced by the square foot, so you can order as much or as little as you need for any job at hand.

LOOSE VENEER

Wood veneered surfaces can be damaged in innumerable ways, but the most often needed repair is to the edges of tops and the corners of drawers and cabinet doors. Often this repair is quite simple, merely a matter of lifting a loose veneer edge, scraping away the old glue from the underside of the veneer and from the surface to which it was bonded. The loosened area can then be reglued, and will be as good as new.

Here are a few hints which will make the cleaning-away job easier: If the piece of furniture you're working on is of recent origin, the veneer will have been applied with contact cement; if it was made before about 1940, the application of veneer to underlay will have been made with one of the old hide or fish-flake adhesives. In terms of the art of surface laminating, contact cement is of fairly recent origin. It's much less susceptible to failure caused by heat, humidity, or other natural forces than were the pre-World War II adhesives, most of which were natural rather than synthetic-based formulations.

If the glue you scrape away feels rubbery, is white or light amber, and stringy in texture, it will be contact cement. If the scraping residues are flaky, grainy, or appear to be nothing more than a dark-colored dust, you're dealing with a hide or fish-flake glue. Both can be dissolved by using a cotton swab soaked in the correct solvent to soften the glue residue, and then by scraping away the film that will be left on both veneer and underlay after swabbing. The best tool I've found for scraping in the kind of tight spots that are encountered in cleaning surfaces of this kind is a #4 or a #9RX X-Acto stencil knife. The blades of both these are sturdy, the handles quite thin. You can get into the tiniest crevices with the tips of these blades.

For softening old glues, use a 28% acetic acid solution diluted with equal parts of water. You can use plain household vinegar, but this is about a 4% acetic acid mixture, and takes a long time to work. Photo supply stores have both 28% acetic acid and glacial acetic acid; if you can get only the latter kind, make your own 28% solution by adding three parts of glacial acetic acid to eight parts of water. Always add the acid to the water; glacial acetic acid is very tough stuff, and a splash of it on skin will burn. You should also avoid inhaling the fumes of either glacial or 28% acetic acid; mix or dilute it in a well-ventilated room, or outdoors. Most natural-based wood working glues and some of the more modern ones can be softened with this solution.

Contact cement can be softened for removal with a chlorethane solvent. Chemical supply houses, paint stores, and some lumberyards stock this material. Use it full-strength, working with a cotton swab on a small area at a time, and scraping away the gummy residue that the solvent will form. It, too, should be used only in a well-ventilated room, or outside.

After the old adhesive has been re-

REGLUING EDGE VENEER

1   To reglue an edge of veneer that has popped loose on a table, desk, or bureau top, slip a putty knife or spatula into the crack between veneer and underlay, and explore with its edge until you've determined how far back the veneer has loosened. Use a second spatula or putty knife to scrape off old glue from both underlay and the back of the veneer.

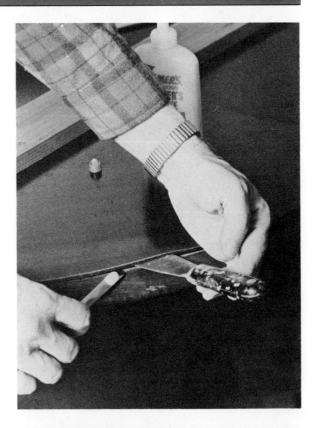

2   Force glue between veneer and underlay and spread it with the blade of the putty knife; press the surfaces together and wipe away all the excess glue that oozes out.

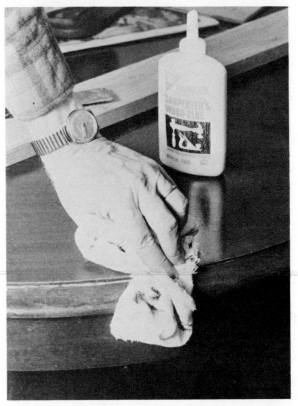

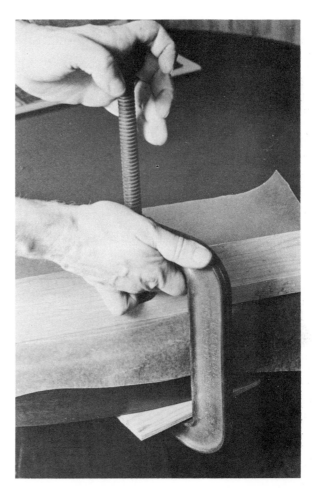

3 Put a sheet of waxed paper or plastic film over the glued area, use a board to spread the pressure of the clamp you tighten over the mend, and let the glue set for a moment. Remove the clamp, wipe the surface free once more, reset the clamp and leave it until the glue dries.

moved, apply fresh glue with a thin strip of veneer or a strip of metal, and clamp the mended area until the glue sets. You'll find one of the aliphatic resin glues the most satisfactory for mends of this type, regardless of the type of glue originally used in veneering the piece. These glues wipe clean easily, and set up quickly. They are also non-staining.

When the glue has dried, you can do any retouching or refinishing necessary to blend areas of cracked varnish with the original surface. The methods of doing this were covered in Chapter 3.

REPLACING VENEER

Replacing a piece of veneer that's been chipped away and lost is another repair commonly required on veneered surfaces.

Do this by squaring off the chipped area with an X-Acto razor saw or a veneer saw, guiding it with a metal straightedge. Or, you can use a Dremel MotoTool for this job. Either method gives you a clean line to which the patch you'll install can be fitted precisely.

No matter how simple the shape of the area to be patched may look, make a pattern before cutting a new piece of veneer to fill the void. Stretch a piece of paper over the void and hold it in place with masking tape. Run a fingertip along the edges of the void where the patch will fit, using enough pressure to crease the paper. Take off the paper and cut the creased lines to make your pattern. The pattern you've made this way will be just a bit oversized, which is exactly what you want it to be.

Now, take the sheet of veneer from which your patch will be cut and work it over the void until you've matched the graining of the veneer as closely as possible to that of the area around the void. This, of course, will make the patch almost invisible. Transfer the pattern to the veneer and cut the piece with a razor saw or veneer saw, then file or sand it to an exact fit.

Your next step will be to find a stain that matches the shade of the one used on the piece of furniture you're fixing. Experiment on scraps of the new veneer until you've gotten a match. Remember, the stain must be dry for you to tell the exact shade it will be. Constantine's powdered stains make matching very easy, because you can add a pinch or so to the stain you've got mixed in order to change its tone just a little bit. Sand and stain the patch before gluing it in place. When the glue's set up, varnish the patch to match the surrounding surface.

This is the basic technique you'll use when inserting a patch in the middle of a veneered piece. The difference is that you'll be working on an enclosed spot, which is going to make things a bit difficult when you begin truing up inside corners. This is one of the jobs for which riffling files were invented, and you'll find one very useful. You can buy these rifflers from several mail-order suppliers, but the only one I know of that doesn't sell them in sets of five or six files is Herter's. One riffler's really all you need for handling even the most complicated, narrowest corners.

Make the pattern for your patch as described a paragraph or two earlier, and fit it into place by filing or sanding its edges until you get a perfect fit. Then, surface-sand, stain, glue, weight, and varnish as already described to complete the job.

A hint or two is in order here. When you're patching a spot away from an edge on the surface of a piece of furniture, cut the grave for the patch in an irregular shape, such as a diamond with the points along the line of the grain, or a serrated edge that looks like a finger joint. This will camouflage the patch and make it almost invisible. If you have a problem matching a pronounced graining pattern on the old veneer around the patch, simply use the graining tool described in the preceding chapter to carry this pattern across the patch. In time, you'll have to look twice yourself to discover where the patch is located.

What you've just completed when you insert a patch such as the one described is really inlaying. It's essentially the same process used in patching a solid wood top as described earlier. However, when you're working on a veneered surface, the grave should be cut no deeper than the thickness of the layer of veneer being patched. Although only a tiny amount of warping can be expected, any patch or inlay should be glued to the same underlay as the veneer around it.

Inlaying is a very ancient craft; it dates back to the days of the Pharaohs of Egypt and the civilization that began in the cradle of history, the Mediterranean countries. Much of the finest furniture which has survived from as far back as 3000 B.C., and much fine furniture today, features inlaid decorative strips or designs, made up of tiny pieces of such exotic woods as ebony, satinwood, holly, or rosewood. In the days when individual artisans made a piece of furniture from start to finish, these strips were cut and fitted a piece at a time; today, you can buy inlay strips ready-made, in widths from $1/16$ inch to $1\frac{1}{4}$ inches, in 3-foot lengths, and in dozens of different designs.

If you encounter a job of restoring a decorative inlay, you can either repair it a

REPLACING VENEER

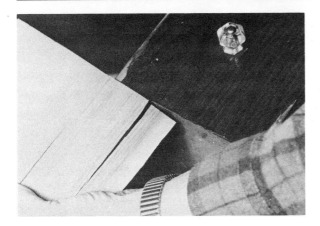

1 Begin the job of replacing a piece of veneer chipped completely off by finding a new piece of veneer that will match as closely as possible the graining of the rest of the surface.

2 Rough-cut an oversized piece of the veneer you've chosen to replace the missing section.

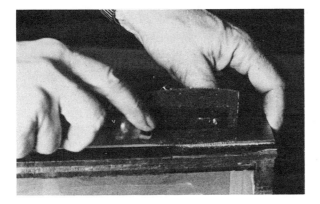

3 Square off the edges of the bare spot, using a veneer saw or razor saw. The shape of the area to be mended doesn't matter as long as it's easily duplicated and the edges are straight and clean.

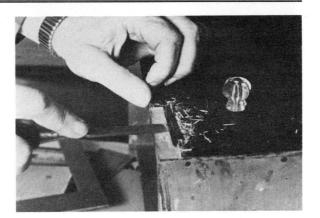

4 With a chisel, remove the veneer remaining in the area to be recovered.

5 True the edges of the veneer left on the piece with a fine-cutting file—X-Acto's minifiles are ideal for this job. If you have a riffling file, use it to get clean-cut corners. At the same time, smooth off the underlay with the file.

6 Butt the new veneer into the patch and edge-sand to match the lines where old and new veneer meet. Then mark the new veneer as shown and cut it just a hairsbreadth oversize.
(continued)

7   Apply glue to the underlay, insert the patch and press it down, and wipe off excess glue.

9   When the glue has set up, edge-trim with a razor saw and smooth with a mini-plane.

8   Use a piece of scrap lumber for a pad, and protect the pad from absorbing any oozed-out glue with a piece of waxed paper between pad and work, then clamp the mended spot.

10   Sand the surface of the patch to bring it level with the surrounding area. Then refinish with stain and varnish.

piece at a time, or remove the entire line of inlay and replace it. Sources of supply are listed in the appendix, and installation of a complete inlay is actually much easier and faster than trying to piece in bits of wood a splinter wide and two splinters long. Simply remove the old strip with a chisel or router and glue the new one in place.

BUBBLES

Wood-veneered surfaces will sometimes bulge up in a bubble because of glue failure. This may be caused by age, heat, or moisture. If the bulge is a small one, you may be able to cure it by cutting through the center of the bulge with a very sharp blade in a skill knife. Cut with the grain,

FLATTENING A BUBBLE

1 Cut across the center of the bubble with the wood grain, then make a second cut at right angles across the grain.

2 With a fine X-Acto knife blade, shave a tiny sliver off one half of the cut, with the grain. Then press the half-bubble flat to see if you took enough off. If you didn't, shave a smidgen off the opposite side and test again.

3 When the spot that bubbled up can be pressed completely flat, squirt glue under the flap and press the edges together. Wipe up any glue that oozes out.

4 Spread a sheet of waxed paper over the glued spot and allow to dry under a heavy weight. Then refinish as required. If a crack is visible, fill it with stick shellac.

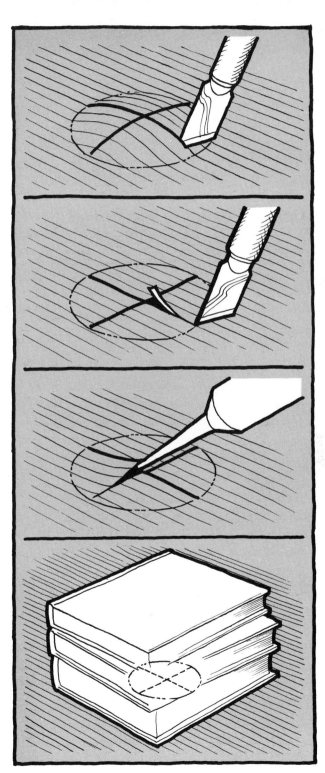

from the point where the bulge begins to the opposite side. When you finish the cut, press down on the center of the bulge with a fingertip and look at the edges of the slit you've made. Rarely will they fit snugly together. Usually, the veneer has swelled. At some point along the cut-line, the veneer will overlap and buckle. This is the spot at which you begin to work.

Raise the edges gently and scrape them delicately, working first on one edge, then on the other. Work from the center of the bulge toward the sides. Don't try to cut, just scrape the veneer with the edge of the skill knife held at right angles to the veneer. After each two or three passes, press down on the center of the bulged area to see if you've removed enough wood to let the edges of the veneer butt together smoothly.

This is a job that can't be hurried. Keep shaving off that infinitesmally small amount of wood from each edge alternately until the veneer finally meets evenly and lies as flat as it did when the piece of furniture was new. When this goal has been achieved, lift the slit edges and carefully scrape away the old glue from beneath it and, if possible, from the back of the veneer. A little mini-keyhole saw blade is the best tool I've found for this. Use the smooth side of the blade rather than the toothed side.

With a strip of cardboard, smear fresh glue under the bulged area. Press the veneer into place and weight it until the glue has set. Wipe the surface of the mend before putting on the weight, to remove any excess glue, and then protect the surface with a piece of waxed paper so the weight won't stick to the tiny thread of glue that will ooze out when the weight is put down. If you've worked carefully, no refinishing should be necessary. If you've taken off too much veneer in your scraping, use stick shellac or stick wax to fill whatever hairline crack shows. If further refinishing is needed, consult Chapter 12.

REPLACING A VENEERED TOP

Inevitably, there are going to be times when you'll encounter a piece of furniture on which a veneered top has been damaged beyond any hope of repair. The piece may be one that you own, or it may be an otherwise good piece that you can buy very reasonably and that you'd like to own. The job of replacing an entire veneered top on a table, bureau, or dresser isn't very difficult; in some ways it's easier to replace an entire top than it is to patch.

Begin by removing the old veneer. This is usually a chisel job, though sometimes in a piece that's suffered from glue breakdown, the old veneer can quite literally be lifted or peeled off by hand. If a chisel's going to be used, select the widest one you have and use it with the bevel on the bottom. Apply as little force as possible; tap very lightly when you must use a hammer or mallet. Try to keep the underlay smooth, for this will save surface preparation later on.

You'll very probably wind up with some strips of glue and perhaps a few splinters of old veneer left on the underlay. Spot-sand these off, then sand the entire top smooth. Fill any dents with wood paste or water putty, and sand them to match the smoothness of the surface. Start with a coarse grits, about #70 or #80, to remove old glue and splinters and to level off any filling you've done. Then go to a finishing paper, perhaps a #100 or #120, for the final smoothing.

Don't skimp on the sanding, if you expect a good veneering job. A smooth, completely flat surface is the key to a good-looking finish, as well as to easy application. This is especially true if you're using one of the new flexible veneers. These are only $1/64$ inch thick instead of the minimum conventional veneer thickness of $1/49$, and even a grain of dust on the surface over which they're applied will look like a billiard ball in the finished job.

These ultra-thin veneers are very easy to use, though. They lie flat much more readily than do most sheet veneers, which have a tendency to ripple across the grain, and after being finished with a coat or two of good varnish, their surface is very mar-resistant. These thin veneers can be cut with scissors, though I don't recommend this. You're better off using a razor saw or a skill knife with a fresh blade. Whichever you choose, guide your cut with a metal straightedge.

After sanding, wipe the surface to which the veneer will be applied with a cloth moistened in thinners, or with a tack cloth. (See Chaper 12, if you don't know what a tack cloth is.) This will remove all vestiges of sanding dust and consequently will improve adhesion. Then you're ready to fit the veneer to the surface. If the top you're working on is too wide to be covered with a single course of veneer, a seam must be planned. The easiest place to put it is in the center, and for the join to look best, the graining of the two veneer pieces should be fairly closely matched.

After you've matched the graining, cut each piece about 1 inch longer than the top they'll go on. Allow a $1/2$ inch overlap for the seam, and another 1 inch on each side. Rough-cut the veneer pieces and lay them on the surface to which they're being fitted, with their graining matched. When they're placed to your satisfaction, hold them with strips of masking tape while you make a few reference marks in the pieces of veneer to guide you in cutting the seam and in joining the pieces on the surface before gluing them.

First, determine exactly where the seam will be in relation to the overlapped areas of the veneer pieces. Then, with a wood block for backing, cut vees in the edges of the veneer pieces, with the point of the vees exactly at the seam line. Now, lift the veneer pieces to a length of scrap lumber that you don't mind scoring with a knife cut or a razor-saw groove. Tape one piece of the veneer to this board so that the center of the vee is along the centerline of the board. Line up the second piece of veneer with the vees matched, on top of the first piece, and hold it in place with short strips of masking tape.

Using a metal straightedge to guide your skill knife or razor saw, cut from the point of one vee to the point of the other. This will give you a perfectly matched center seam. Place the two pieces of veneer on the surface they're to cover and check to be sure you've cut and measured correctly. When in place, the points of the half-vees left on each piece of veneer should meet. Don't trim any overhanging edges of veneer just yet, though.

Check the instructions on the label of the contact cement you intend to use. There are now two types of contact cements: one has a latex base, the other an elastomer base. There are also differences in the latex-based contact cements; some are natural latex, some are acrylic latex, some are neoprene latex. Each has slightly different drying times before bonding is most effective, so be sure you find out whether the contact cement you're using is the natural latex-based type that dries in five or ten minutes, the neoprene latex-based, which dries for bonding in fifteen minutes, or the acrylic latex-based which dries within twenty to thirty minutes. The acrylic latex type, incidentally, can be allowed to stand for as long as two hours without losing its bonding ability.

Follow the label instructions in spread-

VENEERING A NEW TOP

1 First step in veneering a new top is to cut the underlay. Trace the outline on ³/₄-inch plywood and cut it out with a saber saw.

2 After checking the new underlay for fit, trace its outline on a sheet of veneer, and apply masking tape on *both* sides of the veneer, over the saw line. This will minimize splitting or splintering of the veneer.

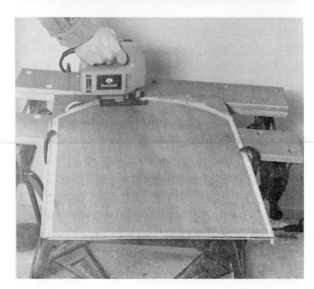

3 One of the tricks to cutting veneer with a saber saw is to use a metal-cutting blade, which has finer teeth than any of the blades normally used in sawing wood. If the saber saw is a variable-speed model, sawing at the highest speed will also hold down chipping and splintering. Cut on the outside of the mark so the veneer will be slightly oversize.

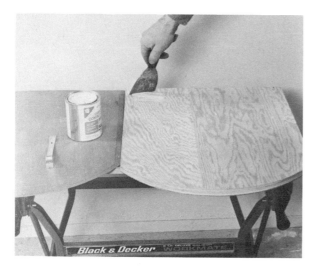

4 When you have checked the veneer and base to be sure they match, and that the veneer is larger by about $\frac{1}{16}$ inch than the base, apply contact cement to both base and veneer.

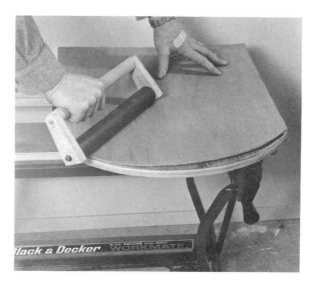

6 After checking alignment again, roll the veneer with moderate pressure, to drive out any air bubbles that might be lurking between it and the base. Then, use heavy pressure for final bonding.

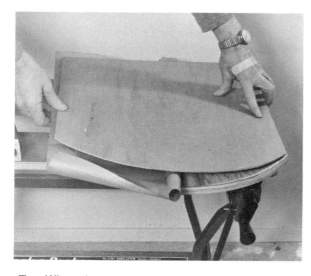

5 When the contact cement is dry, check the instructions on the can for recommended setting-up times before joining. Spread a piece of brown wrapping paper on the base and align the veneer with it. Then, unroll one edge of the paper and push the veneer and base into contact. Use no pressure at this point. The edge contact will keep the two pieces aligned while the brown paper is removed.

7 To remove the overhanging veneer on a curved surface, Stanley's Surform tool called the Shaver is an excellent choice. Then edge-sand and stain.

ing the contact cement on the work, but remember when you come to join the veneer to its underlay that contact cement bonds on contact, and you have no way to make adjustments in the position of the veneer pieces once the glue-spread sur-

faces join. The way to overcome this little problem is to lay a piece of brown wrapping paper on the glue-spread surface of the top, and position the veneer pieces on the paper. Leave one piece of the veneer on the paper and mark along the seam on

When matching the grain of two pieces of veneer being butted together, cut vees at each end of the line on which you plan to saw.

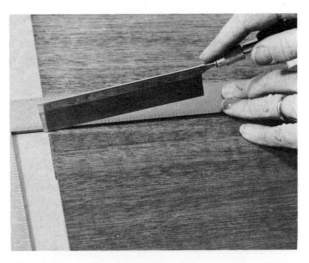

When cutting, match the vees together. If you use a power saw, be sure to put masking tape on both sides along the saw line.

the paper. Fold the paper back under the veneer and press the veneer to the top as you slowly pull the paper out. Smooth the veneer toward the edges as you work.

When the brown paper is free from the work, lay one edge of it along the seam of the attached veneer piece and position the second piece so the seams butt snugly together, then repeat the process of folding the paper under the veneer and pressing it into place, smoothing as you go. Now, get a roller of some kind—a household rolling pin will do as good a job as any other, and in the photos you'll see a veneer roller that I made in about five minutes from an old typewriter platen. Roll the surface with good pressure to insure a firm bond. Finally, turn the piece over on the top, and using a back-up wood block, trim the edges of the veneer smooth with the top it now covers, using your razor saw or skill knife. Hide the edge of the top with a strip of veneer glued to its perimeter.

We've spent a lot of time on this veneering process, because you'll be following the same basic procedure in any application of veneer or laminate. This is true of

the flexible polyvinyl surfacing materials, and it's equally true of the rigid phenol, polyester, and formica/urea laminates. There are a few minor variations in the methods of cutting and applying them, but the measuring procedure is the same, and so is the surface preparation.

To summarize this job, let's quickly run over it step-by-step, abbreviating the captions that go with each picture.

1. Remove old veneer, sand underlay, patch as needed.

2. Match grain of new veneer, if two sections are required to cover tabletop. If only one piece of veneer is going to be used, this step is omitted.

3. Rough-cut the veneer, $1/2$ to 1 inch larger than the tabletop being covered. Use masking tape over the cutline on both sides and cut with the face of the veneer down to avoid splintering.

4. Apply contact cement to both surfaces to be joined; follow manufacturer's directions in allowing set up time for cement, quantity used, etc.

5. Fit rough-cut veneer to top, using the method of placing brown paper between veneer and surface while veneer is being

placed. Roll or tap veneer into firm contact with surface to which it is being applied.

6. Trim veneer around rim of top, apply finish strip if needed; sand, stain, or varnish.

Each of these operations is illustrated, except those involved in the final finishing. You'll find refinishing procedures detailed in Chapter 12. The basic installation steps apply to both wood veneers and plastic laminates, with minor variations.

FLEXIBLE PLASTIC

Because flexible plastic materials are often used to cover kitchen or dinette or recreation room surfaces, and are sometimes used in children's rooms to cover unpainted pieces, or old furniture being recycled for temporary use, let's take a quick look at them.

These vinyl-based materials come in

You can buy a veneer roller such as the one at left, or you can make your own (right). It took less than a half hour, using a discarded typewriter platen, a short length of 1-inch dowel, and a couple of plywood scraps. The homemade job won't win any prizes for beauty, but it works as well as the other one.

rolls and bear a number of different brand names. They're sold by the running foot or square yard, and are really a thin version of linoleum, but are much easier to handle and much more durable. They are cut with a skill knife or linoleum knife and applied with adhesive similar to linoleum paste. Surface preparation is the same as that followed in applying veneers; you want a smooth surface free from bulges or dents. Most of these roll coverings are 48 inches wide, so seamless application is usually possible. Unless the piece you're covering is very irregular in outline, it's usually easier to measure the surface being covered and transfer the measurements to the plastic for cutting.

Apply adhesive only to the surface being covered. The adhesives used with roll coverings set up slowly, allowing plenty of time for fitting. Apply the paste with a wide putty knife or one of the comb-toothed spreaders used with linoleum paste. These are usually priced at less than a dollar. Spread adhesive thinly and comb the surface well to insure complete coverage. Lay the plastic on the surface and smooth it from the center to the edges after it has been aligned. Use a rolling pin or veneer roller; if you don't have either, use a padded block and tap over the entire surface with a mallet or heavy hammer.

When the covering is in place you can easily trim off any irregularities in the edges. A metal border is generally fitted around the edge anyhow, to give the piece a finished look.

RIGID LAMINATES

There are a few small but significant differences between the methods of applying wood veneers and the flexible vinyls and the rigid laminates. The best-known trade name of this latter group is Formica,

COVERING A TABLE WITH VINYL

1 When covering a badly battered tabletop with roll vinyl, the first step is to fill dents, gouges, and scratches on the top with wood filler.

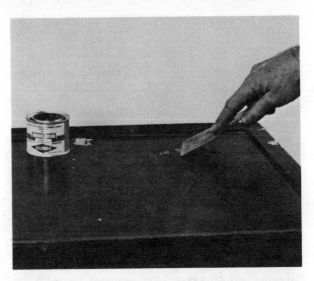

2 Sand smooth with medium-coarse grits to give the adhesive a better footing and get a stronger bond with the vinyl covering.

3 Measure the vinyl, and plan your cuts so the pattern will fit into the available space. Avoid unbalanced lines and unequal spacing of the design. Cut the vinyl and be sure it fits.

4 Spread the top with a thin, even coat of adhesive. Then comb with a serrated-edge tool to assure good adhesion.

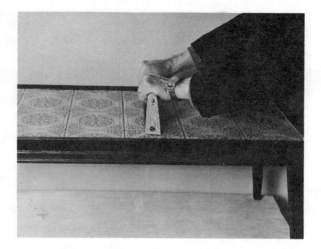

5 Fit the vinyl in place and roll with heavy pressure to remove all bubbles.

which was first in the field with a formaldehyde/urea laminate. All the veneering materials in this group are very similar in durability, and the methods used in applying them are the same. Which brand you choose is a matter of personal preference.

These laminates are very, very tough but relatively brittle until they have been bonded to a thick underlay, such as a tabletop or desk top. They require special attention in cutting, but once they've been cut the rest of the application job is no more difficult than it is when you're handling wood or vinyl. Because they are thin as well as brittle, they must be handled in a manner that avoids cracking them, and cut by using a technique that minimizes their tendency to chip.

Professional installers of these laminates use several types of tools in cutting them. There are skill knife blades designed to score the surface of the laminate, and the pros scribe their scorelines and snap the laminate with ease. There are also friction cutters that in one operation cut the laminate and form the bevel edge which allows the seamless joining of a laminate top and edge at right angles. Both these tools require practice to use

easily. The professionals get this practice every day; the occasional user is far better off cutting rigid laminates with a saw.

A circular saw fitted with a fine-tooth hollow-ground veneer blade is the best choice, but a jigsaw or saber saw with a metal-cutting blade can also be used. In fact, if you've got any curved lines to cut, you'll have to use a jigsaw on them. You can also use a handsaw, a crosscut saw with freshly sharpened teeth. If a power saw is used, place the laminate face down to cut it. If a handsaw is used, place the sheet face up. Regardless of the type of saw you choose, and notwithstanding your confidence in your ability to saw a straight line, you should set up a simple jig to guide the blade. We'll get to that in a moment.

Begin by measuring the surfaces to be covered. Transfer these to the laminate, marking them first on the face, then on the back, and allowing an extra $1/16$ inch in all dimensions. This tiny bit of overhang assures you of getting perfect edges when you reach the step of finishing off the job neatly and professionally.

After you've marked the laminate with sawlines, press a strip of masking tape over each line, centering the tape on the line along which you'll be cutting. Yes, all of them, both on the face and on the back. Masking tape is thin enough to enable you

Rigid sheet laminates of the Formica type must be sawed in absolutely straight lines if you want to avoid time-consuming work on their edges later on. A jig such as the one shown here will take only a few minutes to set up, and will save many minutes of future work. Support the laminate sheet on 1 x 8 boards between sawhorses, with a gap in the supporting boards under the line the saw will travel. Clamp the laminate sheet to a 1 x 4 or 1 x 6 that you've selected for its straight unwarped edges and use this as a guide for the left edge of the saw's baseplate after truing the board's edge parallel to your saw line. Apply strips of masking tape over the saw line on both sides, and cut the sheet face down to minimize chipping.

to see the lines you'll be following, and with a jig you really won't need to see them, for the jig will guide your blade.

To make your jig you need three 1 x 4 or 1 x 6 boards a few inches longer than the longest cut you'll be making. At least one of the boards must be absolutely straight, free of warping. Reserve it for your saw guide when setting up the jig. Lay the other two boards a foot or so apart on sawhorses, and align the marked sheet of laminate to lay across them with the sawline about 1 inch from the edge of the left-hand board. Measure the exact distance from

the center of your saw blade to the left edge of its soleplate. Clamp the straight board to the board supporting the laminate sheet on the left, with the edge of the top board spaced so that when the plate of the saw is firmly against it the blade is on the cutline.

Take your time setting up this jig. Be sure the top board, which will guide the saw, is exactly parallel to the cutline and that the distance from the sawline to this board's edge is precisely that from the center of the saw blade to the left edge of the saw's soleplate. The laminate, remember, is sandwiched face-down between the two boards that form the left side of the jig if you're cutting with either kind of power saw.

If you're using a circular saw, set its blade to make a cut just deep enough to part the laminate. If you're using a jigsaw, be sure the blade will clear the sawhorses supporting the work; it may be necessary to put pieces of scrap lumber under the jig's boards. Now, keeping the saw's soleplate pressed firmly against the edge of the top left-hand board, make your cut. It will be absolutely true. Repeat the procedure when making the rest of the cuts needed to reduce the laminate sheet to the dimensions of the surface on which it will be applied.

This sounds like a complicated setup, but the photos will show you how simple it really is. It actually takes less time to put this jig together than it does to read about it. A jig of this type will save you a lot of grief, especially when cutting laminates or veneers or making long rip cuts in lumber. Yes, I know that most power saws have rip guide attachments, but they're usually only 10 to 12 inches long. A rip guide that would be useful in cutting 4-foot wide panels would be so heavy it would be unwieldy, or so soupy it would be useless.

There are good reasons for applying masking tape to the cutlines you've marked on the laminate sheet and for sawing it as described. Laminates are quite brittle. They tend to chip on the side from which the teeth of a saw emerges when they are being cut. This is why the face of the laminate should always be placed so the teeth will enter it. Any chipping will take place on the back side. Even the sharpest saw blade with the finest teeth is going to cause minor chipping of the sawn edge of this material, and the masking tape minimizes the chipping.

After you've sawed the laminate sheet that will cover the top of your table or dresser or whatever, check its dimensions on the piece itself. You've allowed for a bit of overhang when marking, so there should be a slight protrusion of the edge of the laminate beyond the top on all sides. This is to allow for a neat finish job around the top's perimeter. Usually, this finish consists of a strip of laminate butted to the top sheet, with the edges of both sheets beveled to make the join invisible, or at least very inconspicuous.

If you have a router, there are bits that will finish off the edge of the top sheet of laminate either flush with the edge or with a slight bevel. If you don't have a router and don't want to rent one for this job, work the edges of the top laminate sheet down with sandpaper and form the bevel with a smoothing file. Cut and apply the edge strips before gluing on the top piece of laminate; hold the pieces together with masking tape while you check to make sure you'll have a clean joint.

Finally, glue the laminate sheet to the top of the piece of furniture you're covering. Use the folded brown paper method that was described in an earlier part of this chapter, and use a roller or padded block and hammer to insure good adhesion.

CONTACT PAPER

At the beginning of this chapter, I mentioned that very low-priced pieces of furniture are often covered with wood-grained contact paper. This paper has the virtue of being very inexpensive, as compared to wood veneer, plastic roll covering, or sheet laminates, but this is about its only virtue. It requires the same careful surface preparation that's required for any of the veneers or laminates, and you'll spend almost as much time apply-

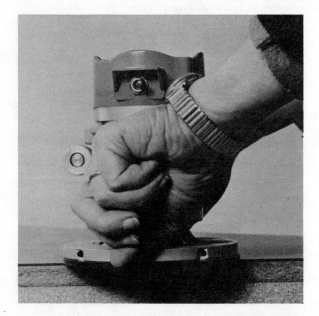

A router with a tungsten-carbide bit is the best tool to use for trimming a laminated edge. If you're not using a self-guiding bit, a rip fence should be fitted to the router.

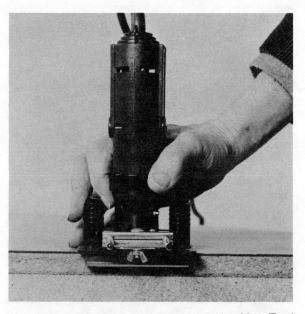

A small-scaled router such as the MotoTool can be used if you feed it gently into the work.

Finish off the edge with fine sandpaper; you're really polishing rather than finishing. The X-Acto sanding block holds the finer grades of finishing paper in a tight grip, which makes sanding jobs like this easier.

ing it. There's no way for you to tell how long a roll of this paper has been in a retailer's stock, and the cement with which it's coated may have deteriorated to the point where it won't adhere well, even on a smooth, sanded surface that has been given a coating of shellac.

Contact paper is very fragile. It abrades easily, and unless applied very expertly and rolled firmly will wrinkle and pull away in time from the surface of the furniture to which it was applied. However, you can often find real bargains in cabinet pieces that are basically well made; they're priced low because they have been covered with this paper. Many times you can convert these pieces to good-looking serviceable ones by removing the contact paper and recovering the piece with wood veneer or with a laminate. Use a warm iron to soften the adhesive and pull off the paper, then put on a covering that will withstand the kind of wear most pieces of furniture get in the average household.

Wood veneers, flexible and rigid laminates all have a place in repairing and restoring furniture. One of the three is often the way to go when you want to improve the looks and extend the service life of a piece of furniture that might otherwise be discarded. The time you spend in learning to work with them won't be time wasted.

5

Chairs

Chairs seem to need repairs more often than other types of furniture, and the reasons for this aren't hard to find. Generally, chairs have structural components that are small in relationship to the loads they're called on to support; even the simplest chair will have more than fifteen separate parts, held together by twenty or more individual joints. Few of these joints are reinforced, and still they're called on to bear loads and endure stresses that aren't distributed in ways foreseen by the chair's designer.

Very few chairs were planned for double occupancy, yet it's fairly commonplace for two people to sit in the same chair. Uneven floors, or positioning a chair with one or two legs on a carpet, the others on the bare floor, mean that all four legs don't meet the floor at the angle planned by the designer. Chairs are moved around more than most other furniture pieces, and are also used as ladders, sawhorses, and other purposes for which they were never intended.

In this chapter we're concerned primarily with wooden chairs of what might best be described as traditional or conventional design. This means straight chairs, often called side chairs. We'll also cover rocking chairs, which are enjoying a tremendous revival of popularity as this is being written. In other chapters we'll explain how to repair the frames of upholstered chairs, how to reupholster chairs, and how to repair chairs made of bent tubular metal, plastic, or wood.

Straight, or side, chairs get these designations from two sources. First, they're designed to hold an occupant in a straight or upright posture. Second, the kinds of chairs we're interested in here are traditionally placed along the sides of a dining table while the host and hostess occupy armchairs at the table's head and foot. Rocking chairs are really nothing but straight chairs with curved wooden slats attached to their legs, so we'll include them here, too.

Face the fact at the beginning that because there are so many styles of chairs, and the lines dividing these styles are so thin and wavering, every job of repairing a chair will very likely be slightly different. It would take an entire book devoted to chairs alone just to describe all the styles, and we'd end in a welter of confusion between Adam, Hepplewhite, Phyfe, Sheraton, Chippendale, Queen Anne, Jacobean, Windsor, Victorian, Empire, Directoire,

Primitive, slatback, ladderback, and so on and on for another page and a half if I were to try listing all the identifiable styles.

We're not concerned here with styles of chairs, but with the best and easiest ways of repairing them. In spite of the differences in style details, many of which are very minor indeed, the assembly of all parts of a chair as well as the parts themselves will always bear a strong family resemblance. The chair jungle isn't as thick as it might seem to be at first glance. Because of this family resemblance between components and assembly methods, a few general rules can guide your approach to repair jobs. And to give you a bit of encouragement at this point, I've never seen a wooden straight chair that can't be repaired by the average home craftsman without the need for any special tools, even when it's necessary to make components to replace those that have been broken.

Before we start simplifying the problem of identification, which is the key to knowing where to begin a repair job, let's look at the way all chairs are made. Regardless of style or the use for which they were designed, all chairs are divided into three assemblies: legs, seat, and back. There will be differences in the components and in the manner in which they're put together, but the similarities will remain. Some styles of chairs have their legs attached directly to their seats; in some styles the rear legs extend upward to form the frame for the back. In some styles the legs will be attached to a skirt and the skirt will be fixed to the seat. In others, there will be stretchers—often called rungs —extending between the legs. The backs in some styles of chairs will be a single wide piece between the back frames. Some chair backs will consist of wide horizontal supports, others will have narrow vertical supports. These back supports

we'll always call splats, no matter what their shape or attitude.

For all their apparent simplicity, straight chairs are really quite sophisticated examples of functional design and construction. The designer of a straight chair generally wants to keep its weight to a minimum, so stresses are carefully calculated. The man who is designing a straight chair faces much the same problem that confronts an airplane's designer. Each component must reinforce other components by sharing the stresses or loads to which the entire piece will be subjected.

One result of this design problem is that when any joint of a straight chair loosens, or any component breaks, even under what might be unusual or unforeseen stress, the entire chair is weakened. The failure of one joint or component can be expected to lead very quickly to the failure or breaking of another. If you don't pay immediate attention to a loose joint or a broken splat or stretcher, you'll have a much more extensive repair job on your hands in the near future.

In order to simplify our approach to repair jobs, let's brush aside such things as the period, style, and name identification of chairs and arbitrarily put them into two categories. We'll call all chairs Type 1 or Type 2 and classify them according to shared construction details.

Type 1 chairs, for repair purposes, will be all those made with separate assemblies of legs, seat, and back. The legs of these chairs almost always have three or more stretchers. The simplest of them have only three stretchers, two of which connect the front and rear legs, and a third running at right angles between the two that join the legs. Alternatively, Type 1 chairs may have four stretchers, one stretcher on each side, one in front, and one in back. The legs may terminate at the top in a skirt which is attached to the seat, or the skirt may be omitted. The back side-frame/splat assembly will be jointed in the seat.

Type 2 chairs will be all those with a shared leg and back assembly; the rear legs will rise to form the back side pieces, and the seat will be attached by a direct mortise joint to the rear legs, or will rest on a skirt assembly mortised into both front and rear legs. In chairs of this type, stretchers may be omitted entirely, as the skirt takes over the job of keeping the legs from spreading. However, you'll occasionally find a three-stretcher assembly in chairs of this type. Seats of Type 2 chairs are often upholstered and rest on corner blocks attached to the skirts; the

seats are held in place by screws run up from the bottoms of the corner blocks.

Even within these two streamlined categories you'll find that construction details vary. The splats, which is the correct name for the pieces that form the backrest, may run vertically or horizontally. There may be only one splat—a single, wide vertical piece—or there may be spindles. Splats which run vertically may be joined to a cross-splat just above the seat, or may be joined to the seat itself or to a back skirt in chairs which have drop-in upholstered seats. However, if you keep in mind the basic construction feature that sets apart the two categories, you'll have no trouble in separating Type 1 chairs from those that fall into the Type 2 group. This feature, of course, is the use of a single member to

This is a Type 1 chair. The top of the back and the splats are assembled as one unit, the legs and stretchers as another, and both are joined to the seat.

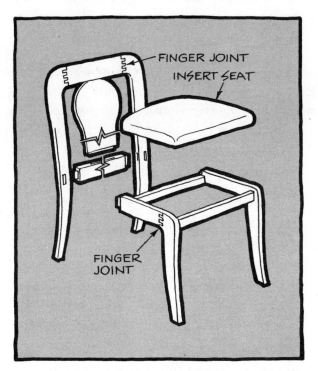

In a Type 2 chair, the back legs, frame, splat, and rear skirt are assembled as a unit, the front legs, front and side skirts form the second assembly. The two are joined to the frame at the back. The seat of this type of chair is usually a separate upholstered unit which is dropped into the frame.

form the rear legs and the back side-frames. This is your one shining beacon in an ocean of variety.

This has been a long preliminary dissertation, necessary because unless we have established some reasonably firm guidelines, we'd bog down later in a mass of repetitive details. Now, let's move on to the repairs commonly required by each of our chair types.

REGLUING STRETCHERS OR SPLATS—TYPE 1

Quite probably, the repair most often needed by Type 1 chairs is a simple regluing job on stretchers or splats. For this, the human factor is chiefly to blame. Youngsters stand on stretchers and jump up and down on them. Adults sometimes use them as the first step up when a chair's being substituted for a ladder. People sitting in chairs tilt them back, which puts a double stress on the rear legs, back, and stretchers; if they hook their feet over the front stretchers while the chair's tilted, the stress is nearly doubled. If you've ever looked closely at an old chair that's spent its left in a rural store or some other place where folks meet to sit and gossip, you'll see that the front stretcher is reduced in size by as much as a third from the abrasion of heels having been hooked over it through the years.

It would be nice if I could honestly advise you to replace a broken stretcher just by removing any stub ends that might be left in its socket and forcing a new stretcher into them, but the job can't be done that easily. The entire leg and stretcher assembly must be taken apart, because if you simply spread it to put in a new stretcher you'll break the glue joints in all the legs. Once a glue joint has been broken, there's no easy way to restore it. Yes, I know about those hypodermic-needle type of "glue injectors," and even tried to use them when they first came on the market. Every loose joint I tried to reglue with one of these injection devices failed again in a week or less. Finally, I gave up trying to beat the problem that's faced woodworkers since glue was first invented: new glue won't stick to old glue, whether it's injected or spread.

There's only one way to make a lasting repair to any glued assembly when the original glue gives way. Take the assembly apart, scrape and sand away the old glue, apply fresh glue to the cleaned wood, and reassemble the pieces. This is true of any gluing job you'll ever encounter in repairing furniture.

At the risk of being unnecessarily repetitive, the strength of a chair comes from a series of components designed to distribute stresses, and when one fails to carry its share of the stress, it leads to the failure of others. Disassembling a chair assembly is seldom much of a problem; you can usually do it by hand, simply wiggling and twisting stretchers or splats or legs from their sockets. If this doesn't work, tap them with a mallet or padded hammer, and if brute strength fails, make a levering jig like the one shown in the photo. It will always work.

When cleaning away old glue, don't overlook the sockets. One of the most useful gadgets I've found for this is the small rotary rasp, a drill accessory you'll find listed in the Craftsman catalog. This is especially useful when you must drill the stub of a splat or stretcher that has broken off in a socket. If a jagged bit of the broken piece is left in the socket, trim it flush so the bit will start straight. Use a bit smaller than the diameter of the socket, then insert the little rasp in the drill hole to clean the shell of the stub and the old glue from the hole.

Round stretchers can be duplicated

from a length of dowel that you can work with a Surform tool or rasp to match the contours and taper of the old one. Finish with file and sandpaper before staining. A contour gauge is helpful here, but most of these gauges are too short to measure the length of a stretcher, or a leg, at one time. Take the contours off in sections, transferring each section by tracing them on a piece of cardboard, then cut the cardboard to make a template. Place the template against the partly finished work from time to time to reproduce the old piece exactly. Shaping a simple taper this way is easy, but a lot of patience will be required to match more elaborate pieces.

Square stretchers and rectangular splats can be made very easily using standard dimension lumber, which you can work with a circular saw or jigsaw. Chairs that have a single wide vertical splat can be repaired by cutting a new splat from plywood of the proper thickness. Oc-

The levering jig shown here speeds the job of breaking the glued joints between chair legs and stretchers.

casionally, you'll run into a chair having one of these wide vertical back splats in which the splat has been milled to a thickness that can't be matched in dimension lumber or standard-thickness plywood. The only practical solution is to use a thicker plywood, cut the splat out and chamfer the ends to fit the mortise slot into which the original splat was seated.

Now and then a leg on a Type 1 chair will break. If the break doesn't come where there's a stretcher socket, the leg can usually be mended. A long vertical split can be glued, and dowels inserted along the break at right angles to the split for reinforcement. If the break is at a socket, you'll have to make a new leg. Use the same method given for making a new stretcher.

Square legs present no problem. A round leg offers a few complications, the most obvious of which is the problem of finding a suitable piece of stock for the leg, as most lumberyards don't stock dowels larger than 1 inch in diameter. Relax, and buy a length of drapery pole. Lumberyards and housewares stores usually stock these poles, which are nothing more than oversized dowels, in diameters of $1^1/_2$ to $1^3/_4$ inches. Cut a section of the required length from the pole and form it with a spokeshave, Surform tool, or rasp to match the broken leg. Work from a template, which has already been described. Turn the work often, reducing the incurved areas a little at a time with a rasp. The Surform round tool and the Mini-file will get into tight curves; work across the grain with them and then go to a half-round file for the final shaping and use a triangular file to finish off the grooves. Smooth with sandpaper.

Naturally, this kind of job isn't going to be finished in a single five-minute work session. Don't take it on unless you are prepared to spend the time and put forth

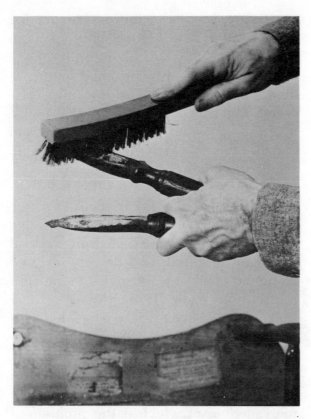

Make quick work of cleaning splinters and fuzz from a split leg by using a wire brush. Unlike sandpaper or a scraper, the brush will preserve the fracture lines so the joint will fit.

After cleaning the joint, apply glue and fit the split sections together. Then clamp the work until the glue sets.

the effort required. The point is that such jobs can be done without using a lathe. But if you want to save time and elbow grease, take the template and a piece of drapery pole to a cabinet shop and have the new leg turned on a lathe. The cost will be small. Of course, if you own a lathe, or have a friend who does, you're home free.

When it comes time to drill holes for the stretchers in the new leg, make a paper pattern to locate the holes into which the stretchers will be fitted. Use the mate to the leg being replaced; a back leg mates to a back leg, front leg to front leg. Take a strip of paper long enough to span the distance from the bottom of the leg to all the stretcher sockets drilled in it, and wide enough to be wrapped around the intact leg being used as a pattern. Mark one side

Reinforce the joint with dowels. For maximum strength, drill the holes at opposing angles rather than at right angles to the leg.

FORMING A CONTOURED SPLAT

1 When forming a round, contoured stretcher or splat that will match others on a chair, make a template to guide you. You'll need a contour gauge to duplicate the piece.

2 Transfer the contours from the gauge to a thin piece of cardboard. If the piece being formed is too long for the gauge to span in one push, gauge it in sections and match the gauge's curves to those on the template.

3 Cut the outline you've traced with a fine-bladed knife such as the X-Acto stencil knife. This gives you a profile of the curves, tapers, and knobs you want to reproduce.

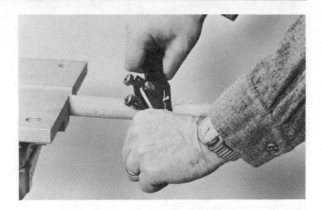

4 On a dowel of the desired diameter, form the primary shape with a spokeshave.

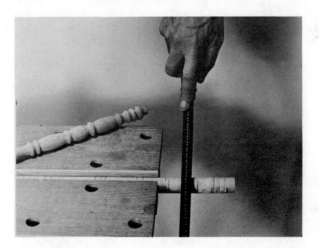

5 Most of the remaining shaping can be done with a Surform tool, though you'll need a triangular file or knife file to form sharply indented grooves.

6 Press the template against the work at right angles and rotate the work. This will keep the curves in order and the grooves at the proper depth and angle.

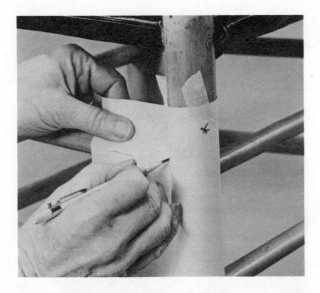

To locate the stretcher holes in a newly shaped chair leg, mark a sheet of paper on one side at the top edge, wrap it around the twin to the new leg, and mark the location of the holes.

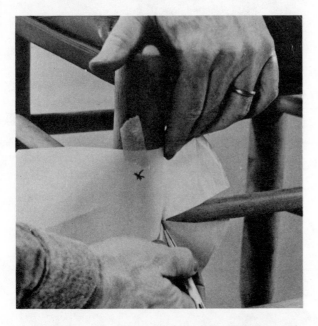

If the stretchers are still in the leg you want to measure, slit the paper at each stretcher and use an X-Acto knife with a fine tapered blade to cut around the stretchers.

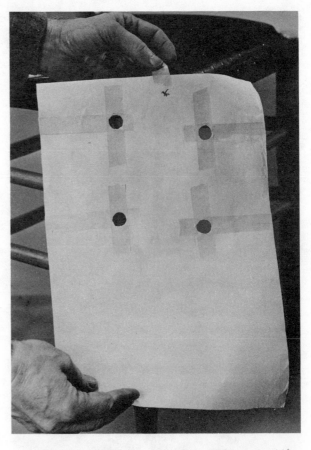

Remove the paper, lay it flat, and put masking tape over the slits. Reverse the paper and wrap it around the new leg with the mark on the inside. The result will be a mirror effect; the location of the holes in the new leg will be reversed, as they should be.

of the paper so you'll know which side is which later on.

Wrap the paper around the old leg. Press your fingertip along the edges of the stretcher sockets hard enough to leave a ridge in the paper. Cut out the rounds marked by the ridges. Now, *reverse* the paper, and with the side that was on the *outside* when you made the pattern, wrap it around the new leg. Trace the holes on the leg. This will locate exactly where the stretcher sockets must be drilled.

If you haven't found it necessary to remove the leg used as a pattern, cut slits in the paper corresponding to the location of the stretchers that are still in the leg and then cut around the stretchers at the point where they join the leg, using a very sharp skill knife with a fine point. Hold the slits together with masking tape, as shown in the photos, so that your pattern will still be true when you transfer the location of the holes to the new leg.

Unless the legs are perpendicular to the floor, which chair legs seldom are, the sockets must be drilled at an angle so the stretchers will be parallel to the floor. The easiest way to determine this angle is to use a carpenter's bevel square. But you can also use a folding rule, even a pocketknife.

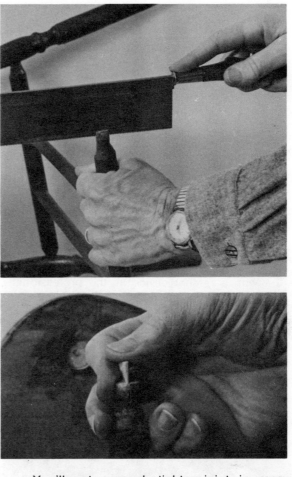

You'll get a much tighter joint in reassembling a mended chair if you use a kerf-and-wedge arrangement in the dowel joints. First, saw a kerf in the end of the stretcher or splat. Then insert a very thin wedge. When you drive the joint together, the wedge is pushed into the kerf, locking the joint tightly.

While a paper pattern will give you the precise location of the stretcher sockets, it won't give you the angle at which these socket holes must be drilled. Chair legs normally slant from seat to floor at a compound angle in relation to the seat, and to fit the stretchers properly the sockets must be drilled at an angle that will keep the stretchers parallel to the floor. Use a bevel gauge to establish this angle for each socket. Lacking a bevel gauge, you can improvise one from a folding carpenter's rule or a pocketknife with a straight-backed blade, as illustrated.

Ideally, if you're replacing a component of a chair you should use the same kind of wood from which the chair was originally made. Both Constantine and Craftsman stock a variety of hardwoods in dimensions that will yield stretchers and splats and small-scaled chair legs. If you feel that you want to substitute another wood, ash can be stained and grain-marked to look like most hardwoods. See Chapter 13 for details on finishing new woods to match old.

When you get ready to assemble the chair with its new components, use the saw-kerf and wedge method to get tight, permanent joints. Cut kerfs in the ends of stretchers and splats with a backsaw or dovetail saw. Make thin wedges to fit into these kerfs. Apply glue to the wedges and inside the sockets as well as on the ends of the new stretchers, slats, and so on. When you reassemble the piece, these wedges will expand the ends of the splats inside their sockets.

Use a web clamp or a rope windlass to hold chair assemblies tight while glue sets

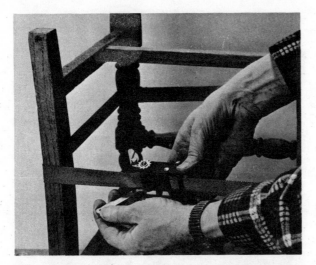

A web clamp, a long piece of sturdy fabric with a ratchet device, is the professional's tool for holding reglued chair legs in place.

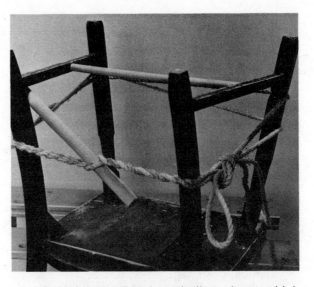

Another expedient is a windlass clamp, which can be made from a piece of rope long enough to go around the job twice. Insert a dowel between the strands of the doubled rope, tighten, and lock the dowel as shown.

This rubberband clamp from Brookstone does a satisfactory job and is less expensive.

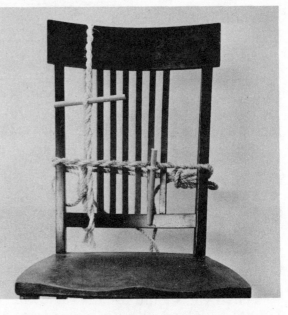

This double windlass clamps a chair back in two directions at the same time.

up. Web clamps are canvas or nylon belts that can be pulled tightly around leg and back assemblies. Stanley and Pony make rachet-tightened web clamps; Brookstone has an inexpensive clamp which is essentially a set of oversized rubber bands. Windlass clamps are made of rope, as illustrated. You need enough rope to go twice around the work. Tie the doubled ends together and slip a length of dowel between the two courses of rope. Twist the dowel and turn it to tighten the ropes. When the windlass is tight, wedge the dowel in place as shown, or tie it to the leg or frame of the chair.

About the only repairs ever required by the seats of Type 1 chairs are those already mentioned in an earlier chapter: chips or

When you're too busy to make a proper repair of a split chair seat, you can use a metal mending plate. Pull the split together with a clamp while you screw on the plate. Regard the repair as only temporary. It won't last as long as a glued split, which can be considered a permanent repair if it's properly done.

cracks or separation at old glue joints. These repairs have already been covered, but one note might be added here in connection with replacing a split board in a chair seat. If such a replacement is necessary, and the chair has a contoured seat, a shavehook is the tool best suited to tailor the new board to match the contours of the rest of the seat.

REPAIRING TYPE 2 CHAIRS

Type 2 chairs are assembled differently from Type 1 chairs. Typically, the chair will be made up of as many as ten or twelve separate pieces. These can be divided into two major assemblies: the front assembly, which consists of front legs and front and side skirts, and the back assembly, which consists of the back legs, back frame, back skirt, and splats. Stretchers are rarely used in these chairs.

If the seat of a Type 2 chair is of wood, it may be attached to the legs with dowels, or to the skirt with glue blocks. Occasionally, a solid seat on a chair of this type will be fitted into a dado that runs

around the inner sides of the skirts. If the seat is upholstered, it will be dropped inside the skirts to rest on corner blocks, to which it is attached from below by screws. In cane-bottomed chairs of this type, the wooden portion of the seat is nothing more than a frame designed to support the strips of cane that form the woven seat. We'll look at cane-bottom chairs in detail a few paragraphs further along, by the way. Right now, let's continue with the main topic, the methods used in repairing typical Type 2 chairs, as these are a bit more complex than the straightforward dowel-into-socket jobs encountered in Type 1 chairs.

Taking off from our usual base, we'd better look first at the two spots most likely to require fixing. These are the joints where the side skirts are attached to the back leg assembly, and the joints where the front skirt is attached to the front leg subassembly.

The break most often encountered in these chairs is at the joint where the side stretcher is attached to the back leg/frame. If this is a dowel joint, the repair is a straightforward matter of levering out the dowels of the unbroken side and replacing the broken dowels by the methods discussed earlier in this chapter. If a mortise and tenon joint has been used here, the job's harder.

Unless repairs have been neglected so long that both rear joints have given way, or one of the tenons has broken, you'll probably be faced with the need to break the second back joint in order to repair the broken one. Using sidewise force is dangerous; it might split the back frame. If you're impatient and don't want to make up a levering jig, which will usually force the joint apart, try working the unbroken sidepiece back and forth rather than side to side. If the joint resists all the pressures you can safely apply, it must be sawed

REPAIRING A SPLIT EDGE

1 Open the split with a saw. Cut a piece of scrap lumber as thick as the kerf, and glue it in the kerf. Tap the patch with a hammer to be sure it's well seated.

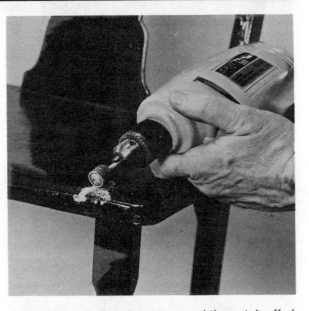

3 Use a sanding drum to round the patch off almost flush with the seat.

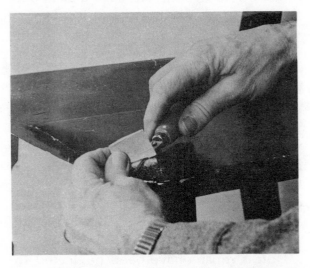

2 After the glue sets, saw off the waste. This little mini-keyhole saw is ideal for the job.

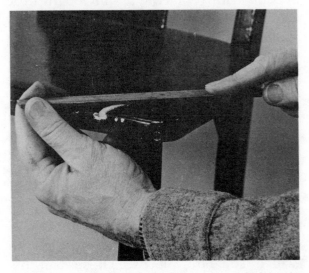

4 File and sand smooth, and refinish the patched spot.

apart. Saw along the back frame line with a mini-keyhole saw or razor saw to cut the tenon off flush with the frame. If you use a saw with a wider blade, you'll have to insert a veneer spacer when you reassemble, and use a dowel joint here in the reassembling process.

Type 2 chair front-leg assemblies are normally made by joining the legs and side skirts with a finger joint, though now and then you'll find this joint, too, is a mortise and tenon. In some chairs, dowel joints are used to connect side skirts to the front leg pieces. The front skirt joints, which are the second most often encountered trouble spots, are generally shallow

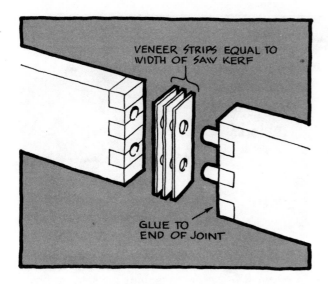

VENEER STRIPS EQUAL TO WIDTH OF SAW KERF

GLUE TO END OF JOINT

When you're forced to saw a joint apart, remember that good furniture is built with very precise measurements. When you reglue the joint, compensate for the space lost as sawdust by inserting veneer spacers the width of the saw kerf.

mortise-and-tenon joints. This is the reason they're inclined to give way; they have relatively small glued surfaces. Clean the inner surface of the mortise and the surfaces of the tenon, apply fresh glue, and hold the chair in a web or windlass clamp until the glue sets up.

A split side skirt is encountered less frequently. The kind of split determines whether repairs can be made by gluing and adding a mending plate. A clean split along the grain can almost always be fixed this way. If the wood is shattered, make a new side skirt and fit it in place.

CANED SEATS

Chapter 11 gives you the methods of reupholstering the seats of Type 2 chairs, which are usually of the drop-in kind. Since caned seats can't be classed as upholstery, let's deal with them now. There are two kinds of caned seats. One is woven on the chair, the cane strands being held by pegs in holes bored around the frame's pe-

rimeter. These holes are carefully spaced, and will usually be useful only if the open-weave style of caning is reinstalled in any of several patterns. This type of caning is tedious and time-consuming and requires a book to explain, so if you need to re-cane a chair seat of this type, I have to refer you to one of the several books that covers the subject. However, using

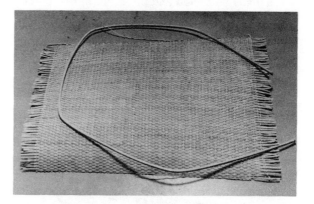

New caning is sold by the running foot in widths of 18, 24, and 36 inches. Several different patterns are available, reproducing all the traditional weaves. The spline needed to attach the cane to the chair seat comes in two widths and is sold by the foot.

INSERTING A NEW CANE SEAT

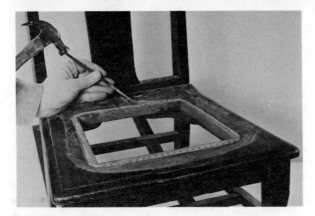

1 Remove the spline that held the old cane in place. The joint of most splines in cane-bottom chairs is at the back center, so make this your first point of attack.

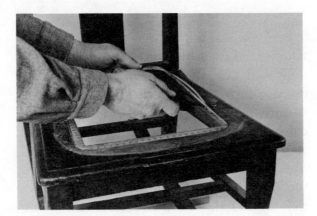

2 Once the spline piece is loosened, it can usually be pulled and pried out in one piece.

3 Clean the spline groove thoroughly, removing all bits of old cane. If the frame of the seat is to be sanded for refinishing, do it next.

4 While you've been cleaning the spline groove, your new cane should be soaking in hot water to make it more pliable. Spread the cane on the chair seat to get an idea of how it's to be placed, then fill the spline groove with glue.

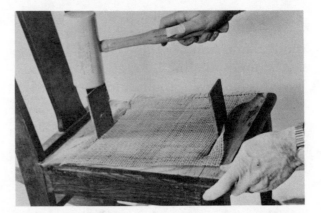

5 Make wedges of ¹/₄- or ³/₈-inch fiberboard to hold the cane in place at the beginning stages. *Important:* Set the front groove first, then the back groove, unless the inner frame is square.

6 A rocker tool made of thin fiberboard will help in getting the cane in the groove. Don't use excessive force: you may split the groove.

7 Start the spline in at the back center. Use a thin piece of wood to drive the spline into the groove, starting at the back center and tapping along as you go. Cut the end of the spline at an angle so that a matching cut at the other end will result in a neat join.

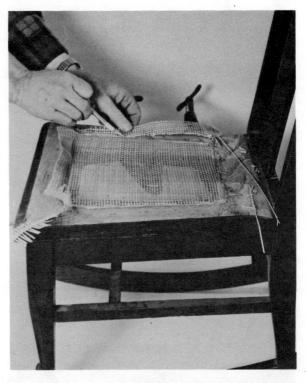

9 Don't wait for the cane to dry before cutting it off level with the seat. Cut while wet, the cane ends will pull below the level of the seat as they shrink in drying.

8 When the spline is in, the job will look like this. You can see the temporary cross braces under the seat, wedged in to keep the groove from splitting out. They were removed when the job was completed.

10 With its new seat installed, the chair is now ready for refinishing.

REPAIRING A CHIPPED CHAIR LEG

1 Plane the broken spot so it is smooth and square. Check the wood to make sure you'll be working on a flat surface.

2 Trace the outline of the bottom of an intact leg on a piece of paper.

3 Align the outline with the broken leg and mark the straight cut needed to saw the replacement end that matches the intact leg. Then transfer this drawing to a piece of lumber the same thickness as the leg.

4 Cut out the piece needed for the repair and glue it to the leg; clamp, and let the glue set.

5 Drill holes for dowels to reinforce the joint. Instead of driving the dowels in with a hammer, force them in smoothly with a C-clamp.

6 Rough-sand with a drum, then finish with fine grits in an orbital sander.

prewoven cane is another thing. The cane piece is simply stretched over the seat and a spline taped into a groove to hold it. The photos show you how this method of caning works.

LEGS

Let's move on to chair legs. Chipping at the bottom of a leg is probably the most common type of repair job you'll encounter. Because the wood grain in a chair leg runs vertically, and legs are often sawed to end in a slight arc or curve, pieces break away along grain lines. Often, if such a chipped-off piece is replaced at once, glue with a dowel reinforcement is all that's needed—a quick job.

When the chipped-off piece has been lost, a new piece must be formed. The broken section has to be squared off, the new piece put on with glue and a reinforcing dowel or two, and sanded to match the contours of the opposite leg. The photos show step-by-step procedures for this job, which isn't at all difficult to handle. The inserted piece must, of course, be stained and varnished or painted to match the finish already on the chair.

ROCKING CHAIRS

Now, let's consider an old type of chair that is enjoying a revival of popularity: the rocking chair. There are two kinds of rocking chairs: the armless "boudoir" chair and the armchair style.

Rocking chairs are one of the few types in which screws are commonly used rather than mortise and scarf or dovetail joints. You will find in most rocking chairs that the arm assembly is attached to the back sidepiece with long screws, which may or may not be hidden with glued-in plugs. In boudoir chairs, the side skirts may also be attached with screws, though a mortise-and-tenon joint is more commonly used here. Screws may also be used to attach the top back piece to the sidepieces, and in chairs having bentwood arms, a T-bolt may be used at the bottom of the arm to fix it to the seat.

Horizontal splats are often attached with screws into a mortise on the back sidepieces. Vertical splats are commonly set into a horizontal splat, though they may be set into the chair's seat. In the leg and rocker assembly, a long threaded rod or bolt may be inserted along the stretchers from side to side as an additional reinforcement. Joints set with screws may also be glued.

There's good reason for this. Rocking chairs take perhaps the greatest stresses of any chair made, not only because they're kept in motion, but because in past generations mothers rocked children in them, and because they're frequently overturned. Oddly, rockers rarely break, but when they do it will more than likely be at the point where the back legs are attached, especially if the legs are inserted into a socket in the rocker itself. For this reason, many rocking chairs have a lap or double-lap joint at this point. Even then, the weakening of the leg caused by the insertion of screws creates a weak joint.

If you want to look on the bright side, this use of screws works in favor of the craftsman repairing a rocking chair. It's a lot easier to disassemble a back or leg assembly that can be loosened by the removal of a few screws than it is by having to tap or lever apart a glued assembly to replace a single splat or stretcher. However, a majority of the rocking chairs that are met with on the modern scene are survivors of an earlier day, antiques or collectibles, and chances are that the passage

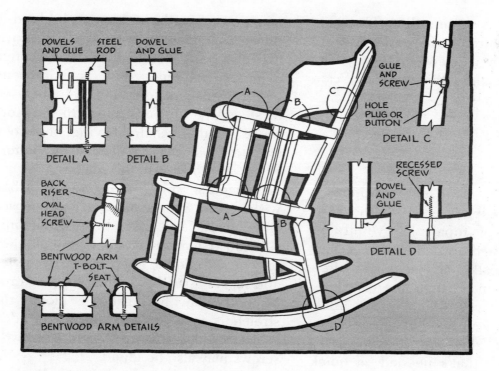

CONSTRUCTION OF A ROCKING CHAIR

Detail A: Arm joints doweled and glued, reinforced by a steel rod.

Detail B: Arm joints doweled and glued.

Detail C: Headrest screwed to back risers, plugged or buttoned.

Detail D: Rockers usually screwed to bottom of legs; sometimes doweled.

of years has wedded those screws so firmly to the wood around them that they'll defy your efforts to remove them with a regular screwdriver. One of those tools mentioned in Chapter 2 can be a real boon at such a time. It's an impact screw-extractor, which quite literally jars a screw loose and enables it to be removed with a minimum of muscle strain. You'll find it in the Brookstone catalog.

With two exceptions, the methods already given in this chapter will enable you to repair or replace any break you might run into in rocking chairs. One of the exceptions is breaks in bentwood chairs, but these chairs are discussed in a later chapter. The other exception is a broken rocker.

There's no way I know of to repair a broken rocker; it must be replaced with a new one. Cutting a new rocker with a jigsaw, using the old one for a pattern, is an elementary job. Your problem is going to be to find the wood from which to saw the

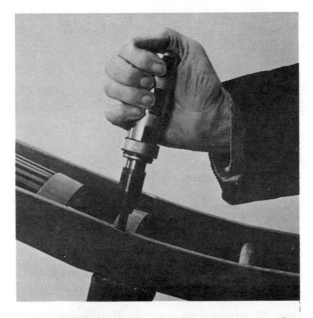

This impact tool, from Brookstone, jars frozen screws free so they can be removed easily without damage to the wood.

Chairs which have screw joints are usually dressed up with a button in the screw hole. Several of the firms listed in the appendix stock both buttons and plugs.

rocker. On most chairs, the rockers are a full 1 inch in width. My only suggestion is that you write one of the specialty supply houses, explaining your problem, and ask them for a supply source. Once you find the stock, fit your jigsaw with an extra-length blade, and cut and fit the rocker to the chair.

Generally speaking, the repair jobs covered in this chapter establish techniques that can be applied to any type of chair repairs. It's up to you to adapt the techniques to specific jobs. The few types of chairs not mentioned in this chapter are covered at the end of Chapter 10.

6

Tables

While there aren't as many types or styles of tables as there are chairs, there are enough to require a quick look at the kinds you'll be most likely to encounter. It's about the only way to be sure that we're all playing in the same ballpark.

Authorities, who're usually people who assume that everybody speaks the same specialized language they do, talk about tables in several frames of reference. The trouble is that every authority uses a different frame. One will describe tables as being of a certain period, another will base his description on the uses to which different kinds of tables were put, the next will base his references on characteristics or styling that is typical of one of the famous cabinetmakers of a bygone era.

Since our purpose here is to look at tables in terms of the repairs they're likely to need, and not to prepare a catalog for an auction sale, suppose we simply agree on a set of arbitrary descriptions that will give us the quickest way of identifying the different kinds of tables at a glance. We'll make up a list that depends on the most obvious characteristics, which in the case of tables could be the leg arrangement or the kind of tops they have. Then, when we run into a kind that doesn't fit into our sys-

tem of identification, we'll handle these on a case-by-case basis.

First, let's set up two chief categories based on the kind of underpinning that establishes the height of the table. We'll refer to all tables that have individual legs at each corner as *legged* tables. Those that are supported by a central assembly we'll call *pedestal* tables, and those resting on a pair of crossed legs at each end we'll call *trestle* tables. The trestle table is so sturdily built that it seldom needs repairs, and so simply jointed that fixing one isn't at all complicated. A second kind of trestle table, almost as sturdy as the crossed-legs type, has a solid support at each end; it may also be referred to as a *refractory* table, but we'll keep it in the trestle class for simplicity's sake.

Any table with a nonexpanding top will be referred to as a *solid-top* model, even if the top is laminated or veneered. Those with tops that can be expanded by inserting leaves will be called *extension* tables, while those that can be made bigger by lifting side or end leaves we'll call *dropleaf* tables. In this last classification we'll include those that have an extra pair of legs that swing out to support the leaves, and are usually described as

These are the five main types of tables, each presenting slightly different repair problems which you're likely to encounter. Each is discussed separately in the text.

gateleg tables. There's a sub-member in this group, which has wing-shaped members that swing out to support the dropleaf, and these bear the common name of *butterfly* tables.

By combining all these scraps of descriptive nomenclature and referring oc-casionally to the pictures that show the different kinds and sub-classes, we should at least be able to agree on what we're talking about when we get into the details of repairing them. My choice of names might be unorthodox, but practical solutions to a problem often are.

We can't always apply this naming system to small tables, of which there is a variety as endless as the grasses of the fields. Consequently, all coffee tables, side tables, end tables, game tables, all of which the furniture trade groups as "occasional" tables, will in this chapter be called simply *small* tables.

Unless your guests include high-spirited women or flamenco dancers who cavort in high-heeled shoes on the top of your dinner table, your small tables will take more of a beating than your large ones. The most frequent repair job legged tables need is to their surfaces and corners, curing the mars made by cigarette burns, stains and dents, and these have already been covered in Chapter 3. When you're beginning any job of repair on any table, large or small, don't crawl around on the floor on your hands and knees while craning your neck to examine the underside of the table to find out what's wrong, or to determine how the factory assembled it. Turn the table over. You'll see things while looking down at the underside of an upended table that you'd have missed if you were twisting your neck peering upward, or lying on your back, and your perceptions will be keener, your judgment better, if you're looking at the table while you're comfortable and not trying to favor a muscle that's being strained. Just imagine how much easier an auto mechanic's job would be if he could flip a car over on its back while he worked on the clutch or transmission.

LEG REPAIRS

Suppose we start at the bottom, then, with table legs, and the injuries to which they're prone. The most common of these isn't really an injury, but a sign of age and use: loose legs. Legged tables share the problem faced by athletes, mail carriers, and racehorses; their legs are usually the first to go.

Large or small, the stresses which tables are designed to stand don't approach those which must be borne by furniture on which people sit, lie, lean, or lounge. Because the components of small tables are more delicately scaled than those of big ones, this breakdown is more frequent on the small kinds. This doesn't mean that the legs of big tables don't suffer. Dragging is the chief cause of this, for moving a big legged table is a two-person job often attempted by one individual. Even if a legged table is dragged for just a few feet, vibrations are set up which cause the table to develop wobbly legs. Warping of a tabletop is something that can be blamed on humidity, but loose legs and loose skirts or stretchers on all tables, large or small, are most often caused by dragging.

There are several ways by which the legs of tables are attached to the tops. In large tables the legs are most often attached to the skirt, which in turn is fixed to the tabletop. There are four ways by which large table legs are commonly attached to the skirts: with metal hanger plates, with inletted glue blocks, with mortise-and-tenon joints, or with rabbet joints. The first two are pictured, because they haven't been illustrated before. In an earlier chapter, mortise and tenon and rabbet joints were pictured.

All these joints tend to work loose with time and use, and the method of tightening them is pretty much the same. Hanger plates, as you can see from the photo, are slid over a double-ended fastener, with a bolt thread on one end, a screw thread on the other. The screw is run in to a corner of the leg, the hanger plate is hooked into saw kerfs on the inside of the skirt, and a nut tightened on the protruding bolt end to pull the assembly together. Nine times out of ten, tightening loose legs on a table

This is an inletted glue block. To break the joint, remove the screws that go into the apron and leg through the block and use a chisel to pry the block loose.

Older tables are likely to have a hanger-plate leg assembly. The plate fits into grooves in the aprons, and a special bolt, with screw threads on one end and nut thread on the other, passes through a hole in the plate to the leg. No glue is used in this assembly; tension does the job. Occasionally, a wooden plate will be used instead of one of metal.

assembled this way is a simple matter of a few turns on the bolt.

Inletted glue blocks are used on most contemporary tables. These are the familiar triangular braces, glued and screwed to the skirts, but when used as a table-leg fastener, the glue block is inletted into the table leg or the leg is inletted into the block. Both ways produce a sturdy joint. Often, screws work loose and allow glue joints to break. A temporary cure is to tighten the screws, but eventually you're going to have to reglue the entire assembly, so cut your losses and do it when the leg first becomes loose.

When mortises are cut into table legs and the skirts attached by a tenon milled in their ends, the assembly is usually reinforced by a brace that runs diagonally across the corner, from side skirt to end skirt. Again, tightening the screws on this brace may result in a temporary repair, but ultimately the loose glue joints in the mortise are going to have to be renewed, so disassemble, scrape clean, and reglue, as described in earlier chapters.

Rabbeted leg-to-skirt joints are also generally reinforced by a diagonal brace, but

A dovetail slot cut at a slant into the wood of the top, with the top of the leg formed to fit the slot and hammered into place, is often used in assembling small tables.

rabbet joints on a table-leg assembly are the least sturdy of all and the most inclined to give. When you disassemble to reglue a loose joint of this kind, set dowels through the rabbet joint. These will prevent, or at least delay, a repetition of the loosening.

All the foregoing ways are used in setting the legs of small tables, plus a few more very rarely seen on big ones. Small legged tables with solid tops may have a female dovetail routed at a slight angle into each corner to accept a male dovetail routed into the top of the legs. Tables assembled this way generally have a set of stretchers or a platform set low on the legs, but this doesn't keep the upper joint from working loose. Tap the joint into its groove, toward the middle of the top, with a mallet or padded hammer to cure looseness.

Many small table legs are set in sockets drilled at an angle into a cross brace or cornerpiece glued to the underside of the top. Even when stretchers are fitted lower on the legs, or when a platform is used in lieu of stretchers, the legs will work loose in their sockets. Disassembling and regluing the entire table is usually the only lasting cure. When the socket is small and the top of the leg has been turned down to fit, breakage is fairly common. If the break leaves the tip on the socket, drill out the stub as described in an earlier chapter and square off the tip of the upper leg, then fit a dowel into the leg to go into the socket. Remember to allow for the slat to which the top of the dowel must be trimmed in order to make a solid joint. The photos show this operation step-by-step.

Repairing fractured chair legs was discussed in detail in Chapter 5, and the only difference between making a similar repair to a table leg is the scale of the components with which you'll be working. To mend a long, clean split, apply glue and clamp the work together until the glue sets. A couple of small dowels inserted at right angles to the split is quick and easy insurance against the split recurring. If the break is at right angles, and can be fitted back together readily, center drill each of the ends, insert a dowel, and reglue. If the fracture has caused extensive splintering of the wood, a splice may be required. Splicing wasn't mentioned in Chapter 5, because I hesitate to recommend it for chair legs, which often are subjected to an oblique stress caused by a sitter treating a straight chair as he would a rocking chair. No splice will endure that kind of strain. Table legs don't usually get such strains, and their larger size makes splicing practical.

If I were to be called on to splice a table leg, I'd use a lapped splice. To make the job easier, I'd cut the wood to be used for the splice from a length of 4 x 4, and make it a square cross-section piece about $1/4$ inch larger than the diameter of the leg. To make a lapped or lipped splice, square off the broken ends of the table leg, and remove a half-section about 2 inches long from each end. Measure an intact leg to determine the length of the splice required. This will equal the amount of wood removed from the leg.

In the wood used as the splice, cut out a rabbet equal to half its thickness, on opposite sides at each end. You've already cut this piece to the correct length. The pictures will show you how these cuts are made, and how the ends of the broken leg fit into the splice. Glue and dowel the leg pieces to the splice, then trim the splice with a Surform tool, spokeshave or block plane to match the diameter and taper of the leg. Finish with file and sandpaper and stain or varnish as required to blend the splice almost invisibly into the leg.

REPAIRING A DOWELED TABLE LEG

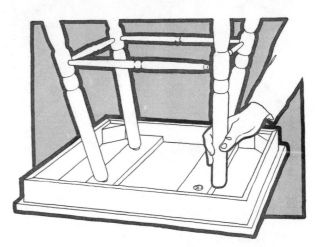

1   On some tables, legs are set in sockets formed in blocks glued to the underside of the top. First step in repairing a broken joint is to remove the leg and gouge out the remnants of the dowel stub.

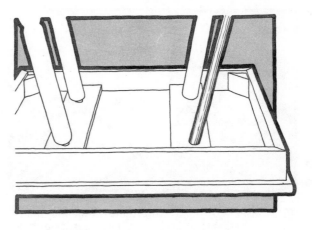

2   Insert a dowel of the proper size into the cleared socket. Trace a line around it, using the block as a guide, to give you the angle at which the dowel must be cut. Measure the length as well.

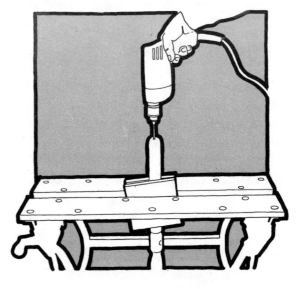

3   Saw off the end of the table leg at the base of the broken dowel. Use a centerfinder, if you have one, to mark the center, and drill a pilot hole, then a hole to accept the new dowel.

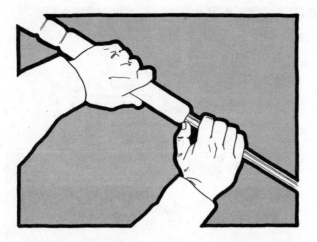

4   Gauge the length of the dowel needed by inserting the unsawed end of the dowel into the hole just drilled. The depth of the hole in the table leg plus the thickness of the block determine the length.

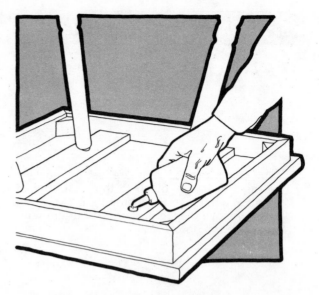

6   Put a generous dollop of glue on the dowel and in the socket and set the leg in place.

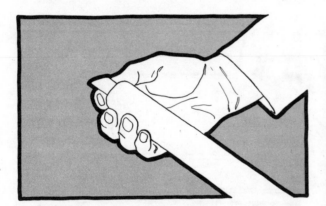

5   Saw the dowel to length and glue it in the end of the table leg. Remember to set its angled head so that the same point of attachment of leg to stretcher can be used when reassembling.

MAKING A NEW LEG

You might prefer to make a new leg, but hesitate to take on a job of cutting a compound taper without a bandsaw, which would cut through the thick stock you'll be using in one pass, or a table saw, which will do it in two passes. You can chicken out at this point, take the broken leg to a cabinet shop, and pay them to rough-cut a new leg which you can finish. Or, you can tackle the job yourself if you have a $7\frac{1}{2}$-inch circular saw, a handsaw, and a little bit of patience. You wouldn't hesitate, of

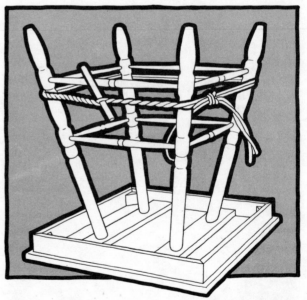

7   Reattach the leg to the stretcher and use a web or windlass clamp to hold things tight while the glue sets.

course, to cut a rectangular cross-sectional taper, because that's a simple job. Cheer up. You can cut either a square or round cross-sectional taper with very little more work.

Sawing out a rectangular cross-sectional taper is the equivalent of what anybody who has and uses a circular saw does re-

SPLICING A BROKEN LEG

1 Measure the length of the broken leg. If the break makes this impossible, then measure one of the unbroken legs.

2 Saw off the broken ends, cutting at right angles to the leg's center.

3 Saw a half-round section about 1½ to 2 inches long out of each piece of the broken leg. The longitudinal cut should be in line with the center of each piece, the connecting cut at right angles.

4 Select a square block of wood, ¼ to ½ inch thicker than the largest end of the broken pieces. Saw rabbets on opposite sides of each end. The rabbets should be as long as the half-rounds taken from the leg pieces. The unsawed center of the block should be equal in length to the missing section of the leg. This piece is the actual splice.

5 After truing up all cuts in the leg and splice to get a smooth surface-to-surface fit, glue the leg sections to the splice. Clamp until the glue sets.

6 Drill dowel holes through each of the lapped sections at right angles to the centerline of the leg and centered in the half-round ends. Glue the dowels in place.

7 Plane off the corners of the splice, and round the block with a Surform tool or wood rasp to match the taper and contour of the leg. Sand, and refinish the leg to match the other three on the table; then fit it in place.

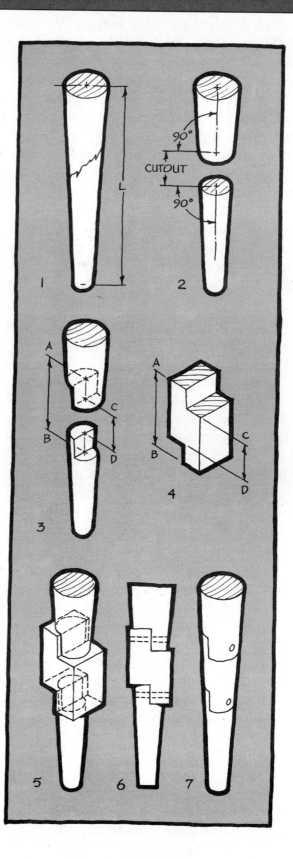

peatedly: make an angled cut on a piece of dimensional lumber. It's just a matter of laying out the taper's converging lines and following them. You would naturally keep the kerf just outside the cutline to make planing off the saw marks and reducing the piece to exact dimension easier.

Cutting a square cross-sectional taper is not much different. You need a piece of stock about $1/2$- to $3/4$-inch larger than the finished leg. It will probably be larger than the 2 x 2 stock lumberyards carry, but smaller than 4 x 4, the next common square lumber dimension. However, in this do-it-yourself era, most lumberyards are equipped with radial saws that will rip a 4 x 4 to the 3 x 3 dimension you're most likely to need. Few of them will go beyond straight rip cuts; you'll be faced with cutting the taper yourself, from the 3 x 3.

In addition to the stock from which your leg is to be cut, you'll need a piece of 2 x 6 about 20 inches longer than the stock. This is your vise and anchor. The stock can't be held in either a vise or C-clamps, though it could be held in a pipe clamp fastened to its ends and the pipe clamp in turn held on the workbench with a C-clamp. But, it's just as easy to toenail each side of the stock to a length of 2 x 6 clamped on sawhorses or a bench, or to make a temporary wedge clamp from the 2 x 6, as described in an earlier chapter, to keep the stock from moving.

First, square the ends. Mark them diagonally from corner to corner to give you a center mark. Center the large end of the old leg on one end of the stock, mark its sides, and extend these marks on the end of the stock to its edges. Repeat this marking on the other end of the stock with the small, or bottom, end of the old leg. Now, to make things easier, identify each mark at the edge of the top end of the stock with a letter and number, moving clock-wise from the top right-hand corner: A, B, C, D, E, F, G, and H, as you go around the perimeter. On the other end of the stock, identify the edge-mark opposite A as A1, then go counterclockwise and tag each mark, B–B1, C–C1, D–, etc. When you get through marking, A and A1 should be opposite one another at opposite ends of the stock, and so should all the other identifying letter-number combinations.

On the sides of the stock, connect the end marks, A to A1, B to B1, and so on around. Put your pencil aside and reach for the circular saw. The blade will be at 90° to the soleplate and extended for the deepest cut of which the saw is capable. This won't be deep enough to go through 3 x 3 stock, but don't worry about that. Of course, if you're using a handsaw, you needn't bother about depth of cut, because it'll do the job in one pass, even though it'll take more muscle and time.

Saw from A to A1. Rotate the stock a quarter turn to the left, which puts the line B–B1 under the sawblade, and much more to the point, gives you the width of the stock on which to rest the saw's soleplate. Before you saw, though, slip a thin wedge in the kerf of the cut you've just made, and be ready to put similar wedges in each succeeding kerf you cut so the stock will retain its original dimensions. If you don't hold the kerfs apart, your workpiece will be inclined to lean a bit.

Now, in succession, saw each mark, rotating the stock a quarter turn and wedging each kerf as the cuts are completed. Visualize what's happening inside that 3 x 3. The sawcuts will have formed the taper you're after, but the waste pieces are still attached to the stock by thin vees at the spots where the taper is largest. The small ends of the new leg are freed. Take a handsaw and free the top ends by following the kerf made by the power saw on each side of the stock. A bit of planing, a

CUTTING A SQUARE TAPERED LEG

1 Mark the ends of a piece of square stock, $\frac{1}{2}$ to 1 inch larger than the leg to be copied, with the dimensions of the top of the leg on one end, those of the small end of the leg on the opposite end. The dimensions should be centered in the stock, as shown, and the lines defining them carried to the edges of the stock and labeled as in the diagram. Carry the end marking down the sides of the stock connecting line *A* on one end to *A1* on the opposite end, *B* to *B1,* and so on around the four sides of the stock.

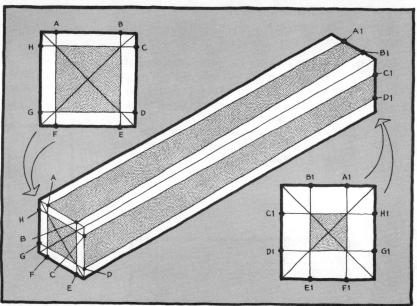

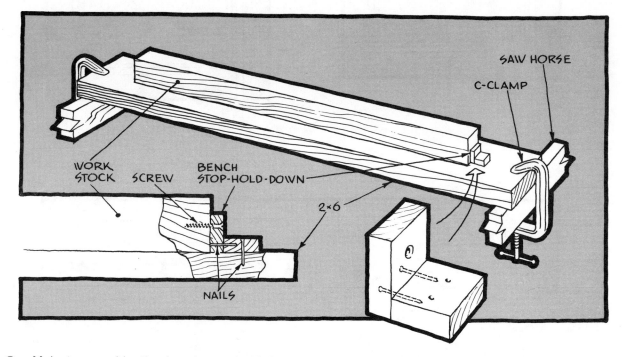

2 Make two combination bench-stop hold-downs out of scrap 1 x 2 lumber or $\frac{1}{2}$-inch plywood. Nail the stops to a 2 x 6 which is long enough to extend several inches beyond the stock for the leg. The distance between the stops should equal the length of the stock. Clamp the 2 x 6 to sawhorses or workbench. Put the stock between the stops and run screws into each end. Back out the screws each time the stock is to be turned, and run them into the stock after turning it. The screw holes left by the hold-down will be invisible after the table leg is installed.

3 With the blade of a 7½-inch circular saw set to make the deepest cut possible, saw along line *A-A1*, insert wedges into the saw kerf to keep the kerf open, and saw lines *B-B1*, *C-C1*, and *D-D1* in turn. Then, saw from the opposite end of the stock, using wedges to keep the kerfs of each cut open.

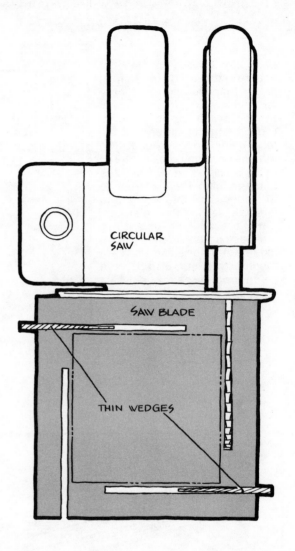

CIRCULAR SAW

SAW BLADE

THIN WEDGES

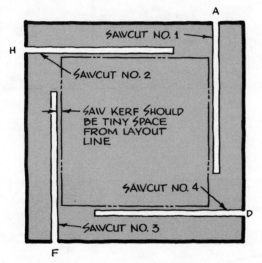

A

SAWCUT NO. 1

H

SAWCUT NO. 2

SAW KERF SHOULD BE TINY SPACE FROM LAYOUT LINE

SAWCUT NO. 4

D

SAWCUT NO. 3

F

DEPTH OF KERF FROM CIRCULAR SAW   PORTION OF NEW LEG STILL ATTACHED TO WASTE - REMOVE WITH HANDSAW   OUTLINE OF NEW LEG

4 When the eight sawcuts have been completed, a thin triangle of uncut wood will remain at the bottom of each kerf, as the cutaway shows. Remove these with a handsaw, following the kerfs made by the power saw. The leg is now ready to be planed to size, sanded, and finished.

bit of sanding, and your new leg is ready to be put in place and finished.

Let's tackle the job of cutting a round tapered leg from 3 x 3 square stock. Begin by tracing the outlines of the large and small ends of the old leg on a sheet of paper. Cut out these two circles and fold them in quarters; when unfolded, the creases will mark their centers. Mark the center of each end of the stock and push a brad through the centers of your templates to center the circles on the ends of the stock. Trace their outlines.

Find the center of each side of the ends of the stock and mark it on the ends. Using a try-square at 45°, establish the point at which a saw cut made at that angle must begin to miss the rim of the circle by about $1/4$ to $1/8$ inch. Mark this line, and using the center marks made on the ends as reference points, repeat the marking on the other three corners. Do the same thing at the opposite end of the stock, which you've already marked with the circle that represents the small end of the old leg.

Let's go back now to old Friends A, A1, B, B1, and so on. Identify each of the eight edge-marked diagonals in turn, beginning at top right, and rotating the stock to the left a quarter-turn as needed. When you've gone all the way around, A, B, C, D, E, F, G, and H, repeat the process at the opposite end, but this time begin your marks with A1 at the top left-hand edge and rotate the stock counterclockwise, to the left. Connect the edge marks along the sides, A to A1, B to B1, and so on.

Yes, the side lines will cross somewhere in the upper third of the stock. Don't worry about it. You're sawing to form a round leg, remember. That means your sawcuts will have to be made first from one end of the stock, then from the other. The only saw I know of that will make these cuts is a jigsaw with a base or soleplate that can be set at 45° on either side—left or right. However, all the modern models of jigsaws from Black & Decker, Millers Falls, Rockwell, and Skil have this feature.

When starting from the stock's end that is marked with the large circle, set the sawblade 45° right, and watch closely to be sure that the blade follows both the top and the side lines.

When sawing from the end of the stock marked with the small circle, set the blade at 45° left and watch the course of the blade as before.

When your cuts are completed—and you may find that you'll have to make two passes with opposite blade settings to go through the widest part of the stock, near the small end of the job—you will have an octagonal-shaped piece with a hump where the cuts made from opposite ends converged. Reduce these with a plane or Surform tool or wood rasp. With the same tools, reduce the corners of the octagon until the work is round. Don't try to take off one corner completely before rotating the stock to work on the next. Make three or four long, shallow plane-strokes on one corner, rotate the stock to the next, and take three or four shavings off it.

When you've gotten the job to the stage where you can't judge by eye how much more wood must come off any corner, cut a series of templates, half-circles of graduated diameters, in a strip of cardboard and use them to help you. If you have a caliper big enough to check the work for round, use it, of course.

Apply a straightedge the length of the work as it progresses to guard against high or low spots. Rotate the work against the straightedge while you look for bumps and valleys. Sand with progressively finer grades of sandpaper until the surface is ready for finishing with stain, varnish, or whatever finish is required to match the table and its original legs.

CUTTING A ROUND TAPERED LEG

1 Make templates of each end of the leg that you want to duplicate. Outline the ends of the old leg on pieces of paper and cut out the circles. Fold the circles into quarters to find their centers. Push brads through the paper at the center of each circle.

2 Find the center of each end of the stock by laying a straight-edge diagonally across the ends and marking the point where the diagonals intersect. Center the brads on the X mark and trace the outlines of the circles on the stock; then with a combination square set at 45°, mark diagonals across each corner about 1/8 inch outside the perimeter of each circle. Identify each diagonal on the edge of the stock with a letter-number combination, being sure that the letter on the second end marked is directly opposite the same letter on the other end; *A* to *A1*, *B* to *B1* and so on around the four sides of the stock.

3 Connect the edge marks along the sides of the stock, with lines from *A* to *A1*, *B* to *B1* and so forth.

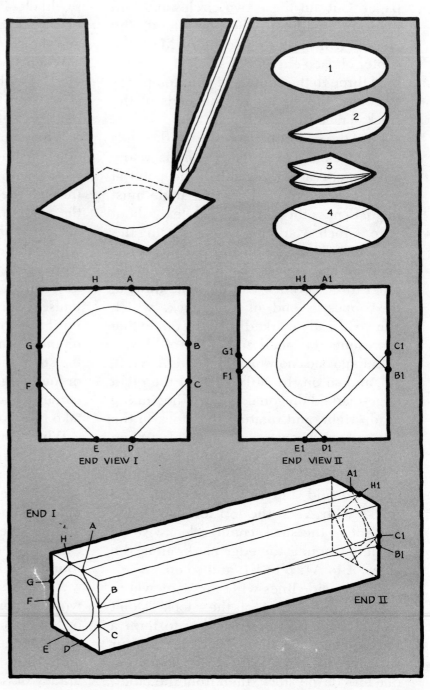

4 Set your saber saw blade at 45° right and saw from *A* to *A1, B* to *B1* and so on until all cuts are completed. For the last cuts, it may be necessary to reverse the blade setting to 45° left and saw from the opposite end in order to give the saw's base a supporting flat surface on which to travel.

5 There will be an octagonal taper with a hump where the saw cuts converged. Remove the hump with a Surform tool or wood rasp.

`**6** With a block plane, work down the corners of the octagon. Make three or four passes the length of each corner in turn, rotating the stock, instead of trying to reduce each corner in succession. When the corners of the octagon have been planed down equally, you will have a 32-sided figure, very close to round. Continue to reduce all corners with the plane until an almost-round is produced, then switch to a Surform tool or rasp.

7 In the final stages of the work, use a caliper to check for roundness. Or cut half-circle templates of stepped-down diameters on a piece of cardboard to guide you.

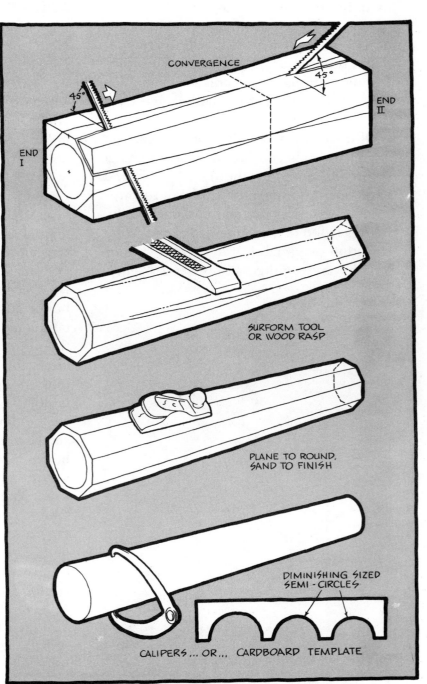

A lot of work for a single table leg? That depends on how you look at it. To risk being repetitive, the job of making a round tapered leg goes a lot faster than the description reads. It's like a lot of other do-it-yourself projects: the money saved by doing instead of hiring or buying may be a secondary consideration. What most of us who enjoy jobs of this kind are after is the satisfaction of proving to ourselves that with simple hand tools we can match or exceed work that's usually done by a machine in a factory.

Of course, if you don't want to take on what you might consider to be a somewhat involved hand job, there's a quick and easy out. Lumberyards and housewares stores, as well as the mail-order specialty houses listed in the appendix, carry a large selection of prefabricated legs in various lengths and configurations. You can al-

ways buy four of these and replace all the legs on the table. Several styles of these ready-to-install legs are shown in the accompanying photo.

REPAIRING STRETCHERS AND APRONS

Now, let's move on to stretchers. These aren't commonly found on large tables, but are commonplace on small ones. They're fixed in exactly the same way you'd fix the stretchers of a chair, as detailed in Chapter 5. The only difference is one of scale; and table stretchers are easier to repair because they're larger.

Continuing to move on higher, we come to aprons, also called skirts. On large legged tables these are generally part of the leg assembly, as we've already seen. On small tables, though, the skirts and legs may be separate assemblies, the skirts being attached to the underside of the tabletops by long screws that go through them in countersunk pilot holes. Less often, the skirts of a small table will be fitted into a dado channel routed in the tabletop's underside as well. These joints are seldom glued. All tables, large and small, are designed to give a bit under heavy loads; this is why such devices as hanger plates and tabletop hangers are used. You will find glued joints on small tables with proportionately small components. These are often assembled by mortising the skirts into the legs and fitting the top into a dado groove that runs around the inner perimeter of the skirts. This method is commonplace in tables designed to accept a glass top.

With age and use, no matter how carefully it's been seasoned, wood shrinks. Screws work loose and drop out, joints open as a result, and tables get loose and wobbly. The cure for loose screws is to replace them with new ones of the same

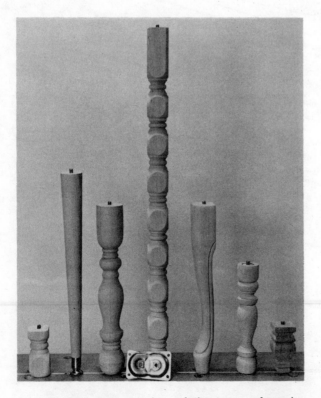

These are just a few of the types of ready-made legs that you can buy as replacements for broken ones.

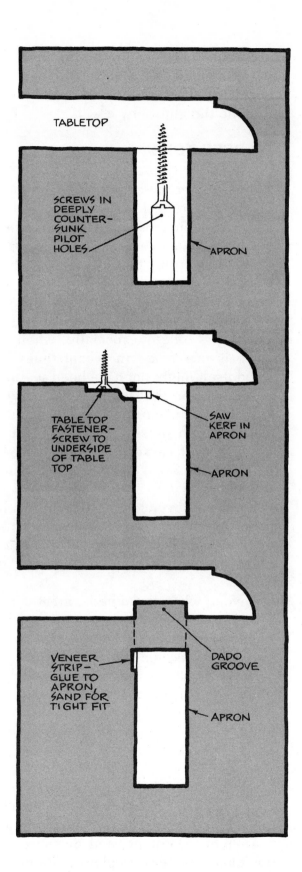

TABLETOP

SCREWS IN DEEPLY COUNTER-SUNK PILOT HOLES

APRON

TABLE TOP FASTENER—SCREW TO UNDERSIDE OF TABLE TOP

SAW KERF IN APRON

APRON

VENEER STRIP—GLUE TO APRON, SAND FOR TIGHT FIT

DADO GROOVE

APRON

Screws passing through the apron into the underside of the tabletop will be found on most small tables and some large ones. Tighten the screws to tighten the apron.

Metal clips that fit into a dado groove in the apron and are screwed to the tabletop are another method of attaching aprons. If the screws are loose, tighten them. If the groove is worn, shift the hangers an inch or so to tighten the apron.

On tables having the apron fixed to the legs, a dado grove may have been cut in the underside of the tabletop to accommodate the apron. A short length of veneer glued to the top inside edge of the apron and sanded to fill out the groove will remove play of the apron in the groove and end looseness.

length, but a size larger in diameter. A dado joint that's never been glued, or in which the glue has failed with age, can be made tight by gluing a strip of veneer to the inner face of the apron, where it goes into the joint, and sanding it until the apron fits tightly again.

Both large and small pedestal tables are almost always put together by attaching a framework to the underside of the top and then screwing the pedestal to this framework. Here again, one or more of these screws may fall out as the wood shrinks away from it, or as the screw works loose when the table is moved from one place to another. The cure once more is a larger diameter screw of the same length.

Pedestal tables seldom have leg problems, but occasionally they'll suffer from opening glue joints. The cure has already been noted: clean away old glue and apply new. An X-Acto razor saw blade will do the groove-cleaning very efficiently

In a typical pedestal table assembly, the pedestal will be attached to a frame that in turn is fixed to the underside of the tabletop. This is equally true of extension-type pedestal tables such as the one shown here and those that lack the extension feature.

and a thin metal strip will work fresh glue into the joint. Use a web or windlass clamp to pull the joint together and to hold it while the glue sets.

WARPED TOPS

There will be times when a tabletop or bureau top or desktop will warp or twist for no apparent reason. The reason's there, of course. In a great majority of cases, the cause of a warping top can be traced to the maker of the piece of furniture, who failed to seal the raw underside of the top with a wash coat of stain, shellac, or varnish. Less often, especially when the piece is one made in recent times, the wood itself might not have been seasoned properly, or in the case of softwoods that have been veneered, a glue void might have set up a stress. Other reasons are a misalignment caused by legs of uneven length or the breakdown of a key joint in the frame.

There are several cures for warping, but none of them is a 100% guaranteed method that will prevent a recurrence unless steps are taken to remove the cause.

Anyone who's examined a great deal of furniture in secondhand stores and antique shops has seen examples of tables, bureaus, desks, and other pieces on which a warped top has simply been turned over, a new edge routed, and the top refinished. Frequently, on the pieces given this treatment, the reversed top will have developed a crack; this is because internal stresses have been imposed on the wood when the arc of the warp was removed by clamping. The chances are that's why the piece found its way to secondhandville.

Another expedient used by those who don't know better is to plane and sand the top to remove the bulge of the warp and make the top flat again. Of course, this

Even a badly warped top on a piece of furniture, such as the one on this antique china cabinet, can be cured if you'll follow the procedures given in the text and drawings. Remember, though, time was required to create these warps, and a bit of patience will be required to cure them.

treatment doesn't really make the top flat, it just makes it look flat. Nothing is done to remove the cause, and the warping is sure to continue. Because removing wood has created a thin spot, the top eventually will crack and have to be replaced—a bigger job than curing the cause of the warping when it first became noticeable.

Nature put the warp there, and nature will remove it for you, if you've the patience. Your first step is to remove the top. Older pieces will probably have been assembled with glue blocks, triangular lengths of wood glued and perhaps screwed along the line where the top and skirt or frame of the piece meet. In more modern pieces, the top may be held by L-shaped metal pieces screwed to the underside of the top and fitted into a saw kerf in the skirt or frame. Occasionally, the skirt or frame and top of a piece may be held together only by glue.

Whatever the method of assembly, the top must come off. Old glues can usually be softened with a strong solution of acetic acid, which is the base of vinegar. In fact, you can use vinegar, though the job will take longer. Make up a 28% solution of glacial acetic acid, which you can get from any photo supply store, by pouring 3 ounces of glacial acetic acid into 8 ounces of water. Always add the acid to the water; if you add water to the acid, a splash will spray your hands with the acid, and they'll sting until it can be washed off. Do your mixing outdoors or in a well-ventilated room, for the fumes will be very strong. Further dilute the 28% solution in the ratio of one part of the acid mixture to two or three parts of water. You may be able to buy a ready-mixed 28% acid. Wet rags in this and soak the glue-line until the glue softens.

If you can't take the glue blocks off this way, use a razor saw or dovetail saw to part them by sawing from their base to the line where top and skirt join. Then, with a chisel, take off the remains of the braces from top and skirt. Metal plate fasteners can be removed by simply taking out the screws.

Once the top has been removed, your procedure will vary according to the season. In warm weather, take the top out to the lawn, and water an area of the grass slightly bigger than the top will cover. Lay the top on the grass with the arch of the warp upward. Forget it for a half-day, give or take an hour or so. The actual time required for the combined action of sun and moisture to flatten the top will differ with weather conditions. On hot, humid days, only three or four hours may be required, but on cool, dry days the top may have to lie exposed for two days or more.

In winter, or during periods of rainy weather, form a base of wet papers or cloths on the concrete floor of a garage or basement. Lay the top on this pad and hook up a sunlamp or two—infrared lamps is their correct name—and adjust them to spread their light evenly over the entire surface of the top. This method takes longer to work than does natural sunshine.

Count on at least one full day, perhaps two, before the top flattens out.

Indoors or out, you can speed the flattening process by using clamps. No C-clamps that I know of have throats deep enough to apply pressure to the right spots, so you'll have to improvise. Cut lengths of 2 x 4 lumber about 8 to 10 inches longer than the width of the warped top. You'll need two pieces for each clamp, and the clamps should be spaced no further than 20 to 24 inches apart.

If you have enough big C-clamps, use one at each end of a pair of 2 x 4s with the top sandwiched between them; the 2 x 4s will naturally be at right angles to the line of the warp. Few of us have as many big C-clamps as will be needed for this, so improvise again. Drill mating holes through each end of each 2 x 4 and insert bolts that can be drawn tight to press the 2 x 4s against the top. Be sure to use washers at head and nut of each bolt. Don't be in a hurry and try to force the flattening with excessive pressure. When you first put in these clamps, finger-tighten the nuts and then tighten them by about three turns with a wrench. Then, at intervals of an hour or two, take a turn on each bolt until the top is flat. Usually, the process will be speeded if you brush the underside of the top with water and use sunlamps for heat. The clamps can be used whether you're working indoors or on the lawn.

If a warped top doesn't flatten out by continued pressure alone, saw-surgery is indicated. Set the blade of your circular saw to cut a kerf one-third to one-half as deep as the top is thick. In other words, if the top you're trying to straighten is $3/4$ inch thick, the saw kerf should be $1/4$ to $3/8$ inch deep. On the underside of the top, saw a row of kerfs $1\frac{1}{2}$ to 2 inches apart. Cut with the grain of the wood, which is almost invariably the long dimension of

the top. Use clamps as described earlier to force the top flat. Work very gently, applying both heat and moisture to the underside to avoid cracking the upper surface of the top.

When the top has been forced flat, cut strips of veneer as long as the saw kerfs and as wide as the kerfs are deep. The veneer should be as thick as the width of the kerfs. Lacking veneer, cut strips of the proper width from the edge of a piece of scrap lumber. Brush the saw kerfs thoroughly with glue and slide the veneer strips into them. Loosen the clamps long enough to slide pieces of waxed paper between the 2 x 4s and the glued surface areas they touch. Tighten the clamps and let the glue dry overnight. Take the clamps off, rough-sand the work surface, and brush it with a wash coat of shellac or varnish to keep moisture from penetrating the wood again.

As complex as this repair seems to be from what you've just read, it's really not all that difficult. It's really the only way to straighten a warped top permanently. On some tabletops, you can simply screw braces on across the grain, spaced 16 to 18 inches apart along the underside. This method isn't satisfactory for cabinet pieces such as bureaus and desks, because any braces big enough to do the job of holding the top straight will interfere with the drawers sliding in and out.

Incidentally, if you encounter a top that has warped enough to cause the wood to crack, straighten the top before trying to deal with the cracks. When the warp is cured, work glue into the crack—or cracks—and use a pipe clamp to pull them closed. Then, put a metal mending plate or one made from hardboard along the length of the crack on the underside of the tabletop. My own preference is to use the thin hardboard and glue and screw it into place.

If you don't have the pipe clamp that

CURING WARPED TABLETOPS

Often, a warped tabletop will straighten out if it's put on wet grass in the bright sunshine.

If the warp doesn't straighten in a reasonable time, say ten hours of exposure on a wet surface to bright sunlight, or if it doesn't flatten out completely, use clamps to speed the job.

Should the pressure of clamping still prove inadequate to straighten the warp, take the next step. With the blade of your circular saw set to cut between $1/4$ and $1/2$ inch, depending on the thickness of the top, saw kerfs at regularly spaced distances on the concave side and replace the 2 x 4 clamps. Cut splines the width of the saw kerfs and glue them in the cuts. Plane the protruding edges of the splines level with the surface.

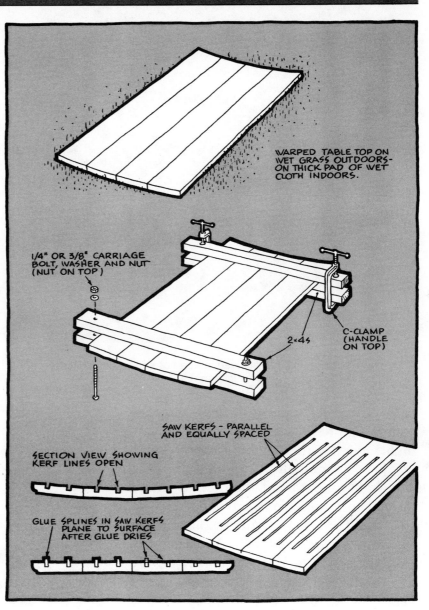

WARPED TABLE TOP ON WET GRASS OUTDOORS- ON THICK PAD OF WET CLOTH INDOORS.

1/4" OR 3/8" CARRIAGE BOLT, WASHER AND NUT (NUT ON TOP)

C-CLAMP (HANDLE ON TOP)

2×4s

SAW KERFS - PARALLEL AND EQUALLY SPACED

SECTION VIEW SHOWING KERF LINES OPEN

GLUE SPLINES IN SAW KERFS PLANE TO SURFACE AFTER GLUE DRIES

makes jobs of this kind easy, you can make a wedge clamp that will do most of the things a pipe clamp will. Wedge clamps were easy to improvise in the days when most workshops had wooden floors. The wall served as one side of the clamp. a 2 x 4 nailed to the floor the proper distance from the wall formed the other end, the work was laid between the wall and the nailed-down 2 x 4, and wedges tapped in place between the work and the 2 x 4 to press the job together. Today, when most workrooms have concrete floors, it takes two to tango.

Cut two pieces of scrap 2 x 4 or 2 x 6 into equal lengths, 3 or 4 feet, whatever fits your needs. Screw crosspieces made of the same material at right angles to these boards on the ends of each board. Cut two more crosspieces and clamp them at right angles to the other ends of the long boards while you drill a pair of holes through

The wedge clamp can be used instead of a pipe clamp for edge-gluing or other wide jobs, but it must be used on the floor or on a large table.

each crosspiece and on through the long board. The easiest size hole to drill is ¹/₄ inch, which will accommodate a 3-inch hex or machine bolt ⁷/₁₆ inch in diameter. The bolts will thread themselves into a ¹/₄-inch hole and no nuts are needed; pressure will hold them firmly in place when the wedges are tightened. You can drill similar holes 8 to 10 inches apart toward the middle of the long boards to give you a variety of openings. Cut wedges of 1 x 4 or 1 x 6 lumber to press the work together. The photos show the finished clamp.

Pipe clamps or wedge clamps are useful for gluing chair seats and other wide flat pieces that have cracked or split along a glue joint. Usually, such splits occur along a glue line, and mending is just a matter of cleaning off old glue, putting on new, and clamping the work to let the glue set. Of course, if the split is the result of a crack in the wood, you'd want to use a mending plate to reinforce the mend.

This detail of one end of the clamp shows how the stopblocks are attached to the crosspieces and the crosspieces scored to give you a quick index mark and assure proper alignment. When you tap in the wedges, do it with a hammer in each hand, striking both wide ends at the same time.

Glue failure in a tabletop or desk top isn't commonplace, but it does happen. If you need to reglue, begin by opening the joints wide enough to allow you to scrape off all the old glue.

EXTENSION AND DROPLEAF TABLES

Now let's look at some of the special problems that afflict multi-function tables: extension tables and dropleaf tables. The slides you'll encounter in extension tables are all pretty much the same. Those on better pieces or newer pieces will be made up of four hardwood boards connected by dovetail joints that run the length of the boards' centers. The outside boards will be attached to one side of the tabletop, one to each half, and the center boards will slide free. When additional leaves are being inserted, the center boards are pulled in the dovetails to span the gap and support the leaves that are being added. Some kind of a pin or block is fitted to keep the slide assembly from being pulled apart when the ends of the table are separated too far. On pedestal-type extension tables, the slide will be sandwiched between the underside of the tabletop and a frame that's attached to the pedestal.

By far the most common need for repairs to these center-split extension tables is the stopblock or stop-pin that keeps the two halves from being pulled completely apart. Blocks that are glued on will simply fall apart when the glue fails, those that

If the table has irregular ends, curved, rounded, scrolled or whatever, cut pads to match the contours. This will be insurance that the pressure of the clamps will be applied evenly as they're drawn tight.

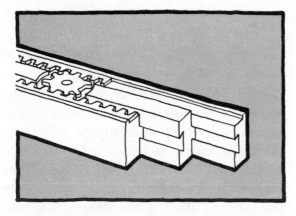

Details of slide construction. It's more practical to replace a slide instead of trying to repair one.

Those stubby dowels or metal pins that protrude from one side of an extension-table leaf have a high mortality. To replace, first drill out the stub of the broken dowel. Clean out the remnants of the dowel and remove the old glue with a narrow chisel. Try not to enlarge the hole.

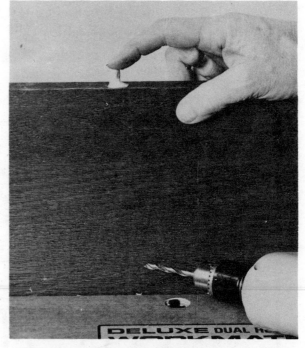

Cut a length of dowel, glue it in place, and taper with a file to make it slide easily into place when it's pushed against the hole in the mating leaf.

have been screwed on will come off after a screw has been loosened from the repeated jarring of the table being opened, pins get bent or loosen and fall out. Reglue the blocks after scraping off all old glue, and anchor them with screws. Put new screws or pins in to replace those that have gotten loose or bent.

Some modern metal-and-plastic tables will have metal extension slides, and if one of these gets damaged or bent, the only cure is a new slide. Constantine and Craftsman carry table slides in stock.

Leaves of extension tables are also subject to damage; usually the damage is a chipped corner, a repair that's already been covered, or one or more broken pins. These pins are designed to fit into holes along the edges of the mating leaf, or into the edge of the tabletop when only one leaf is inserted. Drill out the stubs of the broken dowels and insert new ones. Your chance of finding matching metal pins of the type used on any given table are about nil, as manufacturers invariably order only enough parts of this kind to fill a production run. Replace them with dowels, drilling out the matching holes on the other leaves and the edge of the tabletop to the larger diameter the dowels will require.

The dropleaf is another type of extension table, and the most common damage

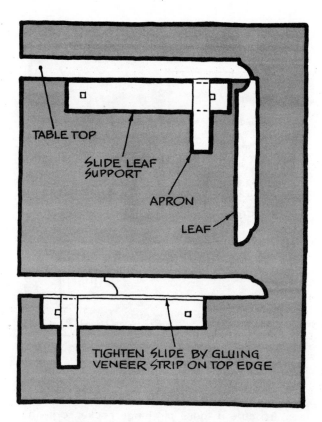

This is one of the three types of supports used on a dropleaf table to hold up its leaves. The slide travels through a slot in the apron. Eventually wear will loosen the slide. The best repair is to glue a strip of veneer on the top edge of the slide.

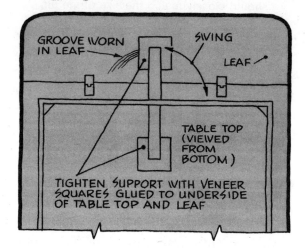

Some swing-out supports for dropleafs simply run along the underside of the tabletop; ultimately these will wear a crescent-shaped groove in the wood, allowing the leaf to sag. Sand the worn area smooth and glue a thin veneer patch over it. If the place is deeply worn, as it may be in an old table, put a second piece of veneer behind the apron to minimize future wear.

it suffers is loose hinges. Often, only two relatively light hinges will be fitted to hold a heavy leaf, and in time the strain put on the hinges when a leaf is raised by lifting it at a corner rather than the center will cause the hinge screws to come loose and perhaps to bend the hinges at the center joints. Replacing the light hinges with a piano hinge, or two or three 6-inch lengths of piano hinge, will end the problem permanently. Replacing old screws with new ones of the same length but a size larger in diameter will cure it temporarily.

Dropleaf tables have slides that extend through the apron to support their leaves when raised. The slide may travel back and forth through a narrow slot cut in the apron, or it may be hinged with a center pin to swing out from a slot the size of the slide. Wear on the slide or the underside of the leaf will cause the leaf to sag when raised; the cure is a strip of veneer glued either to the top of the side or the worn area on the underside of the leaf.

Butterfly and gateleg tables have similar leaf supports. Those on butterfly tables are shaped like a half-heart; on gateleg tables the supports are a full-length leg that resembles a gate. Both are pin-hinged to a stretcher at the bottom and to the tabletop or apron at the top, and these hinges are the parts on such tables that most commonly need repairing.

With use, the hinge holes get enlarged or the pins themselves get bent. In the latter case, the pins must be replaced, and this usually means having new pins turned at a machine shop. If the holes are worn, it's a do-it-yourself job to install metal bushings the length of the pin. Ream the holes with a drill, and enlarge the pins so they will fit snugly with bushings made from the seamless brass tubing available at hardware stores or by mail order from Brookstone. This tubing

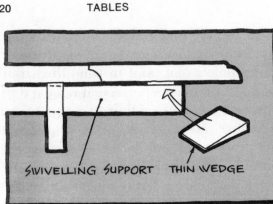

Swivelling support   Thin wedge

On some dropleaf tables with swivel supporting arms, a long thin wedge is glued to the underside of the leaf. The wedge limits the arc of travel made by the support and in effect locks the leaf firmly in an upright position. The cause of a sagging leaf may be wear on the wedge, or it may have dropped off completely. In either case, install a new wedge.

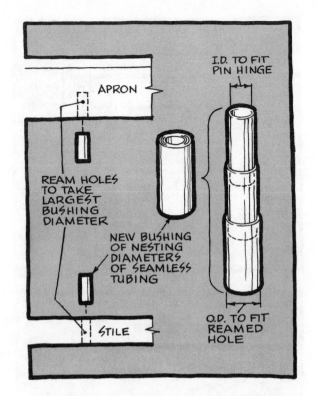

I.D. TO FIT PIN HINGE

APRON

REAM HOLES TO TAKE LARGEST BUSHING DIAMETER

NEW BUSHING OF NESTING DIAMETERS OF SEAMLESS TUBING

STILE

O.D. TO FIT REAMED HOLE

To cure a loose pin-hinge socket, drill the socket a bit larger and get nesting seamless brass tubing in two or more diameters. Cut lengths of the tubing to fill the enlarged socket. The outside diameter of the largest piece of tubing should fit the reamed socket snugly, the inside diameter of the smallest should closely match the size of the pin.

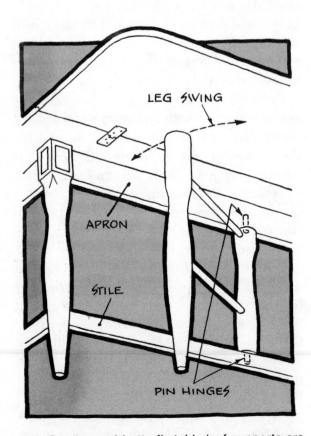

LEG SWING

APRON

STILE

PIN HINGES

Gateleg and butterfly table leaf-supports are generally pin-hinged. A wobbly support may mean that the pin has worn away the sides of its socket.

comes in sizes from $1/16$ to $1/2$ inch OD in $1/16$-inch increments, so successively smaller diameters nest into the next larger size. Cut small-diameter lengths to fit the pins, lengths of larger diameter to fit the reamed holes, and reset the pin.

CARD TABLES, ETC.

There's one type of table I've studiously avoided mentioning until now. This is the ephemeral table, the folding card table with locking braces that in theory will support the legs when they're unfolded. Most of the braces, though, are extremely flimsy and bend quite easily. They can usually be straightened two or three times before they break; then, if you want to keep the table in working order, you'll have to put on a new leg brace.

My advice is, don't bother. Over the years I've wasted more time trying to find the parts with which to repair or replace card-table legs than I like to think about. Usually, by the time a table needs to have its leg struts replaced, it's a model that's been discontinued, for which no more parts are available. The braces were made especially for tables of that model, and were never stocked by the retail stores which carried the tables. A few of the highest-grade folding card tables use standard hardware that you can buy from a few hardware stores and most mail-order specialty suppliers such as Constantine. The sane thing to do is to buy another table.

Game tables such as pingpong tables are quite another matter. These tables are almost always made for heavy duty, and have wooden legs with a standard brace assembly or some kind of locking socket that can be replaced. If a leg breaks it can be fixed with a dowel or splice like any other wooden table leg. You needn't hesitate to take on a repair job involving one of these tables, because sturdiness isn't sacrificed to light weight in their construction.

This chapter isn't the last word in the book on tables. Later, you'll find brief directions for repairing plastic tables, as well as those with marble and glass tops, where such repairs are practical. Almost any well-made table can be repaired unless it's a product of the portable, mobile society of today. If it's a flimsy table to start with, though, don't buck the tide. Discard it and replace it with a table that will endure.

7

Cabinet Pieces

Articles of furniture that have a basic boxlike shape are called "cabinet pieces." The category includes dressers and vanities, desks, wardrobes, sideboards, bureaus, and stands of various kinds, as well as those pieces that have the word "cabinet" in their names, such as a "china cabinet." The family is a large and varied one, but like many families its members have a close resemblance to one another while their differences are often hidden. Consequently, the repair jobs these pieces need are surprisingly similar.

Cabinet pieces are three-sided boxes with drawer fronts or a door forming the fourth side, which is generally the front of the piece. A few pieces combine drawers and doors, and cabinetmakers of an earlier decade used to spend a great deal of time and exercise a lot of ingenuity in fitting one or more concealed drawers or doors into their pieces. This pleasant whimsey seems to have faded about the beginning of the present century. If you encounter a piece with such a feature, you can be certain that it's an old one.

HARDWARE

By far the most frequent components of cabinet pieces that call for attention are the pulls, hinges, latches, and locks. The job of replacing a pull is usually a matter of five minutes with pliers or a screwdriver. Most pulls are attached by a bolt which extends through the drawer or door face and kept tight by a nut inside the drawer. The most common problem here is that the retaining nut often gets lost and there's no replacement with the right threading or of the right size. For temporary repairs, wind dental floss around the bolt and an oversized, wrong-thread nut can generally be screwed on. Pulls which are attached with a bolt inserted from inside the drawer can also be fixed temporarily this way.

In an earlier chapter, I mentioned briefly the problems involved in replacing visible hardware on furniture. To save you from having to thumb back, the recommendation made there was to look for an identical replacement as long as your patience

Replace old bent and twisted hinges with a single strip of piano hinge to end hinge troubles on dropleafs of any kind.

held out, then to replace all the visible hardware. In replacing, look for pulls with bases just a bit larger than the old, or install escutcheon plates to minimize the refinishing that will be called for if a smaller-based pull is substituted.

Hinges haven't changed in a century either as to style or size, so they present no real problem. Take along a matching hinge with the one you're trying to replace, and you'll probably be able to find an exact duplicate at the first hardware store you visit. Locks are another matter. While Constantine, Craftsman, and a number of other mail-order houses give very precise dimensions and specifications for cabinet locks in their catalogs, you won't always be successful in finding a duplicate for those on some pieces. Usually, your best bet is to visit a professional locksmith, who will be able to order the duplicate you're looking for.

Going back to hinges, the most common problem with these is the shrinkage of wood around the screws holding them in place. This can be cured by shaving some thin chips off a piece of scrap lumber and dabbing them very lightly with glue on one side. Insert three or four of these shavings, thin edges down, in the hole, start the screw in it, and trim the chips off flush. Then remove the screw and refit the hinge.

Secretaries, desks, and dropleaf sideboards also develop hinge problems, especially if the pieces were originally fitted with several small hinges along a fairly lengthy span. Replace old, bent and twisted hinges with a single strip of piano hinge to end this trouble permanently.

Surface cracking, checking, and the warping of tops has already been covered in detail in earlier chapters. This includes surface repairs with wax or shellac sticks and wood paste filler, dents, marred places in the finish, and replacing edges or corners that have been damaged.

Improvised clamps of metal angle braces serve on small jobs.

Locking-jaw pliers are another substitute for C-clamps. Be sure to pad the surface on which they're applied or the serrated jaws will mar it.

INTERIOR REPAIRS

Splitting of the thin backs and dust shields on the bottoms of cabinet pieces can be cured either by fitting a new piece of thin veneer, or by gluing a long strip of veneer over the crack. You'll have to remove the cracked piece and lay it on a flat surface where it can be weighted while the glue sets up.

A badly damaged or broken drawer runner can usually be fixed without disassembling the piece, if you don't object to working in cramped quarters. You'll seldom be able to apply clamps on a cracked runner in order to hold a glued repair job. The runner will have to be taken out, or a thin strip of veneer used to close the crack and a couple of small screws used to pull the crack closed. Sometimes, you can improvise a thin clamp from a pair of L-shaped metal angles, by inserting a bolt through the bottom holes. See the illustration for details.

After making the mend, use paraffin, wax, or slick tape on top of the runner to

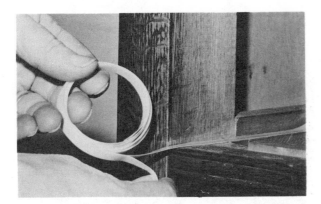

Slick tape is made from thick nylon or teflon with an adhesive applied to one side. It's designed to be applied to drawer runners to keep drawers from sticking.

A glance will tell you that no skilled cabinet-maker made this repair to the broken edge of an antique drawer. However, the repair does the job for which it was intended. The bottom, where drawer and runner meet, is straight and true.

make the drawer glide more easily. This remedy can also be used to ease sticking drawers. Often the sticking is caused by either a cracked runner or by wearing on the bottom edges of the drawer itself. Use a small plane or chisel to smooth the cracked or splintered area, and glue strips of the required thickness to the drawer edges or runner. Old pieces often show signs of this kind of repair. Another good way of judging the actual age of a cabinet piece is to check the drawers for this kind of mend as well as for hand-cut dovetails.

LEGS AND CASTERS

Legs on cabinet pieces are usually integral with the corner frame uprights, or have been made integral by joining the leg and frame with a mortise-and-tenon or finger joint. Methods of repairing split or cracked legs on cabinet pieces are the same as those already covered in the chapters dealing with chairs and tables; the difference is only one of scale. Again, if replacing a broken leg proves impossible, replace all four with prefab legs in the desired style. Often, you can begin with a prefab leg and use a Surform tool or a rasp to form it to match existing legs.

This is as good a place as any to discuss casters. Casters and glides are very important on cabinet pieces, and neglecting to fix or replace a single broken caster may result in great damage to the entire piece. Any cabinet piece that is allowed to sit very long at an odd angle is subjected to strains for which the designer made no allowance in computing stresses. Such treatment can result in warped sidepieces, drawers that have been squeezed out of true, and cracked or broken frame members.

Matching casters in old pieces presents much the same problem as that encountered in matching pulls. You'll have to do some looking, as a general rule. Unless the piece is a modern one, it will be fitted with wooden or porcelain casters, which have just about been replaced by casters with plastic wheels. However, you can get modern metal casters which are not only better-looking than plastic ones, but last longer. If shiny metal casters look incongruous on a piece of period furniture, reduce their obtrusiveness by painting them flat black.

Unquestionably, casters and glides sometimes do detract from the appear-

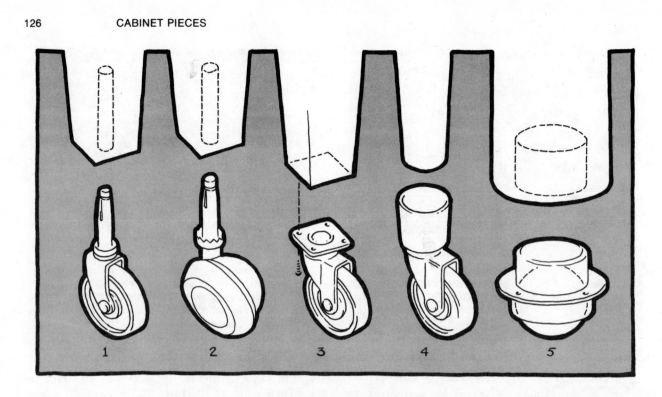

From these five types of casters, you should be able to find the style best suited for replacements. (1) Shafted, the most common, is fitted into a sleeve pushed into a hole drilled in the furniture leg. (2) Shafted, but with a ball that swivels more readily than a wheel. (3) Platform. (4) Cup caster. (5) Ball-bearing inletted into the leg.

ance of a piece of furniture that is an important element in a room's decoration. Compromise. Put casters only on the back legs. You can mount them on the legs, in which case you'll need to shorten the back legs by an amount equal to the height of the caster after it's been installed, or you may be able to offset the caster behind the leg by installing it on a wood block attached to the leg. If the latter method is used, an inconspicuous glide can be put on the front legs to keep the piece level. With casters on the back legs, you need only to tilt a heavy piece at the front to move it out of the path of the vacuum cleaner. This is a lot easier on your back than lifting a heavy piece of furniture, and it's easier on the furniture than dragging or pushing it on casterless legs.

Another compromise that you can make is to fit a period piece with cup casters, which become a decorative accent. A

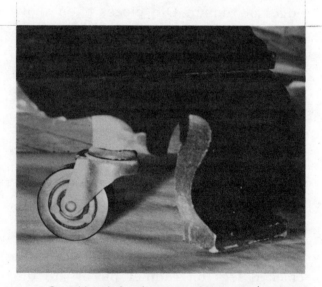

On skirted furniture, casters can be concealed by being mounted on a woodblock glued and screwed to the frame behind the skirt.

skirted cabinet piece can be equipped with invisible casters in two ways. One is to glue a block of some close-grained wood in the corners behind the skirt, and set the casters in this block, where the skirt will hide them. If this isn't possible because of the way the piece is made, a second alternative is to fit the legs with a special ball-bearing caster that is countersunk into the legs; only about $1/2$ inch of clearance above the floor is provided by casters of this type. You'll find them in the Constantine catalog.

On cabinet pieces that aren't too heavy, Teflon-footed glides may be a satisfactory solution. These slide easily on floors and don't mar their surface, yet allow a moderately heavy piece to be moved easily. Some types of glides are adjustable, and can be set to keep a piece level even if the front legs rest on a rug and the back legs on the bare floor. And glides of any kind are much less obtrusive than casters.

SIDE PANELS AND FRAMES

With the easy jobs out of the way, let's talk about those that are more challenging: repair and replacement of side panels and the mending of frames that have suffered breakage or joint failure and thus weakened the entire piece. The best take-off point when we consider these jobs is from the way most cabinet furniture is made.

All cabinet pieces are assembled around a framework. Panels that fit into rabbet joints close off three sides, and included in the framework are runners for the drawers and stiles for the doors that form the front. Back, side, top, and bottom sections of cabinet furniture are usually put together as individual units. In pieces that will be visible on all four sides, all three side panels will be finished. These are called "free-standing" to distinguish them from pieces that are intended to stand against a wall. On other pieces that back panel is generally left unfinished except for a wash coat of thinned shellac or stain to retard checking or warping.

Unless you're working on a very old cabinet piece, or an exceptionally well-made modern piece, the sides will be veneer. On older pieces, the sides of cabinet furniture were made from solid wood sawed to about $3/16$ inch thickness. Beginning in the 1840s, veneered sides began to appear, as the supply of the big hardwood trees that could provide boards up to 3 feet wide began to be depleted. These older veneer sides were usually two plies of almost equal thickness, with the grain of the inner ply of softwood running at about a 45° angle to that of the outside piece, to minimize warping. By the turn of the century, the predecessor of today's plywood was being used for cabinet sides, and all modern pieces have either a $3/16$- or $1/4$-inch section of plywood in the sides.

Methods of curing minor cracks and checks with stick shellac or stick wax have already been detailed; this is the treatment you should give solid wood sides. Veneers can be reglued with modern adhesives; just weight the reglued section well on a flat surface until the glue sets up.

A cabinet side that has suffered major damage may have to be replaced. In this case, you'll need to take its frame apart, and usually the quality of the piece dictates the method by which the frame was assembled. Better pieces will have frames joined with a mortise-and-tenon, or dowel-pinned lap, or tongue-and-groove joints. Less well-made pieces will have simple lap joints; schlock pieces may have simple miter joints or unpinned lap joints. If you must saw or chisel a joint apart, work on the inside of the frame, where repairs can be made that will be invisible when the piece has been reassembled.

Side panels in quality pieces are usually held in a dado joint, without glue. This is because all wood, even plywood, expands and contracts throughout its life in response to atmospheric conditions, mois-

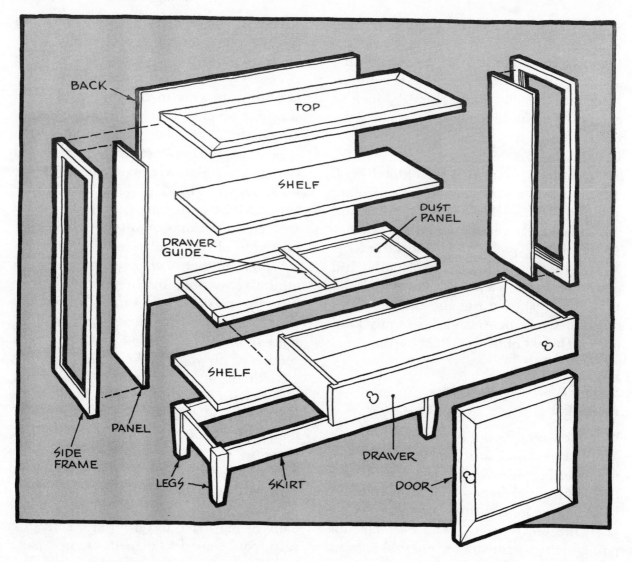

BACK

TOP

SHELF

DUST PANEL

DRAWER GUIDE

SHELF

DRAWER

SIDE FRAME

PANEL

LEGS

SKIRT

DOOR

Exploded view of a typical cabinet assembly. Small details have been omitted because they vary from one piece to the next. The *frame* may be fitted into a dado joint routed in the underside of the *top;* the *shelves* and *drawer runners* may be fitted into rabbets routed in the frame, or these parts may be set on glue blocks. The piece may have doors or drawers, or both.

ture and heat. When solid wood panels were used as cabinet furniture sides, their ever-changing dimensions caused the piece to develop loose joints and the problem was solved by installing the sides in dado grooves. In later years, with the development of better seasoning methods and glues and finishes, the practice began to change, but some makers still follow the old way.

Instead of holding the sides in a dado groove, furniture makers today use a simple rabbet joint with a spline strip on the inside. The side panels of the cabinet piece you're working on, then, may either be held in a dado groove, or in a rabbet with a spline strip, or they may be glued into a rabbet in more modern pieces. In some schlock furniture, side panels are simply tacked in a rabbet running the perimeter of the frame members.

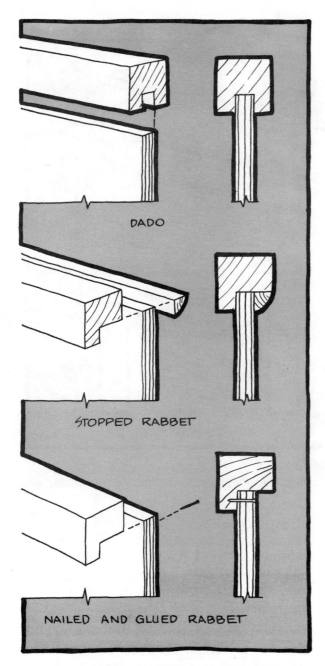

DADO

STOPPED RABBET

NAILED AND GLUED RABBET

Several methods of fitting panels in frames. In better-quality pieces panels are fitted in dado grooves without glue (top). Almost equally common are panels set in rabbets with a quarter-round stop glued or braded to the frame (center). On lesser quality pieces, the panels may be glued and nailed to the rabbet (bottom). In schlock furniture the panels will be held in place with brads and there may be no rabbets.

Still, the strength of a cabinet piece remains in its frame, and in pieces such as desks and dressers the drawer runners will have been fitted to become part of the frame. This is fairly complicated construction, and very rarely will a well-made cabinet piece need repairs to its frame. However, if you're faced with the job of replacing a side panel, be prepared to do a substantial amount of work. If a frame member must be replaced, the same amount of labor will be called for. And, if the frame of a cabinet piece requires repair to any joint because of glue failure, go on the theory that the failure of this joint is a clue to general glue deterioration, and disassemble and renew the glue throughout the piece.

Just how hard the job will be depends on the kind of joints used in the piece you're going to repair. This is the first thing to investigate. If the joints are mortise and tenon, each one must be broken with a chisel or sawed apart. When the piece is reassembled, splines or dowels must be substituted for the tenons. If the joints are doweled, old dowel stubs must be drilled out and new dowels inserted when the piece is reassembled. Lap joints can be broken quite easily, so can mitered corner joints, even if they have been keyed. See Chapter 1 for the ways to make and break each of these commonly used furniture joints.

Disassemble the frame section, then, and cut a new panel if panel replacement is your objective. Pre-sand and pre-finish the panel; it will save you time later. And, to repeat, always work on the inside of the section when you do the disassembling.

If a panel must be replaced in a frame that has simply been rabbeted and the panel tacked or glued in place, the job is a lot easier. It involves just about the same amount of work as changing a picture in a frame, and takes roughly the same amount of time.

It's seldom possible to repair a broken frame member on a cabinet piece. Usually

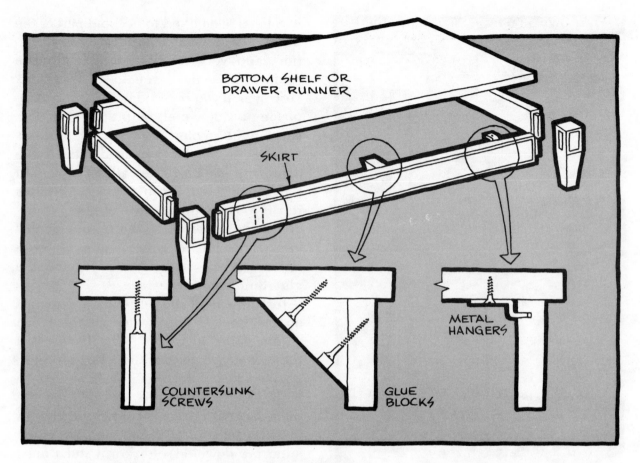

Most common methods of assembling cabinet bases. You may also encounter hanger plates and corner glue blocks.

it's necessary to make a new section to replace any member that has been badly split or splintered. You may be able to make the new piece a bit more simply, using a rabbet joint rather than a dado for the edge of the panel, which will simplify the reassembly. If you do this, use brads and glue to fit a small piece of quarter-round along the inner edge of the frame member to substitute for the omitted half of the old joint.

SKIRTS

Skirts on cabinet pieces are very easy to remove and replace in a majority of cases when this repair becomes necessary. The common method of attaching skirts to cabinet pieces is with a few screws placed in deeply countersunk holes that pass through the skirt into the bottom frame member. The apron may or may not be glued to the frame as well. Seldom is the apron joined to the legs or to the frame members at the sides, though this may be done with dowels on better-quality furniture. In the latter type of construction, it's almost always necessary to remove the legs in order to repair or replace the skirt. This puts the job into the major repairs category. If the skirt can be repaired with a mending plate on the back, it's better to go this route. Methods of minimizing surface damage will be found in an earlier chapter.

Your own ingenuity, perhaps aided by some of the construction details and repair suggestions in this chapter, should guide you in deciding which repairs are worth making when weighed against the time and materials involved. There are few shortcuts you can take in repairing really seriously damaged cabinet pieces. Frame members can only be replaced when broken, and this applies almost universally to each component in a cabinet piece.

Yes, there are a few money-saving shortcuts you can take. For instance, when replacing a visible component, you can usually veneer a piece of inexpensive lumber instead of fashioning the new piece from costly, hard-to-find hardwoods. You can often find suitable hardware in secondhand furniture or rummage stores that will be more suitable for a piece than new hardware, after you've refurbished the used items. You can even build up your own veneers at a fraction of the cost of commercial veneers, using the veneer and crossbanding materials that such firms as Craftsman and Constantine can supply.

Complete step-by-step details of such jobs as making veneered paneling are a bit outside the scope of this book, but the suppliers of materials have instruction leaflets that will give you these.

Finally, there are two thoughts I'd like to leave with you as this chapter ends, because so much of the emphasis here has been on the negative aspects of this branch of furniture repairing. Actually, it hasn't been all that negative—merely factual. Repairing cabinet pieces is a challenge that will try your best skills, but what's a challenge for if not to be met? What good are skills unless you use them after you've developed them?

Don't let the idea of any job of furniture repairing, even such fairly complicated jobs as making new frame members for a good cabinet piece, intimidate you. Just take your time, work out ways of solving the problems you know you're going to meet, and solutions will almost always present themselves.

8

Beds and Other Frames

Writing about straight chairs in an earlier chapter, I noted that if furniture was rated according to the stresses each kind was expected to handle in everyday use, this kind of chair would be at the top of the scale. Applying the same scale to other pieces, and rating straight chairs at 10 on the stress scale, I'd give beds a rating of about 9, and couches, divans, and upholstered chairs a 7 or 8.

Though there is seemingly no kinship between beds and upholstered furniture, a bit of analysis will show that they have one thing in common. All of them are basically frames, designed to carry the weight of one or more people on a number of intra-braced and relatively small-scaled boards. Consequently, there's a general relationship between the repairs they require and the methods of carrying out these repairs. The chief difference between beds and upholstered pieces is that most of the framework of beds is visible, most of the frames of upholstered pieces are hidden.

Some beds of the "modern" era don't fall into the category of framed pieces. Waterbeds, for example, are so heavy that they usually pass most of their weight and the weight of their occupants directly to the floor. The type of bed which consists of a free-standing headboard and a metal frame supporting springs and a mattress isn't a true framed piece of furniture. Neither of these types is considered in this chapter. If your waterbed springs a leak, you need a vulcanizing job from your friendly tire repair shop; if the metal framework of your free-standing headboard bed breaks down, it's a job for a welder.

Because their use-stress patterns are so much alike, repairs to framed pieces are also quite closely related. The splices and reinforcing techniques that have been detailed for other kinds of furniture often won't prove useful in repairing frame pieces; this isn't because these splices aren't strong enough, but because frame furniture encounters different kinds of stresses that are imposed on it from different angles. In many cases, frame pieces can be repaired, but there are some kinds of damage that call for replacement rather than mending of a badly damaged component.

Beds are designed more simply than the frames of upholstered divans or chairs.

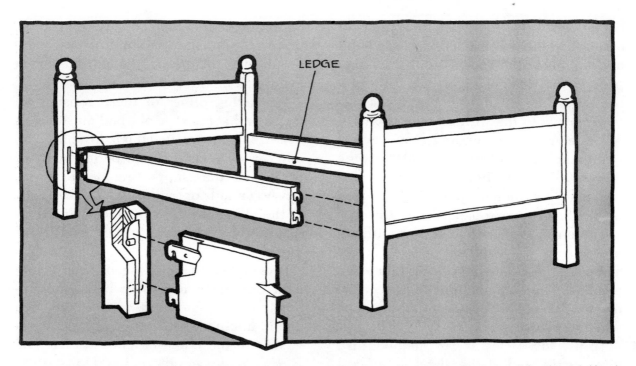

LEDGE

In conventional wooden bed assembly the legs are integral with the headboard and footboard. Headboard and footboard are connected by sidepieces with hooked fasteners that slide into slots and engage metal cross-pins. Ledges attached to the sidepieces support the bedsprings and mattress.

Most traditional beds get their strength from the size of their components rather than from the system of interlocked and braced joints found in upholstered pieces. At the risk of being repetitive, traditional beds are in essence very sturdy frames and little more. Decorative trim and details are secondary.

Traditional wooden beds, the only kind we'll deal with here, usually consist of four primary pieces: headboard, footboard, and a pair of sidepieces. Whether or not slats are used in a traditional bed depends on the type of springs the sidepieces support. Some kinds of springs have cross members equivalent to slats; other types require slats to support them. Sidepieces are fitted to the headboard and footboard by double-flanged metal inserts that lock into strong metal pins inserted in the side frames of the head- and footboards. There are several other kinds of bed fasteners, and we'll meet them a bit further along.

LEDGES AND SIDEPIECES

All beds having sidepieces support either slats or the frames of box springs on a slat-ledge that is glued and screwed to the inside of the sidepiece. The ledges and the sidepieces themselves are the most common source of problems in such beds. Because few manufacturers provide any method of securing the slats or the frames of the springs to these ledges, the sidepieces may react to the weight put on them by bowing outward as time goes on. When such bowing reaches a certain point, the slats fall off the ledges, or the weight of the spring frames becomes concentrated at the ends of the ledges instead of being distributed evenly along their length.

When this happens, the overstressed ledge may split and break in spite of the screws and glue that attach it to the sidepiece. At best, the falling of one or two center slats triggers the dropping of others, and the bedsprings develop a habit of dropping to the floor. Usually this happens in the dead of night, when the unconscious movement of the bed's occupants moves the springs even slightly.

There are two quick and easy ways of realigning the sidepieces and keeping them in alignment. Both ways require that the mattress and springs be removed before beginning repairs. After this has been done, a clamp of some sort, either a pipe clamp or a windlass, is used at the center of the siderails to bring them into parallel. The slats should be spaced so that they do not bind against the sidepiece when in place.

To use the easiest repair method, drill through the end of the slat and siderail ledge with a small bit—about $3/16$ or $1/8$ inch—and cut off the tip of a 10 penny common nail so that when dropped into the hole its point will not protrude from the bottom of the ledge. Do this at each end of the two center slats. The nails will hold the slats firmly in place and will stop the sidepiece from bulging any farther. However, if the bulge in the sidepieces is extreme, this method shouldn't be used, for there's a danger that the pull of the warped sidepieces may cause the nails to split the ledge piece.

Instead, on beds where the sidepiece bulges outward more than $1/4$ inch, use a turnbuckle repair. Drill pilot holes for stout screweyes at the center of the sidepiece; the point of the screw should penetrate at least half the thickness of the sidepiece itself after passing through the ledge. Install eyes on each sidepiece and run a length of picture-hanging wire with a turnbuckle in its center through the eyes and secure the wire ends by wrapping them around the wire itself. Adjust the turnbuckle by tightening it until the sidepieces are parallel. On beds having very

badly bowed sidepieces, two or even three turnbuckle assemblies may be required to distribute the pulling effect evenly along the sidepieces.

In making either of these repairs, remember that the slats of a bed must have a little bit of room in which to shift. You don't want to fasten them permanently or firmly to the supporting ledge, with screws or nails or glue. Don't jam the ends of the slats into the sidepieces so tightly that they can't shift a tiny bit, perhaps as much as $1/16$ to $1/8$ inch.

Broken ledges are the second most common damage suffered by beds of traditional design. The cause has already been given: unequal distribution of the weight of slats or the frame of a box spring. The cure is to replace the ledge. Don't try to splice it. Figure the weight this ledge carries: springs, mattress, covers, bed occupants, and the reason becomes apparent. Cut a new ledge from good straight-grained lumber and attach it to the sidepiece with screws and glue. Space the screws so they'll go into spots other than old screw holes, and plug the old screw holes with pieces of dowel. This is a good precaution to take, by the way, when replacing any component of a framed piece. Old screw holes left unplugged create weak spots in wood framing members that must bear strains.

Sidepieces will sometimes split at their ends, where saw kerfs have been cut to accept fasteners and the wood further weakened by drilling for the fastener pins. If the split is a clean one, you can sometimes repair it by gluing the split edges together and then putting on a hardboard mending plate with small screws and glue to cover the entire length of the split. Naturally, the mending plate would be attached to the hidden inner face of the sidepiece.

A sidepiece that has suffered major damage, such as a jagged break or a split that

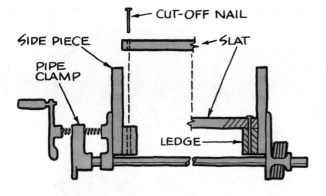

One way to cure bowed sidepieces which allow bed slats to fall out is to pull the sidepieces parallel with a pipe clamp. Then drill through the two center slats and the ledge and drop a nail into the holes.

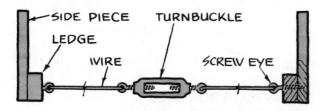

Another method of curing bowed sidepieces is to insert a sturdy screw-eye on the inside of each ledge, being sure the screw is long enough to go into the sidepiece itself. The eyes should be centered and directly opposite one another. Run a wire between the eyes, with a turnbuckle in the middle. Adjust the turnbuckle until the sidepieces are parallel. Badly bowed sidepieces may require two or even three of these adjusters.

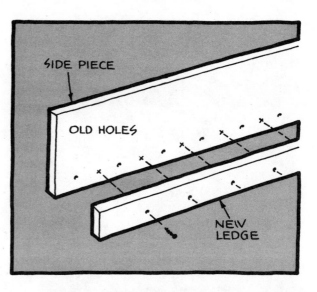

Split or cracked ledges should be replaced, not repaired. When replacing a rail, drill pilot holes for new screws. Then plug the old holes with short pieces of glued-in dowel to maintain the strength of the sidepiece.

has splintered the wood, should be replaced with a new board that can be finished to match the other components of the bed. This is especially necessary if the cause of a split sidepiece lies in the area where the fasteners have been inserted. Sometimes the need to replace a split sidepiece can be averted by changing the type of bed fastener used. There are three types of fasteners, and the only one impossible to use on a split sidepiece is the kind that has a plate inserted in a saw kerf in the sidepiece; this plate locks into pins inset in the footboard and headboard.

Pictured are two other kinds of bed fasteners with which old fasteners can be replaced. One type is mortised into the ends of the sidepieces and the female locking plate mortised into the head- and footboards. The mortises which accept the locking teeth won't have to be deep enough to weaken either sidepiece or leg. This type of hanger can also be mounted on the surface of a block attached to the inside of the sidepieces and legs of the head- and footboards.

Mortising or inletting the second kind of bed fastener isn't recommended. Mount this type on a block of wood securely attached to the inner faces of the sidepieces and the head and footboards. Replacing original kerf-set fasteners with either of these surface-mounted styles of fastener will go beyond simply replacing the old fasteners, which were the source of your trouble to begin with. By surface-mounting them, you add strength to a repair job done on a split sidepiece with the mounting block used for the new hardware.

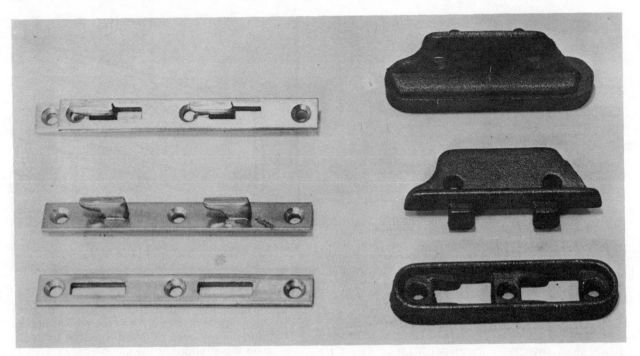

Replacement bed fasteners are made to be surface-mounted (left) or either inletted or surface-mounted (right).

Surface-mounted bed fasteners should be installed with the female fastener on the bed frame and the male fastener on a block of wood that has been glued and screwed to the sidepiece. Recess the wood block so the siderail will butt firmly to the bedframe when it's in place.

HEADBOARDS AND FOOTBOARDS

Headboard and footboard styles of traditional wooden beds vary widely. Generally, they are made by inserting slats or a plywood or veneered panel into dados cut in a frame; the legs normally form the sides of this frame. Repairing headboards and footboards is actually similar to repairing the frames of cabinet pieces. The chief difference is that the headboards and footboards are more accessible, and this makes the job easier. Refer to Chapter 6 for the methods to be followed in replacing or repairing the panels or frame of a paneled head- or footboard.

Similarly, go back to Chapter 5 if you're faced with fixing a slatted head- or footboard. The job is essentially the same as that of restoring a battered chair to useful life, and you'll use the same techniques and tools that would be employed in splicing a chair or table leg or a set of splats or

If you're repairing a split bed frame, mount the second type of fastener on the surface. If the sidepiece has split, the male half of the fastener should be mounted on a wood block glued and screwed in place, and offset to clear the female half. Open a slot for the hooks before mounting the female section. If you're installing one of these fasteners in a bed with intact legs, it's perfectly safe to inlet the base into the frame.

stretchers. For restoring the upholstery on a headboard of the modern free-standing upholstered style, turn ahead to Chapter 11 for methods, materials, and tools.

LEGS

Let's look just a bit more closely at legs. Wooden bed legs, straight or tapered, are often long in ratio to their diameter, and are especially vulnerable to breakage in two spots. Breaks most often occur at the bottoms, or tips, of bed legs, where the wood has been drilled to accommodate the stem of a caster or glide. Next in frequency are breaks at the points where

the leg begins, the spot where a saw kerf has been cut and holes drilled for the pins on which fasteners lock. This latter type of break and the ways to repair it have just been covered.

Obviously, if the bottom of a leg has been splintered by the collapse of a caster, and the caster's stem has torn out a chunk of wood along one side of the hole in which it was inserted, a simple gluing job isn't going to produce a repair strong enough to support the stem of another caster. Sooner or later, no matter what kind of adhesive you've used, no matter how many dowels you've inserted to strengthen the split, it's going to give way again.

Quite often a little shopping around will turn up a preformed leg of the kind pictured elsewhere that can be shaped with a Surform tool, or with rasp and sandpaper, to match the other legs. This replacement can be set into the frame with a large dowel, using the methods described and illustrated in Chapter 6.

There's another kind of repair that is faster and equally successful, if you can't find a suitable preformed leg, or don't want to take on the job of making a new leg from scratch. Glue the split-out section back in place, if this is possible, and reinforce it with a dowel the size of the caster stem glued in the hole where the stem fitted. Remove the casters from the other three legs and install a set of cup or platform casters, preferably the former.

Cup casters aren't fitted by inserting a stem into the ends of a bed leg; instead, their upper section is shaped to accept a round or square leg tip. You'll usually have to do a bit of sanding or filing to get a snug fit, of course, but you'll have a quick and permanent repair. Plate or platform casters have flat tops on which the legs rest and are held in place with screws driven in from the bottom of the platform.

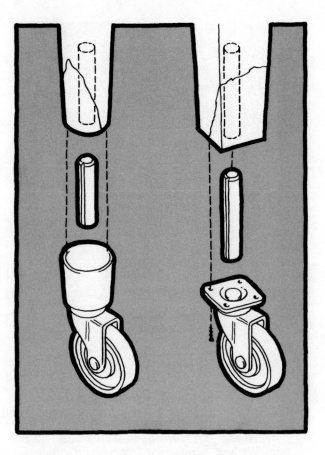

Left: When a shaft-type caster collapses and breaks open a bed leg, repair the tip of the leg by gluing the break, and at the same time inserting a glue-coated dowel in the hole. Then, replace the shaft casters on all legs with cup casters. *Right:* Fit square bed legs with platform casters after making the necessary repairs as described earlier. This type of caster is screw-mounted; check catalogs for the size and style that will most closely fit the legs of the bed to which they will be fitted.

A bed leg will seldom break at a point other than the two just noted. Very rarely, a leg will split at the point where a mortise or dado has been cut to accept a panel or splat, but breaks of this kind are generally above the stress points where the side-pieces or the casters are fitted. Breaks of this kind are minor and can be safely mended with glue, clamps, and a short piece of dowel for reinforcement, as described in earlier chapters.

UPHOLSTERED PIECES

Now, let's move on to upholstered pieces and see how the frames of these can be repaired. Many a good upholstered couch or chair has been prematurely discarded because its owner hesitated to dig into the piece's innards and uncover the frame, where a joint failed or a board cracked and split. The job of getting to the break isn't really all that difficult. If you'll turn ahead to Chapter 11, you'll learn which sections of the upholstery fabric need to be removed, and in what sequence, to reach any part of the frame of any upholstered piece. Your first job is to remove as much of the upholstery and padding as is necessary to get to the section of the frame that needs to be fixed.

Dealers in secondhand furniture have an especially warm spot in their hearts for the legs of both upholstered chairs and couches. These are the components most likely to give way on these pieces, and any dealer in used furniture will tell you that more than half the upholstered pieces he buys at 10¢ on the dollar of their real value are sold because a leg has snapped off. Oddly, the legs of upholstered chairs and sofas are the easiest parts of all to repair.

This is true whether the legs are integral with the sideframes or attached sep-

Buy preformed legs to replace broken ones on low-slung upholstered chairs or sofas. If necessary, install mounting blocks to accommodate the new legs. Glue and screw the blocks to the frame of the piece.

arately to plates in the corners of the piece. The quickest and easiest way to fix a broken leg on an upholstered divan or chair when the leg is part of a side member is to saw the other three legs off flush with the bottom of the piece, insert a triangular block in each corner if necessary, and install four new preformed legs of the type that attach to metal plates screwed on the bottom of the piece. Replacing a leg—or four legs, for that matter—on an upholstered piece fitted with legs of this type at the factory is a matter of twenty minutes' work, after you've found a set of new legs compatible with the style of furniture.

In addition to legs, chairs have two break-prone spots and sofas have four such points. The points are the same in both chairs and sofas, though the frequency of breakage at a given point will vary between the two pieces. In upholstered chairs, the two spots which most often break are the front rail, which supports the seat, and the frame of the armrest. In eight out of ten cases, these breaks will occur at the point where the front rail is jointed to the arm upright and the armrest will fail in the joint that attaches it to the frame of the backrest.

Sofa or divan frames are also prone to give way at these two points, though on sofas the joint where the armrest joins the backrest will give way most often. Next in frequency is a break on the front rail, or apron, of the framework. It's followed by breaks of the front vertical frame member at the point where it joins the armrest frame. The fourth spot where sofas are likely to break is at some point along the back. Usually, the break will occur at a joint, but almost as often a sofa built without a vertical frame member at the center of the back will crack or split somewhere along its length.

None of these breaks needs to be a cause for tears and lamentation, or for consigning the piece to the junk heap. Rather, it should be a signal to reach for the toolbox and glue pot and set about fixing the break.

Frames of most modern upholstered furniture are assembled in three sections. These are the two arm assemblies and the back assembly. The three assemblies are joined together and the piece completed by adding the front frame or apron rails as individual pieces. Both the side and the back assemblies are braced by separate members called tack strips, to which the upholstery fabric is fastened. These strips aren't commonly installed on the front of the piece, as the top and bottom rails serve as tack strips.

Corners where joints meet are reinforced by glued and screwed blocks in better-grade furniture. In less well-made pieces, the joints are doweled, and in schlock furniture they may be lapped, glued, and

TROUBLE SPOTS IN CHAIR FRAMES

This front view of a typical upholstered chair frame shows the location of the joints most likely to require repair. The worst trouble-spots are the joints (circled) that connect the bottom frame to the arms.

From the side, two common trouble-spots can be seen. One has already been mentioned, the arm support where it joins the bottom frame. The other is the back armrest where it joins the upright frame member.

From the back, the frame looks like this. The weakest spot seen clearly here is the back tack rail, the vertical member in the center (arrow), which tends to become loose at the bottom.

A close-up shot of the first potential trouble-spot shows a single dowel holding the arm upright to the side frame. There would be no visible evidence if blind dowels were used in addition to glue when joining the frame members to the arm upright. However, unless two dowels are present in both front and side frame members, the joint is very weak.

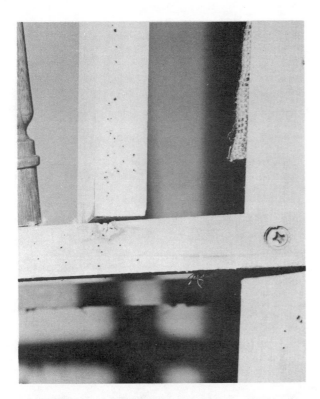

Notice in this close-up shot of the back armrest joint that a single screw holds the armrest to the frame. If you're wondering why, note the curve of the armrest. Using a screw saves hand labor that would be needed to finish off a protruding dowel at this point.

Another weak spot is created by this gap between the armrest and the member supporting the ornamental arm-ends. Lacking visible evidence, we can assume that the ends are glued and doweled to the support, but lack of a connection between support and armrest creates a potential trouble-spot.

held together with screws. In low-grade schlock pieces, joints are butted and nailed. This kind of joint is an almost certain guarantee of trouble. It's apt to break almost at once after the piece begins to be used.

A joint in a piece of upholstered furniture that is weakening and about to give way will almost always give warning in advance of the actual breaking. The piece will be soupy when it's moved, or will creak alarmingly when someone sits down on it. In the last stages, before the joint gives way entirely, the piece will wobble almost at a touch. If you take steps to mend the impending break at once, you'll save a lot of work later on.

A weak dowel joint or glue-block joint should be taken apart and reglued, after its meeting faces have been cleaned of old adhesive. Pipe or windlass clamps are usually required to hold the frame together while the glue sets up. If you find dowel joints that aren't strengthened by the addition of glue blocks, this is the time to add the blocks at the points shown in the sketches.

After a joint has broken, cracked, or split dowels must be pulled out or their stubs drilled out, and new dowels fitted with glue and clamped to dry. Most of these repairs can be carried out without disassembling the piece completely, and often without taking off any more of the upholstery than is needed to reach the trouble spot.

If a frame member breaks at the ends, it should be replaced. If the break occurs at

A loose joint can sometimes, but not always, be reglued without stripping all the covering from an upholstered piece. It was possible to reach the frame-leg joint shown by removing only a short length of the back upholstery, in order to scrape the broken joint and reglue it.

Here are two similar broken boards. One can be mended, the other will never mend satisfactorily. If you encountered these breaks in the frame of a piece of upholstered furniture, which would you mend? Which splice?

a point 8 inches or more from a joint, at or near the center of the board, it can usually be repaired. Clean splits can be glued, clamped, and then when the glue is dry, reinforced with a plate made of $1/8$-inch hardboard glued the length of the split and an inch or two beyond each end. Hold the plate in place with small screws in addition to gluing it on. Plates installed in frame members being hidden by the upholstery don't need to be very fancy jobs. The only thing to look out for is using a mending plate so thick that it will cause an unwanted bulge in the upholstery when the padding and fabric are restored to their places.

In critical areas, where any mending plate is going to be too thick, use a spline instead of a mending plate to reinforce the mend. Cut a saw kerf in the edge of the glued board, starting about 2 inches beyond the split and going 3 to 4 inches into it. Cut a similar kerf at the other end of the split on the opposite edge of the board.

If you picked the top break as mendable, you're correct. Its long diagonal shear line and clean grain ends mark it as being glueable, though it will need a mending plate, spline, or dowel for maximum strength. The knot in the lower break creates cross grain which splits unevenly. A break such as this must be spliced.

Fit strips of veneer into these kerfs. It may be necessary to use two or more thicknesses of veneer glued together to fill the saw kerf snugly. Glue these splines in place.

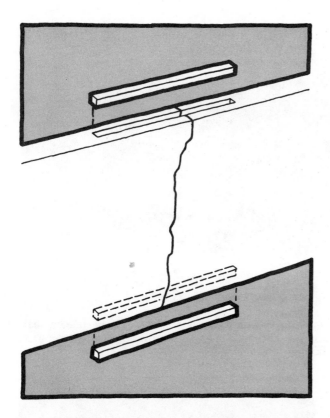

A clean, almost square break is most easily reinforced by edge splines fitted into grooves cut on each side of the board. Both the break and the splines should be glued.

A long diagonal break is best strengthened with splines on opposite faces of the board. The broken ends should be glued.

Some types of breaks can't be cured as simply as a long, clean split that hasn't caused a great deal of splintering along its length. Breaks that occur on either side of a knot are especially hard to rejoin. Such breaks need to be removed and a splice placed in the board. Saw the board off square an inch or two beyond each side of the break. Measure the gap carefully after sawing. Make a template for a tongue-and-groove joint and trace the template on the ends; they should receive the tongues of the splice. Use the template to cut the splice, and be sure to allow for the saw kerf when cutting. You may have to do a bit of fitting, using a smooth-cut file, to get a tight joint. Glue the joint in place, and after the glue sets add a dowel through the tongue at each end of the splice.

RECLINERS AND DIVAN-BEDS

Frames of reclining chairs and divan-beds that have patented mechanisms concealed in them present some special problems. No two of these are ever exactly alike, unless the pieces are twins made by the same manufacturer. Usually, the failure of a frame member will cause some sort of bending or twisting of these mechanisms; sometimes the reclining or folding mechanisms themselves malfunction and cause a break. You can always tell if a break has been caused by the malfunction of a reclining or folding mechanism, because there will be grooves, scratches, or scored places on the inner surface of the frame caused by the aberrant mechanisms.

Unless you have a router with the necessary templates to cut dovetail or finger joints, the easiest splice to make with a saber saw or handsaw is a tongue-and-groove joint reinforced with dowels. Cut a cardboard template and use it to scribe the splice and the joints.

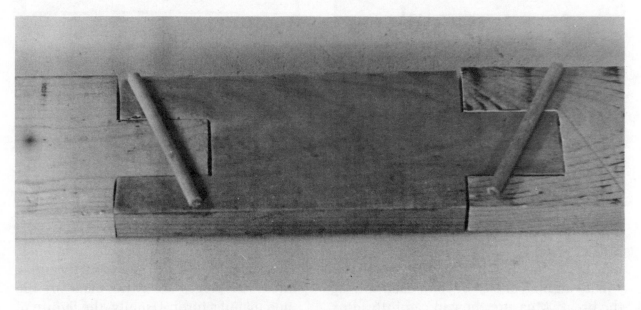

After the splice is glued, drill the edges to insert a locking dowel through each tongue at approximately the angles shown here. If formed correctly, this splice is virtually unbreakable.

Almost invariably, the metal arm-and-springs lashup that goes into any given reclining chair or folding divan-bed is a device patented by an individual furniture manufacturer and fabricated by the maker or to his special order. Getting instructions for repairing these devices is a frustrating proposition, and trying to repair one in a home workshop without really knowing all the details of its functions is pretty much self-defeating. Usually, the store that sold you the furniture will have a repairman trained to do this job. Cut your losses and call him.

This doesn't apply to platform rockers. They've been around so long that almost all the patents on their rocking mechanism have expired, and a number of firms make complete replacement units. The mechanism of a platform rocker is a very straightforward arrangement of paired springs fixed between top and bottom plates which are attached with wood screws to the bottom of the chair and to its platform. These rocking mechanisms can be bought as a unit and installed in a few minutes. If a platform rocker gets out of whack, it's less costly and much easier simply to replace the spring assembly than it is to try to repair it. Constantine, among others, sells these replacement units.

As was noted in the beginning of this chapter, the stresses that framed furniture pieces must withstand are great. If you expect a repair to stand up, it must be carried out properly. Tight, well-glued joints, closely fitted dowel and splice mends are as necessary in repairing as they were in making the piece. The job that's well done will endure forever; the one that's scamped will have to be done again.

9

Outdoor Furniture

Outdoor furniture can be placed in three general categories: metal-plastic, all-metal, and all-wood. The first is the best description I could dredge up for those tubular aluminum framed folding pieces that have plastic webbing or cords or tubing for seats and backrests. A few makers offer outdoor pieces made from molded plastic, or with molded plastic seats and backrests on a tubular metal frame, but let's rule out any possibility of repairing this type. You'll learn the reasons a bit further on in the section devoted to plastic furniture in general.

METAL-PLASTIC

Outdoor furniture that falls into category one has a continuing problem that falls under the heading of maintenance rather than repairs. This is the job of replacing the webbing or cording or tubing every two or three years. Like most plastics, this material tends to deteriorate with prolonged exposure to sunlight, and must be replaced periodically. Luckily, the job is very simple. The webbing on pieces using this kind of material is sold in kits, each kit containing enough yardage to do a chair or a recliner.

A screwdriver is the only tool required. The old webbing is removed—and all the sheetmetal screws and washers taken off should be saved for reuse—and new webbing cut to the proper lengths, using the old pieces as patterns. Apply all the vertical strips at once to save work in reweaving the new lengths. Fold over the ends of each strip, push a screw and washer assembly through the fold, and drive the screw into the predrilled hole. That's all there is to it.

Both cording and tubing are wrapped around the frames and fastened at the ends with a washer and sheetmetal screw in pre-drilled holes. Again, use the tubing or cording that's been removed to measure the lengths you must cut. It's a half-hour job to replace the seat and back on tubular furniture of this type.

Straightening a bent or crushed section of this tubular outdoor furniture is almost as simple a job as replacing the webbing. You need two pieces of scrap 2 x 4 lumber about 8 inches longer than the bent or crushed section, and a pair of sturdy C-clamps. A circular saw is also needed.

Set the saw blade at a 45° angle and the depth of cut to about $1/2$ inch. Saw a V-groove in the center of one side of each

Flat plastic webbing is replaced on tubular metal outdoor furniture by cross-weaving the plastic strips. Each strip is secured to the frame by a sheetmetal screw at each end.

Tubular plastic webbing is anchored to the frame by a sheetmetal screw and wound in a simple spiral around the frame. An alternate over-and-under spiral can be used if you want to spend a bit of extra time on the job.

piece of 2 x 4. Center the bent section of tubing in the groove of one piece of the 2 x 4 and place the V-groove in the second piece on the opposite side of the bend. Put a C-clamp on each end of the bent section and tighten the clamps alternately to squeeze the tubing straight.

If the bend doesn't straighten out, pad the convex arc of the tubing in its center with several folds of heavy cloth and tighten the clamps again. You may have to add several thicknesses to the cloth and repeat the clamping several times until the tubing is completely straight.

Crushed areas should be clamped with moderate pressure, then the boards replaced at a 90° angle to the first pressure line and tightened again. For the third go, rotate the grooved boards 45°. Repeat this until the crushed area is straight. This treatment won't always snap the metal back into a true round, but it will restore the original shape of the damaged section and give it most of its original strength.

Very badly crushed areas must be removed and a splice inserted. You can buy skillcraft aluminum in solid rounds and in diameters that will nestle snugly into almost all sizes of aluminum tubing. Some sizes of tubing will accept hard-drawn aluminum electrical conduit. Since the frame diameters of this kind of furniture differ from one maker to the next, as do the thicknesses of the tubing walls, you'll

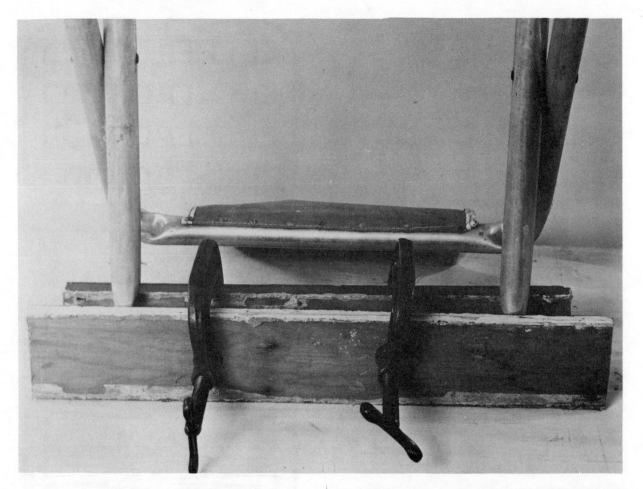

If the frame of a piece of tubular metal furniture is only slightly bent, saw V-grooves in two boards and clamp the frame between them, tightening the clamps alternately. A pad of folded cloth inserted between the tubing and boards at the center of the bend, on its convex side, will speed the job.

have to do a bit of looking to find the right repair material to be used as a splice. You can use wooden dowel if you can't find aluminum bar or tubing of the right diameter.

Saw off the tubing on both sides of the area that you intend to splice. Cut your splice at least $1\frac{1}{2}$ to 2 inches longer than the gap it is to fill, and slide the bar stock or tubing or conduit in place. Drill for a short sheetmetal screw where tubing and insert overlap, and drive the screw in to hold the splice together. If you're using a wood dowel for a splice, choose dowel the same diameter as the outside diameter of the tubing, and form a shoulder as wide as the wall of the tubing is thick. Use a Sur-

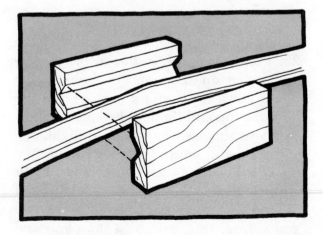

form tool or file to rough in the shoulder and sand to make it fit exactly inside the tubing. Drill for a wood screw, or use epoxy to hold the splice in the tubing.

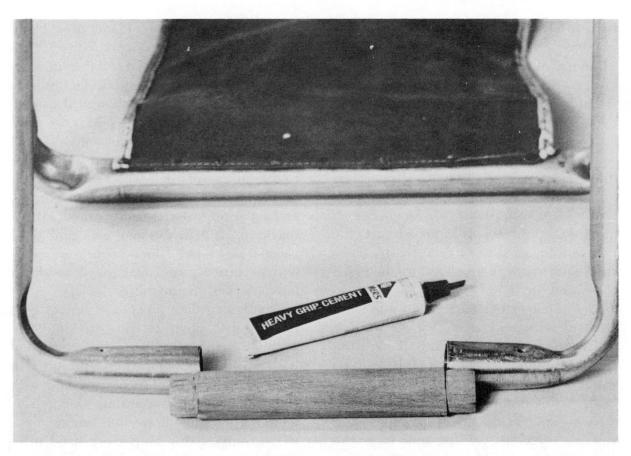

Badly crushed sections of a tubular metal frame must be spliced. Measure the length of the splice on a dowel having an outside diameter equal to that of the tubular aluminum frame, and allow 1 to 2 inches on each side to fit into the tubing. Shoulder the ends as shown.

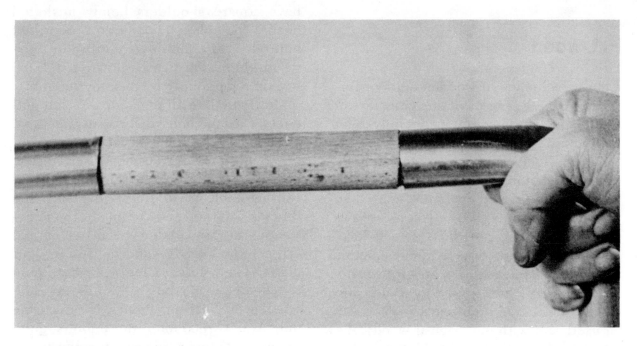

Use epoxy to hold the shouldered ends in the tubing. Or drive a screw through the tubing into the shouldered ends of the dowel.

ALL-METAL

All-metal outdoor furniture is expensive, but practically indestructible. If cast-metal outdoor pieces are given even a minimum amount of maintenance, they will last forever and seldom need repairs. This minimum maintenance would consist of a fresh coat of paint every two or three years for aluminum pieces, and annual inspection and painting for cast-iron pieces. If the inspection reveals signs of rust, the rust should be cleared away with coarse steel wool or a wire brush before the piece is painted.

Any repairs that cast metal furniture might need would be a job for a welder, and outside the scope of this book. Both cast aluminum and cast-iron pieces can be welded, if a leg should break or a crack develop in any of the members. In this case, let your fingers do the walking—unless you're skilled at welding and have the equipment to handle it—to the Ws of your yellow pages and call in an expert to do the work.

ALL-WOOD

Finally, we come to wooden outdoor furniture. Usually, pieces in this group are of frame-and-slat construction, not only to let them drain readily after a rain, but to allow the wood to expand and contract in the changes of humidity, which affect furniture that is kept outdoors much more than they do indoor pieces. The woods used in outdoor furniture are those which have shown their ability to resist the weather's ravages. Redwood is the prime favorite, followed by cypress, yellow pine, and cedar. Rarely will such hardwoods as oak be used, and with the tropical woods like teak and domestic woods like black walnut always in short supply, you'll seldom find outdoor furniture made of a wood that's really difficult to work.

Redwood, cypress, and cedar require no protective paint. Redwood, in fact, rejects both paint and varnish, though it can be successfully stained. Redwood is the most weather-resistant of all the softwoods; it neither swells nor warps, and is immune to the attacks of such wood-tunneling insects as termites and borers. Pine, cypress, and cedar require stain and varnish to give maximum life in outdoor use, and their varnish coats need to be renewed every two or three years. Oak used outdoors needs a yearly varnishing.

Wooden outdoor pieces are generally of the simplest possible construction. Most of them are of straight-line design, joined with lap and rabbet joints, assembled with carriage bolts. If you're not familiar with this kind of fastener, a carriage bolt gets its name from the horse-and-buggy days when bolts of this kind were used principally in wagons and other horse-drawn vehicles. Carriage bolts are threaded for only about one-third of their length, and have square shoulders below unslotted heads. The bolt is tapped into a predrilled hole, its sharp shoulders cutting into the wood below the head, allowing it to be run up tight simply by turning the nut.

However, like all metal objects left outdoors, carriage bolts rust out in time, and grow loose. They're the very devil to get out so that a new bolt can be inserted. The best way I've found to remove a rusted carriage bolt is to douse the nut and threads with kerosene or one of the penetrating oil preparations such as Liquid Wrench, and let it stand for twenty-four hours. Then, force a locking pliers onto the head of the bolt and use an end-wrench or crescent wrench to attack the nut. You'll encounter these bolts quite often in outdoor pieces, for the main repairs most wooden outdoor furniture

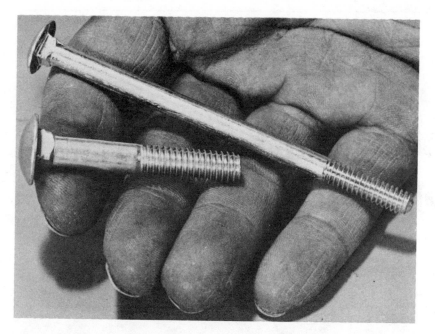

Carriage bolts, which have a square shoulder below the head, are almost always used in assembling wooden outdoor furniture. If you need to replace hardware on a piece of this type, get bolts a size larger in diameter, but the same length as the ones removed.

call for is removal of loose fasteners and their replacement.

Not only rust, but the swelling and shrinking of the wood fibers around them cause fastener failure on outdoor pieces. This is true whether the fasteners are carriage bolts, machine bolts, screws, or nails. Zinc coatings, bluing, and other protective metal finishes all give way to the weather sooner or later. When they begin to rust, remove them at once and replace them with new ones. Much of the time, after you've removed the fastener, you'll find that another of the same size won't fit snugly, so be prepared to go up one step in size when you fit the replacements.

Glue joints are seldom found in wooden outdoor pieces. When you do encounter one, you can be virtually certain that a waterproof glue has been used, and a broken board or slat glued to a frame member with this kind of glue creates a joint that requires a pry-bar to break. You may even have to chisel the broken section of a board in the back or seat of an outdoor piece away from the frame.

Replacing almost all components of outdoor wooden furniture is seldom hard. Nine times out of ten, it's merely a matter of sawing a new, straight piece off a board of the proper dimensions and bolting, screwing, or nailing it in place.

10

Bentwood, and Other Special Problems

This chapter is devoted to odd jobs that you're likely to run into, to furniture made of woods used unconventionally, and to pieces made of materials or incorporating materials other than wood.

Some of the materials and processes that we'll look at in the following pages include furniture of bentwood and molded laminated wood, plastic, cane, glass, and marble. Some of them are survivals or revivals of once-popular furniture styles, others represent totally modern technology.

Bentwood furniture is as good a type as any to begin with. Bentwood chairs and sofas date back to the 1850s. The style reached its zenith in the 1890s, then was revived in the late 1960s. Today you'll find bentwood furniture not just in antique shops, but in the catalogs of the big mail-order houses as well as on the floors of furniture dealers' showrooms.

You can carry out some repairs to bentwood furniture, even without the steaming-chambers and bending jigs used in

its manufacture. The kind of repairs that are possible without this factory-type equipment is limited; you won't, for example, be able to replace one of the recurved back pieces in a chair, but you can replace a leg or mend one of the splits which often occur in the main components. When breaks take place in the reinforcing members, they are usually relatively clean, and often can be fixed with glue aided by an inserted dowel. These two are the most common jobs called for by bentwood pieces.

Splits in bentwood furniture occur most frequently in the backs and reinforcing braces below the seat, and the split will begin nine times out of ten at the point where a curve begins to straighten out or to reverse itself. Your first concern is to stop the split from growing. Do this by wrapping a couple of layers of masking tape around the member about an inch above the split, then tighten a hose clamp over the tape. Now, you can go to work.

Toss some strips of cloth in a pot and

cover them with water; bring the water to a boil. Use kitchen tongs to wrap a succession of these strips of cloth around the split area; this is as close as you'll be able to get to the steaming the member underwent before it was bent into a curve. After a quarter-hour or so of applying fresh strips as soon as the one in place has cooled, go to step two. Place a fresh strip in place and hold a hot iron to the cloth until no more steam rises from it. The split should now be soft enough to work with.

Apply glue to the inner surfaces of the split and pull them together with a second hose clamp. If it's a very long split, use another clamp to pull down the tip of the split. With a small drill bit, predrill for brads between the clamps; drill so the brads will cross in an X inside the wood and about $1/8$ inch apart. Finally, put a brad in a predrilled hole at the very tip of the split section. As soon as the glue and the wood are both dry, remove the clamps, sink the brad heads below the surface of the wood, and refinish as is needed to hide the mend.

When repairing a split, don't disassemble the piece. Do scrape away all paint or other finish from the area in which you'll be working, and if the split is an old one, clean the surfaces that are going to be glued.

Most breaks in bentwood chairs will occur where a brace or a major member such as a leg has been drilled to accept a screw. Use a short conduit connector, available from electrical supply houses and electrical contractors, as a sleeve to hold the wooden member together. Smear epoxy generously over the broken ends and on the inside of the connector. Force the broken ends into the connector and push them together firmly. Hold the mends together with duct tape, which has greater tensile strength and better adhesive qualities than masking tape, while

the epoxy sets up. Then, drill through the connector and replace the screw. Paint the mend after doing any necessary fairing of the ends with a smooth file and sandpaper.

Legs of bentwood chairs are usually doweled into the rim of the seat. Breaks here can be mended like those on any other chair leg, by drilling out the stubs of a broken dowel and gluing in a new one. Legs that have been broken can be spliced, and new legs shaped from a length of tapestry or curtain round. See Chapter 5 for details of these repairs; they're the same on a bentwood chair as they are on a regular straight chair.

Laminated molded furniture is akin to bentwood in one respect: both are formed by being shaped in jigs under heat and with great pressure. Laminated pieces are far from being new; the Eames chair which set the style for furniture of this type in the 1930s is a direct descendant of the Victorian period's flare-back, curved-arm, molded-seat laminated rocking chairs. These early examples of laminated molded furniture were popular in their day, but few have endured. The technology of adhesives was somewhat primitive then, and glues of the period did not age well. They tended to fall apart after a few years of use and exposure to climatic vagaries.

Pieces molded in the period before resorcinol and polyvinyl adhesives came into use often suffered from peeling and separation of the veneer plies, something which very, very rarely happens to modern molded laminated furniture. With age and use, tiny cracks may appear along the lamina lines, and these can be cured by forcing a very tiny amount of a resorcinol glue into these voids. No clamping is needed. If the piece is of light-colored wood, you can safely use a polyvinyl or aliphatic resin glue. Use the tip of an X-Acto knife blade to get the glue worked

REPAIRING A SPLIT BENTWOOD BACK

1 Weakest spots in bentwood chairs are the sharp bends in their backs and arms, where the wood is inclined to split.

2 Begin the job of mending a split by disassembling the chair. Three screws hold the inner backrest. Remove them.

3 Wind duct tape in a tight spiral above the split to keep it from splitting further while you work.

4 Wrap wet rags around the split area and apply heat with an electric iron set at highest temperature. It may be necessary to rewet the rags and apply the iron two or three times before the wood is pliable enough to work easily.

5 Apply glue to the inner faces of the split and use lightly oiled hose clamps to pull the split closed. Wipe off all excess glue and try to avoid getting glue on the clamps, though the oil should keep the clamps from sticking to the work.

6 Remove the clamps one at a time, starting with the one at the top of the split. As each clamp is removed, predrill for a small finishing nail or brad at the angles indicated and push the brad in with a C-clamp.

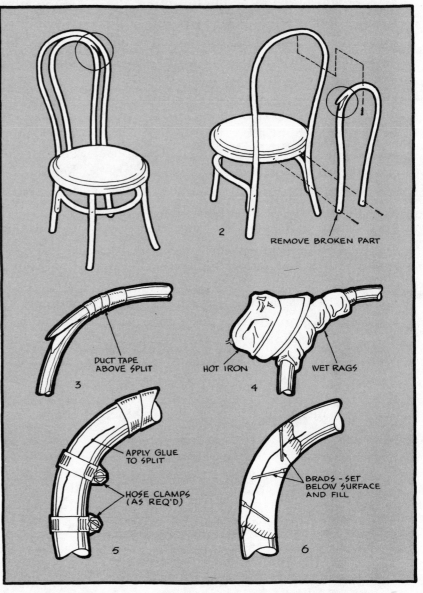

into the crevices, and after it has partly set, wipe across the edge of the piece with a moist cloth to smooth out the glueline.

Older laminated pieces can be repaired by the methods detailed in Chapter 5.

PLASTIC FURNITURE

As noted earlier, plastic furniture has been with us for a long time. Plastic components began to appear on wooden and metal pieces during the Art Deco period of the 1930s. They were followed quickly by pieces made entirely of plastic, and the number of such pieces continues to increase.

There are many plastic formulas, and it's often difficult to determine exactly what type of plastic has been used in a piece you might want to repair. In furniture, the most widely used transparent plastics are the acrylics sold under the trademarked names of Lucite and Plexiglas. Strips, sheets, rods, and angles are bent into various shapes before being assembled into tables, chairs, stands, and display cabinets.

Luckily for the person repairing these pieces, both Lucite and Plexiglas are joined with a thin, transparent solvent widely sold in hobby shops. Its trade name is Weld-On 3. This liquid instantly and momentarily dissolves an edge that is to be joined; a thin film forms where the solvent has been brushed, and if the piece is put into contact at once with the piece to which it is to be attached, the two pieces will bond invisibly and the solvent will set up in about two to three minutes.

However, if you're going to rejoin a broken bond on a piece made from either of these transparent acrylics, I'd suggest that you study the piece for a few minutes before using the solvent. Figure out exactly how and where the bond is to be made, and even more important, how the firm contact between the pieces is to be maintained for the two or three moments required for setting. I've found duct tape to be a great help in providing a third or fourth hand when making this kind of repair. It adheres well, and strips clean, and will not stretch easily as masking tape does. But since no two of these repairs present exactly the same problems, that's about all the advice I can give you.

When we come to the opaque plastics, we're really going into *terra incognita*, the unknown territory indicated by white spaces on ancient maps. Remember, there are some 20,000 or more formulas for plastics of the types being used in furniture today. The Weld-On 3 liquid already mentioned will join some of these, but not all. Epoxy will join some, but on many of the newer plastics epoxy cannot form a bond;

their surfaces are too slick. Little as I admire them, the new cyanoacrylate monomer adhesives can often be used when others fail. Or, you might try using one of the contact cements, if you have great steadiness of hand. Keep in mind that contact cements set when the surfaces touch, and there's no parting the bond.

Both of the leading transparent plastics, Lucite and Plexiglas, have relatively soft surfaces and are subject to scratches. In almost all cases, scratches can be buffed out unless they're deep enough to be classified as gouges. If the surface of a Lucite or Plexiglas piece suffers a really deep gouge, the best way I know of to mount a salvage operation is to use a router or a Dremel Moto-Tool and incise a decorative design that will incorporate the gouged area somehow. It's a far-out way to go, but it beats junking a good piece of plastic furniture because of a single marred spot.

Shallow scratches or rubbed areas are another matter. These usually yield to buffing. If the area is small and the scratch not too deep, you may be able to buff it into invisibility by hand. Use a soft cloth and the mildest possible abrasive—toothpaste or tooth powder. If you use toothpaste, don't moisten your buffing cloth. If your choice is tooth powder, use the least possible amount of moisture required to make a thick paste. Rub across the scratch, using only moderate pressure.

Moderately deep scratches can usually be buffed out more easily with a power tool. An electric drill or flexible shaft fitted with a soft cloth wheel can be used if you keep the pressure on the wheel very light. Too much pressure will create a depression in the material instead of polishing away the scratch. The ideal tool to use is the little Dremel MotoTool, fitted with a cloth wheel which is available as an accessory. Pass the buffing wheel across the scratch, keeping it in constant motion,

Use a cloth buffing wheel in an electric drill—or, better yet, a Dremel MotoTool—to buff away a scratch in marble. Buff in short strokes across the scratch, keeping the path of the wheel well coated with buffing compound.

rather than trying to work along the scratch as you'd erase a pencil line.

When working on either of the transparent acrylic plastics, use no abrasive coarser than the finest grade of rottenstone. When you use this buffing technique on glass, you can safely use pumice to begin with, then switch to rottenstone, and finally give the surface its polish with toothpaste. Paint suppliers handle both pumice and rottenstone, usually in two or more grades of fineness.

Always do your buffing in a back-and-forth motion, across, not with the scratch, whether you're using toothpaste, rottenstone, or pumice. Feather your strokes, using almost no pressure at all at the edges, and only a tiny bit more as the buffing wheel goes across the scratch itself. On the deepest scratches in glass, you may find it necessary to begin with pumice, follow up with rottenstone, then finish the job with toothpaste. Scratches in thick glass, like the heavy plate used for tabletops, are the easiest to remove. If you're

going to use the buffing technique on thin glass such as a cabinet door, take the door off and lay it on a flat surface after you've built up a pad to support the glass. Use magazines or books, and lay the glass on a layer of cloth.

MARBLE

Marble tabletops can be buffed to remove scratches, but the job can't be done by hand. Marble is a very hard material, and it will take time for even a shallow scratch to yield. Pumice is the best buffing agent to begin with; then restore the polish to the worked-over area with a final buffing using rottenstone.

Stains in marble tabletops can also be buffed away, but it's usually easier to remove them chemically. Get a small bottle, two or three ounces, of commercial-strength hydrogen peroxide. Many drugstores carry this in stock, as it's used frequently in hospitals. You're looking for a 35% peroxide solution instead of the 10% solution sold for home use.

Wet a pad of clean cloth with the peroxide and press the pad over the stained area. Dribble a small quantity of household ammonia into the pad after it's in place. The solution will bubble for a few minutes, and the smell will be terrible. When the bubbling stops, the bleach has exhausted its life. Lift off the pad, and if the stain won't go away when you rinse it with plain cold water, give it another peroxide-ammonia treatment. Two or three applications of the bleach mixture, with a rinse between each, will usually get rid of even the most stubborn stains. After the stain has been banished, buff the treated area with a felt pad to restore its polish.

After you've restored the surface of a marble tabletop, either by buffing away a scratch or bleaching away a stain, protect it with a commercial sealer. Don't use wax; it may discolor the marble. Some hardware and paint stores carry commercial marble sealers, but if your inquiries at retail stores are fruitless, look up the nearest friendly tombstone maker. He'll have a supply on hand and will probably be willing to sell you the small amount you'll need for home use.

Imitation marble is an entirely different ballgame. The polish on this man-made material is formed by chemical action when the plastic mixture from which it is cast is curing in the mold. Compared to real marble, the imitation material is relatively soft. It cannot be buffed; all the buffing will do is to remove the polish and scuff up an area around the scratch. Once the thin surface finish of imitation marble has been broken, there's no way I know to restore it to its original condition. The most successful method, using Gudebrod's Hard'N Fast Epoxy fishing rod coating, leaves a very visible patch mark,

though it does protect the surface from further damage.

If you use this epoxy formulation to cover a scratch on any imitation marble surface, follow label directions carefully in the mixing, and be sure to use a pinpoint or the tip of a cocktail pick to burst the small bubbles that form when the epoxy sets up. These bubbles don't always rise to the surface as the epoxy cures. The greater the care you take in feathering out the edges of the patched area, the better and less visible your repair will be.

Deep gouges, broken corners, and major cracks in imitation marble can generally be repaired with a polyester plastic autobody filler. This material resembles epoxy in that it cures by catalytic action, and if you work carefully you'll wind up with a surface that can be sanded and buffed to a very smooth, glasslike finish, which must then be tinted with an epoxy enamel to match the rest of the surface. The kind of plastic I've used most successfully is called SnoWhite Lite N'Easy, and it's available at auto-supply stores.

Incidentally, I've experimented with this material in filling big gouges in furniture and on floors in traffic areas, but these experiments have all been too recent to form a judgment as to its ultimate durability and satisfactory service. It may be possible to use it in repairing badly damaged pressed-metal outdoor furniture, for the substance bonds well to almost anything. However, I've already learned that it isn't suitable for very small repair jobs, such as filling hairline cracks. There are several other brands on the market besides the one mentioned in the preceding paragraph, all similar but slightly different, so it might be that some brand I haven't yet tried will be useful in repairing small areas.

While on the subject of plastics... The metallic-coated plastic film that's become

Finials appear on bed posts, table aprons, chair seats, and elsewhere. Because they're located at such extremities, and generally attached by a glued dowel, finials are often broken and lost.

so popular as a sunscreen for automobile windows makes a very passable substitute for a broken bureau mirror. The cost of mirrors is exceedingly high as this is written, and the price of having a good plate-glass mirror re-silvered equally high. A broken bureau or decorative mirror can be replaced with a sheet of double-strength window glass backed with this plastic film at a fraction of the cost involved in buying a new mirror or having an old one renovated.

There's only one secret to working with this film: surgical cleanliness. Use distilled water, and have all containers in which the water is warmed completely free of any trace of grit or dust. Wash the glass to which the film is to be applied with a detergent and rinse two or three times with a completely lint- and dust-free cloth or with a chamois. The glass should be cut to size in advance. Soak the film in very warm, almost hot water, and separate it from its backing. Both the film and the glass to which it is applied should be quite wet. Use a squeegee with a soft blade to apply the film, and after it's been fixed to the glass, go over the film with a soft, wet sponge, pressing quite hard, with long, even strokes. Use a black cardboard between the back of the glass—the film is on the rear side when framed, of course—and a back-up sheet of stiff hardboard.

This job is one I haven't done myself, but I've seen the result of a friend's work on a large bureau mirror, and am passing on his advice. The finished mirror won't be as brilliant as a mirror professionally silvered; it will have a softer tone and will reflect a flatteringly tempered image.

FINIALS

Now, getting back to wooden furniture, there's one more odd job that comes along occasionally, that of replacing those little decorative finishing pieces called finials. You encounter them on quite a few pieces of furniture, especially the increasingly popular period pieces of the 1890–1920 era.

REPLACING A FINIAL

1 Use a contour gauge on one of the remaining finials to get a profile—called a template—of its contours.

2 You can turn most finials on a hand drill, by cutting the dowel stock to fit into the chuck of the drill. The diameter of the stub needn't be precise; the chuck's jaws will center the stub by biting into it.

3 Clamp the drill in a stand and use a rasp, then a file, to shape the dowel *(continued).*

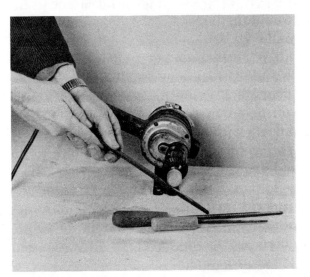

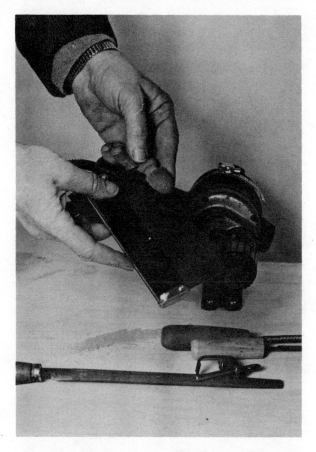

4   Stop the work now and then to check the work against the gauge by rotating it against the profile. Finish by sanding with medium-grits—about #150.

5   Saw off the stub, drill the end for a dowel, and attach the new finial. Finish it to match the rest of the piece.

Most finials are small and can usually be reproduced successfully without lathe work, if you have a 3/8- or 1/2-inch drill. Use a length of dowel stock a bit larger in diameter than the finial to be reproduced. Score its circumference with a saw cut about 1 inch from one end and of a depth that will form a peg which will fit into the drill chuck when the excess stock above the cut is removed with a chisel. The peg doesn't have to be perfectly round, the jaws of the chuck will hold it and center it quite satisfactorily. Put the drill in a bench stand—the one illustrated is made by Arco—and use a mill bastard file to rough in the contours. Follow the outline of the finial being reproduced by using a contour gauge or template.

After the work has been roughed in, reduce it to exact dimensions with successively finer grades of sandpaper. Start with about a #60 grit, go to #100, and finish with #6/0 cabinet paper. Don't use excessive pressure in either filing or sanding. The job goes very quickly if you've made a good, even-sided peg to chuck into the drill. If the peg has any taper, you'll have to stop now and then to reset it in the chuck. Finish the completed finial to match those on the piece of furniture on which the ornament is to go.

If you're concerned because some of the foregoing repair techniques don't go into minute detail, please abandon your worries. To reiterate a fact of life that can't be stressed often enough, no two jobs of furniture repair are exactly alike. This is especially true of the kind of jobs dealt with in this chapter, on pieces that are not the routine products of mass-production methods. When you undertake any kind of furniture repairs, you'll find you have to do some individual thinking about materials, supplies, and procedures, and frequently you'll have to do a bit of experimenting, a sort of on-the-job training, for a specific repair project.

Don't ever be afraid to experiment, or look on trial runs as wasted time. They aren't. They're your assurance that when you go to work on the job itself, you'll do it faster, better, and much more easily, because you've solved a lot of problems in advance.

Who knows? In your experimenting, you might come up with fresh approaches and new ideas that everybody else has overlooked.

11 Reupholstering Furniture

Note, please, that the title of this chapter is REupholstering, not upholstering from scratch a piece of furniture that has been stripped of its original covering.

There are between seventy and eighty recognized styles of upholstered furniture, all different in smaller or greater degrees. Obviously, it's impossible to cover each style in full detail in a single chapter; to do this would require an entire book. Complicating the situation is the fact that like so many traditional crafts that go back several centuries, upholsterers have highly individual work habits. No two upholsterers will cover identical pieces of furniture in precisely the same way, even though the finished pieces will to all appearances be twins.

Don't expect to find uniformity of technique in the workmanship of upholstered pieces you might be redoing. Each factory has its own methods, and each worker in each factory has his or her own trade tricks. It's not unusual to encounter matching pieces of furniture from the same factory which will vary in the hidden details of their upholstery jobs. This is equally true of upholstery work done in independent shops. No two shops follow the same procedures to obtain the same

finished look, though the work done by both will be totally satisfactory.

Before going into the techniques of reupholstering, let's take a quick look at expedients. The first that comes to mind is the use of slipcovers to give tattered upholstered pieces a new look. It's a poor expedient at best, for no matter how carefully a slipcover is fitted, it will not give a chair or sofa the stability or appearance of a piece that's been reupholstered. Nor have you done anything to improve the life of the tattered fabric below the slipcover. The old upholstery will continue to deteriorate, and within a relatively short time the slipcover will look almost as bad as the tattered fabric it hides. Using slipcovers is about the same as painting a dented fender and calling it a repair job. Sooner or later, the job will have to be done properly, so save the money you'd put into slipcovers and invest it in a genuine reconditioning.

Sewing ripped upholstery is another temporary expedient. Unless the rip is in a relatively new piece, the fabric won't hold stitches; in fact, a new rip will probably open up because of the stitches. Again, save effort and go the whole way—reupholster.

162

Vinyl sheeting used in upholstery can be mended, often very successfully, with the little kits which fuse a patch of new vinyl into place. In repairing vinyl this way a thermal bond adds new material to a strain-point which was the original cause of the vinyl ripping in the first place.

These kits are very easy to use. The rough, ragged edges are cut from the area around the tear, and the liquid vinyl spread in the gap. Then the liquid is fused and solidified by the application of low heat. The most common error in making repairs of this kind is failure to apply heat for a long period. Most of the vinyl repair kits I've seen recommend a three-minute application of heat, but you'll have a better repair if you apply the heat for five to six minutes. Follow the illustrated steps to make vinyl repairs with these kits.

Now, let's get on to the matter of reupholstery. By using the methods detailed in this chapter, anybody can reupholster any piece of furniture without having had previous experience. However, for the techniques described to be successful, you must follow each step exactly as given, and you must begin with a piece of furniture that is reasonably intact. Rips and tears don't count. As long as you have the original upholstery fabric to use as patterns for cutting new material, your job will be a success.

TOOLS

There are a few specialized tools needed for reupholstery work. You can buy a kit, such as the one illustrated, which contains all but one of the essential tools, or you can invest in only those tools you'll need the most which are shown in another photo. These basic tools are a good pair of scissors, a tack puller (technically, a tack claw), an upholsterer's hammer, a mallet, a small diagonal pliers, large and small curved needles and a button needle, and most important of all, a trigger-operated stapling gun.

You'll notice that the kit contains a few extras: a web stretcher and fabric pliers, an awl, and an upholsterer's knife. Because web-supported springs have just about been replaced by helical or zigzag springs, called Z-springs in the trade, a stretcher will seldom be needed. You can make an awl out of an old icepick by snapping off the shaft about $1\frac{1}{2}$ inches from the tip and sharpening it to a truncated point; the fine needle-pointed tip on a new ice pick will snap off the first time it's used. Scissors will do all the work an upholstery knife does, and a screwdriver can be used to handle any work the kit's ripping tool would do. Fabric pliers are needed only when a piece is being upholstered for the first time; in reupholstery work they're on the surplus tool list.

From a practical standpoint, a kit such as the one shown will provide you with single-purpose tools which will seldom be used, or for which substitutes can be improvised from regular shop tools. On occasion, you may need such other single-use tools as a button maker, or the special clamp used to install helical springs, or hog-ring pliers with which to fasten loose coil springs. These items can almost always be rented for the few times you'll need them to do a job that will take an hour or less. There's no point in cluttering up a home workshop with limited-use tools that gather dust 364 days a year and are used for thirty minutes on the 365th day.

Most upholstery shops will rent special tools for you to use in the evenings or on weekends, when the shop is closed. Arranging for rentals is easier if you agree to buy some or all of the supplies you'll need from the shop. Local fabric shops or sew-

PATCHING VINYL UPHOLSTERY

1   Obtain a kit for this job. Trim away loose edges of the rip with fingernail scissors.

2   Fill the gap with liquid vinyl. If you're dealing with any but primary colors, you'll have to blend the shade needed, using the twelve or so colors usually provided by such kits.

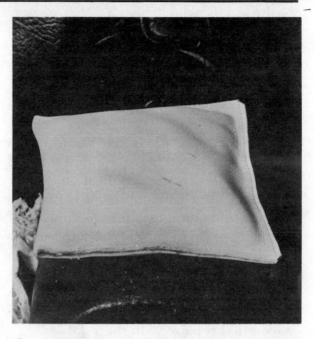

4   Immediately after the heat source is removed, whisk away the shield and weight the graining paper. Here a jeweler's sand-filled leather bag is used. You can use any flexible weight that adjusts to a curved or yielding surface, such as a sack of flour or salt.

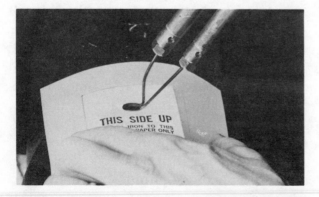

THIS SIDE UP
IRON TO THIS
PAPER ONLY

3   Cover the liquid with a graining paper, included in the kit, and cover the paper with a cardboard or thin metal shield with an opening slightly smaller than the paper. Then, apply heat. I've found that a soldering iron at low heat is more effective than a household iron at high heat, but you must keep the heat source in constant motion for five to six minutes.

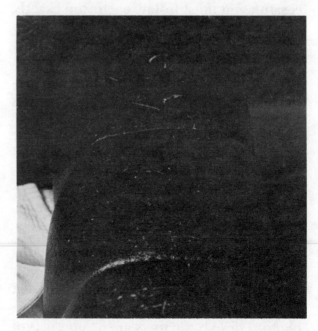

5   For best results, the patch should be allowed to cool, then polished at once with a polish designed for use on vinyl.

ing centers may have tools you can use in their shops for a small fee.

When it comes time to sew your new upholstery fabric, you'll find that a standard home sewing machine will handle all but the heaviest-weight materials quite satisfactorily. You'll need one accessory: a cording foot, often called a zipper foot, with which to sew welting, but this is a standard item available from any store that sells your make of sewing machine.

SUPPLIES

When you use the reupholstering technique that is explained in this chapter, your list of essential supplies can be kept very short indeed. To understand the

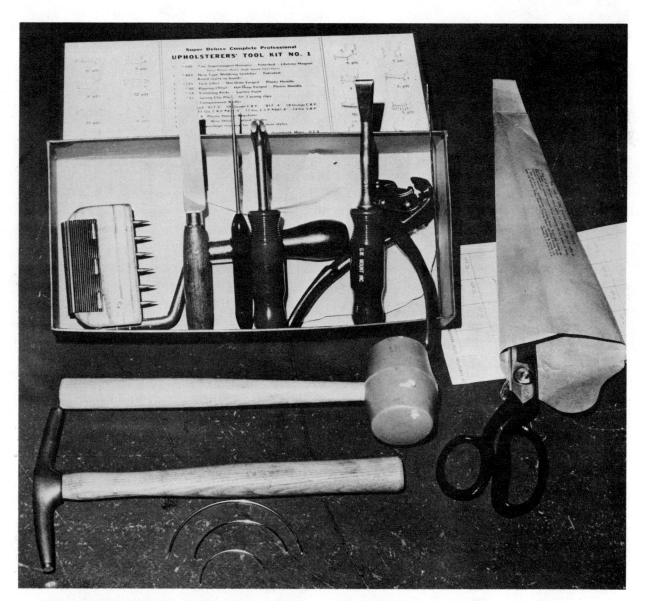

Upholstery tool kits are available from several suppliers listed in the appendix, but all of them contain some items you'll never—or very seldom—use. The typical kit shown here has curved needles, upholsterer's tack hammer, mallet, shears, webbing stretcher, upholsterer's knife (which is sharpened at its flat end), awl (or regulator), tack claw, footed chisel, and pliers for clinching hog-nose rings. It lacks the tool that will save you the most time: a good stapling gun.

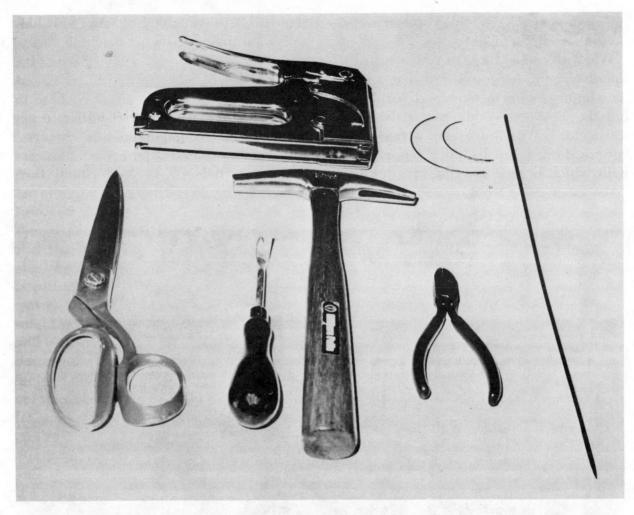

Here are the essential tools, all of which you'll need and use: shears, tack claw, upholsterer's tack hammer, diagonal-nose pliers, curved needles, buttoning needle that doubles as a regulator, and—most important—a stapling gun.

terms that you'll encounter on the supplies list, study the accompanying sketch and the glossary that follows. The sketch shows a cross section of an upholstered piece with the layers of materials that give it form separated for clarity. The sketch will also give you an idea of the sequence in which the materials are applied to the frame. The glossary defines the terms you'll encounter.

Starting from the frame, which in most cases is also the anchor or tack rail to which each layer is attached, and to which the springs and webbing are fastened, the bottom layer is *burlap*. Its purpose is to hold the padding firmly and protect it from the springs. *Padding* is cotton or rubber hair or foamed sheeting; old and now seldom-used materials included horsehair, sisal, moss, tow (made by shredding the stalks of flax plants), and one or two others which you may encounter in older pieces. *Muslin* is a tough, close-weave cloth stretched over the padding to hold it in shape and provide a smooth foundation for the final layer of *upholstery fabric*. *Welting* is a decorative strip made by sewing upholstery fabric around a flexible tube of hollow plastic or heavy cord; it also has a functional use you'll encounter

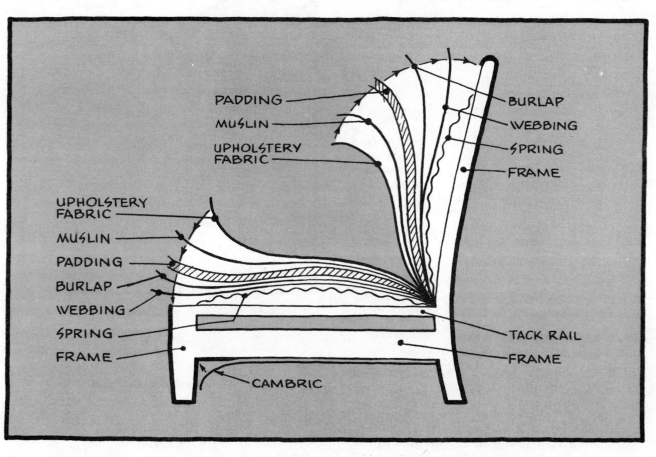

This is a cross section of a typical piece of upholstered furniture. Consider the frame as one unit, and see the text for detailed explanation of the functions of each layer.

later on. *Cambric* is the thin dustcloth covering the bottom.

There are some occasionally used materials or supplies which also need defining. *Tack strips* are narrow widths of cardboard studded with tacks; in use, the edge of a piece of upholstery fabric is folded over the strip and tacked to a piece of furniture so that the fabric is attached with no visible fastening. (See the photos for clarity.) *Gimp* is decorative braiding used to cover a tacked edge; it's put on with *gimp nails* that have tiny, almost invisible heads. *Upholstery nails* have domed heads and are used to attach material to a frame and dress up a visible seam or folded edge. *Buttons* in upholstery terms are domed shells covered with upholstery material in a special press. They have a

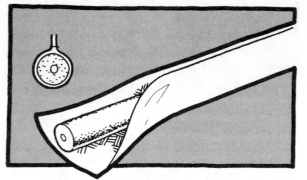

This is a cutaway of welting. It's formed by sewing a strip of upholstery fabric around a core that today is a plastic tube, but was once a heavy manila cord.

looped eye on the back which is pulled into the upholstery fabric.

Except for upholstery fabric and welting cord, you will need very little in the way

This is a tack strip. It's made of thin cardboard with tacks pushed through it at intervals; a special metal tack strip is also available for curving surfaces. The purpose of the strip is to give upholstery fabric a clean line with no visible means of support.

TACK STRIP

of new materials. In most all cases, you will be reusing the underlay materials already on the piece you're reworking. You may need a small quantity of cotton batting to fill in low spots, and the muslin may need replacing. If the padding is one of the foam materials, it may be shredded or hardened, but in most cases a thin covering of cotton batting will allow it to be reused. Only underlay materials that have absorbed unpleasant odors (urine from babies or animals, for example) will need to be replaced. Count on reusing the burlap, the padding, the cambric, and, of course, the springs. It is easier to make new welting than to spend a lot of time ripping up old welting to salvage the cord.

Your list of supplies and materials, then, will normally be limited to staples, tacks (and be sure to get chisel-edged upholstery tacks instead of round carpet tacks, which will split the tack rail), welting cord, and upholstery twine and thread. If you are replacing buttons, you'll need a small roll of the special very strong button cord made for this purpose. Upholstery thread is also made for the specific purpose of sewing thick fabrics. All these can

be bought in spools of various sizes. Tacks and nails with decorative heads may be needed in the final finishing; this will depend on the furniture.

FABRICS

Upholstery fabrics usually come in 54-inch widths. For an average fully upholstered chair, you'll need $5^1/_2$ to 6 yards, depending on its size. A chair without upholstered arms will require $4^1/_2$ to 5 yards. The average fully upholstered, three-cushion sofa requires 10 yards. Two-cushion sofas generally call for a half yard less, and those without fully upholstered arms or no arms at all, $6^1/_2$ to 7 yards. Over-sized pieces may require 11 or 12 yards. Normal-sized chairs or sofas with channel backs will need from $1/_2$ to 1 yard extra material.

For upholstering the seats of straight or side chairs, the simplest and easiest of all upholstery jobs, a piece of material 16 inches square will handle most insert seats, a 24-inch-square piece will take care of seats upholstered fully. It's with this most basic upholstery job that we'll begin.

One admonition before we actually begin working. In all the upholstery jobs described in this chapter, follow the steps in the sequence given, no shortcuts, no variations. Unless you do this, you may find yourself having problems as the job progresses. The sequence in which each piece of upholstery fabric is applied is worked out to assure that all tacked or stapled edges are concealed by a piece of fabric added to the piece in a later operation.

By using the methods and sequences described, you can reupholster any piece of furniture of any style. A big sofa is as easy to handle as a small chair; the difference is one of size, not methods. The bigger piece will require more time to finish and call for more materials, but the method of carrying out each step and the sequence in which the steps are carried out won't change. So, let's go to work, taking the simplest jobs first, and going on to those which are a bit more complicated.

INSERT SEATS

Easiest of all reupholstering jobs is that of replacing an *insert seat* in a straight chair. These seats are pieces of plywood cut to fit between the skirts, padded, and covered with fabric. In most cases, the seats are held in place by screws driven up through corner bracing blocks. The first step is to take out the screws and push up on the bottom of the seat to get it out of the chair.

Next, remove old upholstery fabric with a tack claw or the tip of a screwdriver. If you encounter any staples or tacks left from earlier upholstering, remove these, too. Save the old fabric, and use it as a pattern to cut new fabric. Check the padding; if it is cotton, it may be packed and needs to be covered with a thin layer of new padding.

Check the new upholstery fabric by stretching it over the seat base to make sure it fits and that the pattern is properly aligned. Staple or tack one side of the new fabric to the underside of the seat base, being careful to retain the alignment you've established. Pull the opposite side of the fabric taut and staple it to the underside of the base. Check the appearance of the top; if there are wrinkles or stretch lines showing, you may have to remove and replace a few tacks or staples to cure them.

Turn the back edge of the fabric under and tack or staple it, leaving enough space at the corners to form the finishing fold. Pull the front edge of the fabric taut and staple or tack. Check for wrinkles or stretch lines and make any adjustments required in the positioning of tacks or staples. Fold the front corners in a simple miter, by tucking the side fabric in and up to the edge of the seat base and pulling the front fabric down in a straight line along the edge of the underside. Staple each front corner in turn, fold and staple the back corners,

Cure any wrinkles or stretch lines in the fabric by relocating staples or tacks. In seats with a sharp taper, you may find it is necessary to make a tuck in the excess fabric along the sides; staple or tack these folds. Trim off excess material at the corners. Find the old screw-holes in the underside of the seat base with an awl or icepick, and screw the seat back in place on the chair.

FRAME SEATS

Occasionally you'll encounter a straight chair having a frame rather than a solid insert seat. Usually, these are older pieces with pouf seats. (These are seats that have high padding.) The padding may be put on over springs or webbing. If the web-

REUPHOLSTERING AN INSERT SEAT

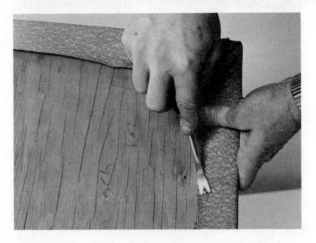

1 Remove the seat from the chair and remove the tacks or staples holding the fabric.

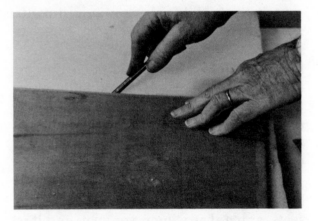

2 Use the seat—usually of plywood—as a pattern to cut foam padding. The foam used in chairs of this type is $1\frac{1}{2}$ or 2 inches thick.

3 Cut the foam with scissors or a skill knife. Other padding materials such as cotton batting can also be used.

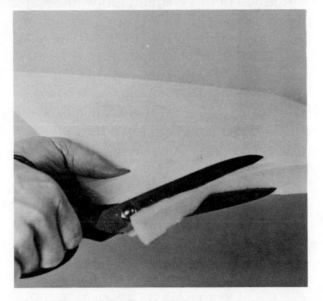

4 Taper the edges of the padding at about a 45° angle. If you feel more at home with scissors, use them. Whether you cut with a skill knife or scissors, the foam will cut more easily if you put it in the freezer compartment of your refrigerator and let it get stiff before cutting.

5 Using the old fabric as a pattern, cut the upholstery fabric to size.

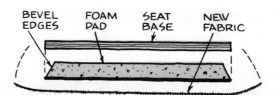

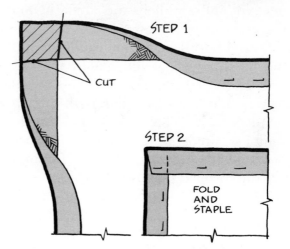

6 Center the pad on the underside of the upholstery fabric; the undercut side of the foam should be *up* (see drawing). Put the seat base on top of the pad, and fold the front edge of the fabric over seat and pad, and staple every 3 inches. Stretch the back edge of the fabric over the pad and seat base—it should be tight but not taut—and staple it after being sure its edge is parallel with the edge of the front fabric fold. Pull each side in turn over the pad and base and staple. Leave about 3 inches free at each corner for folding.

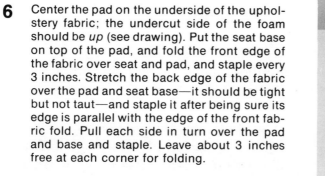

7 Finish corners with a simple over-fold. First cut fabric as shown by dotted lines. Then fold turnovers onto base, snip off excess fabric, and staple.

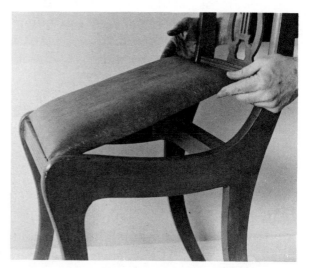

8 The newly upholstered seat can now be returned to the chair.

bing or springs are in bad shape, it's easier to replace them with a piece of plywood or hardboard than it is to put in new springs. Cut the hardboard to fit the shape of the inside of the frame, or cover the entire frame. You should use one of the newer, more resilient padding materials than cotton when replacing the seat. Your best choices are foam or fiberfill, which is made of synthetic filaments and closely resembles cotton. If a loose padding is used, a muslin cover should be put between it and the upholstery fabric to hold the padding in place.

Muslin is also required if you're installing a foam rubber seat, but its application is slightly different from that used in installing a seat padded with fiberfill. We'll deal with fiberfill here and cover the foam pad seat later.

Over fiberfill or cotton padding, apply the muslin just as you would the outer upholstery fabric, but don't close the corners immediately. There will probably be places where the padding has bunched under the muslin, resulting in bumps or low spots. Use a small dowel or buttoning needle to push bumps smooth or to carry additional padding to low spots. Professionals use a long, stiff needle-like wire called a regulator for this job, but a buttoning needle or small-diameter dowel will do an equally good job. Prod the bumps smooth or poke in tufts of additional padding to fill lows until the muslin is smooth and the padding firm and even.

Install the new fabric next. Use the old upholstery as a pattern, but check it first to make sure that the fresh padding hasn't enlarged the seat by raising it; if this is the case, cut an inch or so larger than the old upholstery. Apply the fabric as described in earlier paragraphs, tacking or stapling the sides below the frame, then the front, finally the back. Again, leave the corners

open in order to add small bits of padding with a dowel or buttoning needle if these are required to give a smoothly stretched seat. Push the padding in between the muslin and the upholstery fabric. Then replace the seat in the chair frame.

ARMCHAIRS

You'll use basically the techniques described above in reupholstering a partly upholstered armchair, one with an upholstered inset in the back and a padded seat. The most common reason chairs of this style require reupholstering is failure of the webbing and springs used in older pieces. Generally, only the seats of such chairs fail, and it's much easier to install a piece of plywood for a seat and use foam padding than it is to recondition old springs. However, the back should be worked over and fresh webbing installed while the job is being done. It will have to be stripped of the old fabric anyhow, and little extra time will be required to renew the webbing. A foam pad can be installed at the same time in the back.

Begin the job by cutting and installing the new solid seat. It should fit snugly inside the frame of the skirts, level with their top line, and can be attached by screws driven through pilot holes from the bottoms of the corner braces. Drill a half-dozen $1/2$- or $3/4$-inch holes in the seat to allow air to escape when someone sits down.

Cut the foam seating to size. Whether you're using rubber or synthetic foam, choose a thickness that fits the size of the chair; a small delicate chair should have a seat made of 3-inch foam while a big chair can stand a seat pad 6 inches thick. If you want a straight-edged seat, attach strips of muslin to each edge with contact cement. The strips should be about 1 inch wider than the thickness of the foam. If you want

REUPHOLSTERING A POUF INSERT SEAT

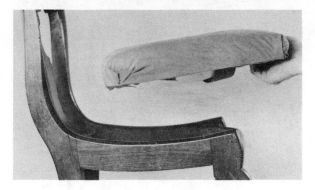

1 Pouf, or puffed, upholstery on some insert-seat chairs is traditional, and only a little more complicated. Here's how the badly sagging seat in this antique side chair is renewed with fiberfill under velvet.

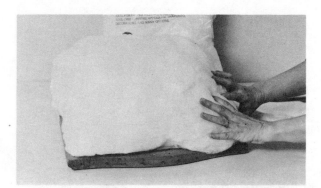

2 Remove the old upholstery, discarding worn padding and webbing. Replace webbing by a solid seat cut to fit the frame. Here, ³/₈-inch hardboard was used for the seat. Place a pile of polyester fiberfill on the frame to determine about how much is needed. This will govern the cutting of the new fabric.

3 Using the old fabric as a pattern, cut the muslin and the upholstery fabric about 2 inches larger than the old fabric to allow for the puffier seat.

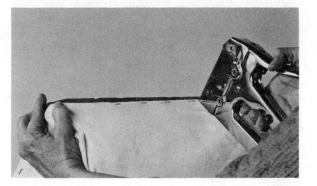

4 Staple muslin to the back frame first, then the front. Next, staple one side but leave the fourth side open.

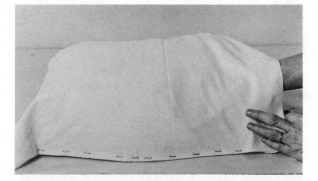

5 Check if more padding is needed. If so, it can be added through the open side and evenly distributed. Then staple the open side, except for one corner.

6 Tightening the muslin may show that still more padding must be inserted. It can be added with a dowel, to distribute it evenly and remove low spots that show up when the muslin is tightened.

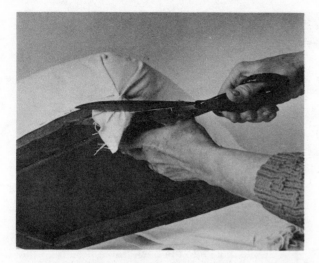

7 When final staples are put in to fasten the muslin, trim excess fabric from the corner.

8 Install the upholstery fabric, pulling its edges under the frame and stapling in the same order as the muslin: back, curved front, sides.

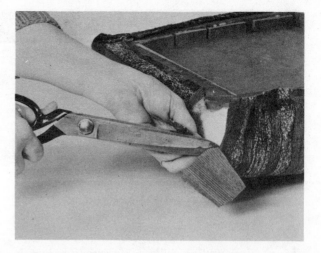

9 Finally, make miter cuts in the corners and close them by folding and stapling.

10 The new seat.

a rounded or pouf seat, cut each edge of the foam at an angle. The angle will determine the arc of the curve rising from the edges of the finished seat to its center. A long oblique cut will give a gradual rise, a 45° cut will give a more abrupt rise. Attach strips of muslin with contact cement to the top of the foam above the angles cut from the edges.

In both straight-side and pouf seats, the muslin strips are then tacked to the sides of the skirts. On pouf seats, the muslin strips will pull the sides down into an arc.

Tack or staple a covering of thin plastic sheeting over the seat. This will keep the inner surface of the upholstery fabric from binding on the foam and creating pellets of material rubbed off the padding. Make relief cuts in the plastic sheeting to allow it to be pulled down smoothly around the arms.

Install webbing in the opening of the chair's back. This can be done in either of two ways. You can tack each strip of webbing individually, or you can tack or staple a single course of webbing around the

REUPHOLSTERING AN ARMCHAIR

1 A 6-inch pad **made** by joining layers of 1¹/₂-inch foam with contact cement gives a firmer seat than does a single 6-inch foam slab. After rough trimming, the pad is tried for size, then trimmed for the last time.

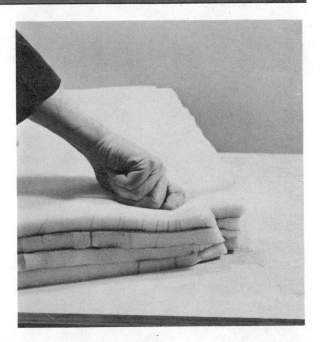

3 Four sides of the pad are tapered 45° with a skill knife.

2 A new solid support for the upholstered seat is installed, replacing rusted-out, broken springs. The base is of ³/₄-inch plywood. Holes were drilled to allow air to escape when someone sits down.

4 Muslin tacking strips are attached to each edge of the upper surface of the pad with contact cement. The strips will pull the tapered sides down and, when stapled, form the pad into a symmetrical dome.

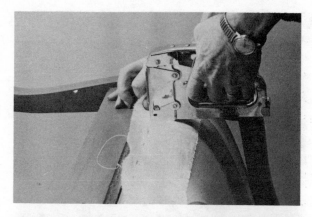

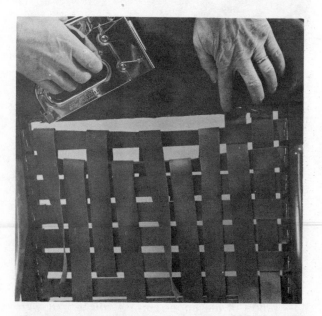

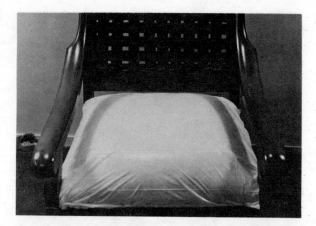

7 A sheet of plastic film is stapled over the pad, to minimize shredding caused by friction between foam and fabric.

5 While the edges of the pad are forced into their curved contour, the muslin is fixed to the tack rail with staples spaced about every 2 inches. The front edge is stapled first, starting at the center. Then the chair is turned on its face and the back strips are stapled. The sides are completed in the same way.

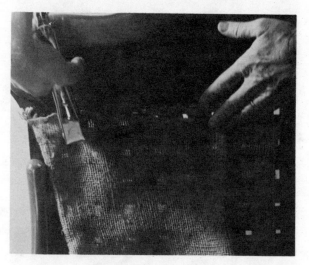

8 Burlap is measured and stapled to the inside back to distribute strains equally on the webbing.

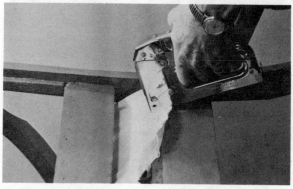

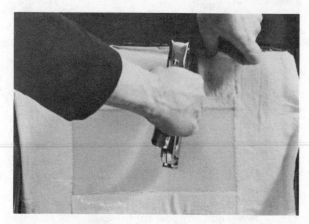

6 The new webbing is attached to the back. All horizontal strips are stapled first, then the vertical strips are woven and stapled.

9 A 3-inch-thick back pad is cut to fit the opening inside the tack rail. It is stripped with muslin applied with contact cement along the edges and stapled next.

10 Upholstery fabric, rough-cut to the approximate dimensions required, is fitted to the inside back and marked for final trimming, then stapled to the tack rail.

11 The seat fabric is rough-cut, then stapled to the frame.

12 Each corner is folded experimentally between frame members and pad, and creased to establish the depth and position of relief cuts. The cuts are made at the front arms on each side, then on the back frame members. See drawing above for details on making relief cuts.

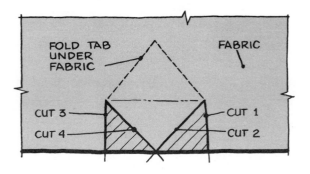

To make frame relief cuts, tuck the upholstery fabric between pad and frame member and push down until your fingers contact the horizontal frame member. Hold the fold with the fingers, pull out the fabric, and make cut 1. This cut ends about $^1/_2$ inch before the crease. Make cut 2 to meet cut 1, then tuck the fabric between frame and pad for a second time to establish the width of the final two cuts. The distance between the tops of the Vs should equal the depth plus the width of the frame member, less approximately $^1/_2$ inch. If unsure, make the first cuts too short rather than too long. The Vs should be spaced to allow the two slanted edges of fabric to be folded over before tacking, and deep enough to allow no wrinkles to form around the corner. Tuck the triangular tab under the fabric before stapling.

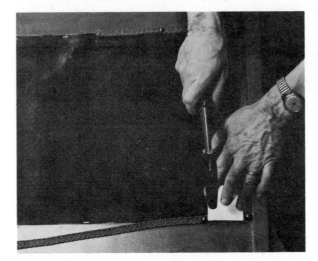

13 The outside back is applied and covered with a gimp strip, a pliable braid of very soft weave. It can be applied with glue, special gimp nails with tiny heads, or, as here, with dome-head upholstery nails. Gimp covers the raw edges of fabric and staples driven along the tack rail. It can be worked along curves and around corners without being miter folded or cut. The strip of cardboard insures uniform spacing between the nails. A gimp strip is used on the inside back, too.

14   The finished chair.

inner perimeter of the back's opening and sew the cross strips to its edge. If a thick upholstery fabric is going to be used, tacking or stapling each strip individually is perfectly satisfactory, for the thick fabric will hide the small bulges made by the doubled ends of the strips. If a thin fabric is being used, then the single line presented by a perimeter strip is preferable.

When weaving the webbing in place, attach the horizontal strips first, and gravity will help you when you're installing the vertical strips. Use a simple over-and-under weave, taking alternate vertical strips over, then under, the top horizontal strip when beginning the course. Tack or staple (or sew, if you've gone that route) the vertical strips at the bottom. When installing webbing, always fold the ends before tacking or stapling.

Don't try to stretch the webbing tightly on the back frame. This is necessary only when webbing is going to support coil springs. The tension should be uniform, but the strips should not be pulled tightly, you're not tuning a guitar or violin. A little give in the back webbing will prolong the life of the job.

Cut the foam for the back, and attach muslin tacking strips just as you did for the foam placed on the seat. Tack the foam in place and cover with plastic sheeting. Now, you're ready for the upholstery.

Use the old fabric as a pattern when cutting the new material. Check the old covering first to make sure it's the right size to cover the fresh padding. Cut the new material a bit larger than you think you'll need, if you have any doubts. You can always trim off excess fabric, but it's not easy to add a strip to a piece that's been cut too skimpily. Don't make corner relief cuts when you cut the new fabric. Wait until you've tacked the sides in place to do this. You don't yet know how much stretch the new fabric will have, and there's a danger of cutting too deeply.

Tack or staple the new seat fabric in place. Attach the sides first, then the front, finally the back. Check pattern alignment if the material has a pronounced figured or striped design. Large figures should be centered in the seat as nearly as possible, stripes should run from back to front in even courses. After the fabric has been tacked or stapled along the sides, either on a tack rabbet at the top of the skirts or on the bottom edges of the skirts, cut relief strips and tuck the edges under, then pull the corners tight and tack or staple along the arms.

If the chair you're working on has a tack rail at the top, you have three choices of a method of finishing off the job. One is by running gimp strip along the rail and gluing or tacking it in place. The second is by blind-tacking, using a strip of cardboard through which tacks have been pushed at intervals of about every 2 inches, folding the raw edges of the upholstery fabric around the cardboard, and driving the tacks by tapping them through the fabric. The third is folding the fabric around a strip of cardboard and using upholstery nails to hold the fabric in place. This is a matter of your own individual taste. If you decide to finish with upholstery nails, you can space them evenly along the edge of the upholstery fabric or place them so that the heads touch to make a continuous line, and if you use gimp you can glue it on or attach it with gimp nails, which have heads so small that they're virtually invisible.

Just in case you got lost when we turned that corner, *gimp* is a flexible ornamental braid material available in several styles and a number of colors. It's designed to conceal edges such as the one we've just been discussing. Upholstery nails are oversized tacks with large domed heads; they're also called *metalline nails*.

Installing the back fabric is a repetition of the job of putting the fabric on the seat. The foam is cut and muslin strips cemented to it, then tacked or stapled to the tack rail. If you plan to have a buttoned back, the buttoning must be done before the outside back fabric is installed. The number of buttons used will depend on the size and shape of the upholstered area, but as a rule four buttons spaced at the corners of an imaginary square and a fifth button in the center makes a nice appearance. You'll find full details on the making and installing of buttons in a paragraph a few pages further on.

After buttoning the inside back, install the outside back fabric and the job's finished.

FULL UPHOLSTERED AND HALF-BACK

Let's go on now without any further discussion to the steps involved in reupholstering what was once called "overstuffed" furniture. We'd better begin by agreeing on the identification of the different pieces of fabric required to recover a fully upholstered piece. These pieces will be referred to by name or intiitals from this point on, so it's important that you note their names as well as the sequence in which they're handled. This sequence isn't always the one you might think it would be. It's the sequence in which each piece of upholstery fabric is removed, and when reversed, the sequence in which each piece will be replaced on a chair or sofa.

Before we think about this, though, start by removing the cushions from the piece of furniture to be worked on and put them aside for later attention. Seat cushions are

This is full upholstery. The entire piece is covered with fabric; the seat and back cushions, upholstered separately, are removable.

This is half-**back** upholstery. The **back** cushions are integral with the inside back piece and only the seat cushions are removable.

always covered on both sides, but about one-third to one-half of all chairs and sofas have back cushions which are integral with the back upholstery fabric, sewed to this fabric. Furniture in which all cushions are removable and reversible is called *full upholstered.* Furniture in which the back cushions are not removable is called *half-back furniture,* though the term hasn't quite the same meaning that it has in football. But, if you want to be whimsical and name a piece of half-back furniture after your favorite running back, do so by all means. In a piece of half-back furniture you obviously can't remove the back cushions, so let's just ignore them for the time being. We'll get around to them a bit later.

Our upholstery fabric nomenclature begins at the bottom, with the piece of lightweight fabric tacked or stapled under the seat. Its purpose is to keep dust from creeping up into the seat from below, and it's called the *cambric.*

Go now to the piece of upholstery fabric that covers the back of the chair or sofa.

This is the *outside back*, abbreviated as *OB.*

Next come the *outside wings*, which we'll shorten to *OW*, and as there's one on each side we'll wind up with an *LOW* and an *ROW*, left and right. Wings aren't on all chairs; pronounced wings are a holdover from the days before central heating protected people sitting down from drafts. But any fabric in the wing position, even if it's just a narrow strip up the side of the back, is called the wing in upholstery terms. If you encounter a chair or sofa with no wing fabric as such, don't worry about it. Allowances will be made to cover the area.

An occasional piece of furniture will have a strip of fabric that runs from the outer edge of the front arm on one side to the outer edge of the opposite arm, around the back. This might be a single strip, or two side pieces and a front piece, and it may be pleated, ruffled or plain. As it's between legs and bottom, it's called a *skirt.*

Now comes the fabric that stretches

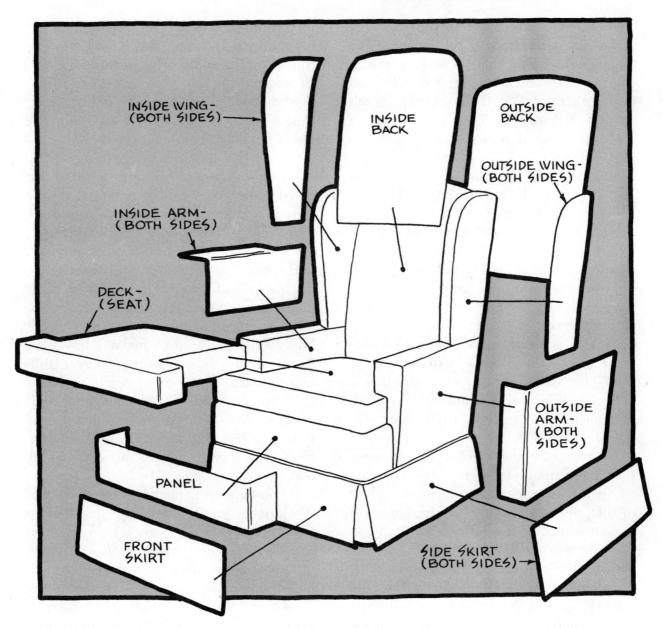

Each piece of upholstery fabric has its own name and place.

from front to back on the outside between arms and skirt. These pieces are the *right outside arm* and the *left outside arm* —*ROA* and *LOA*.

Below the seat on the front, there's a narrow piece of fabric that extends to the bottom of the frame. This is the *front panel—FP*.

So far, so good. We've gone around the chair on the outside—and remember,

these same pieces of upholstery fabric carry the same names on sofas, too—so now we'll move to the inside fabric.

Begin with the wings, if the piece has these embellishments. They are the *right* and *left inside wings—RIW* and *LIW*. This applies to a thin strip of fabric, if that's all the piece of furniture has in this area.

Some upholstered pieces have arms

covered with a separate strip of material that's not connected to the material between arms and seat. These are *arm covers—LAC* and *RAC.* Don't worry if you find a chair or sofa without these; just omit them from consideration.

On most full-upholstered furniture, the fabric covering the arms begins below the seat and overlaps the arms. These pieces of material are the *right inside* and *left inside arms—RIA* and *LIA.*

Next, there's the seat. It will usually be a U-shaped piece of upholstery fabric with a square center section of muslin, and will lap over the front to be attached to a tack strip or the frame. The entire assembly is called the *seat* or *deck, S* or *D.*

Finally, we come to the *inside back* covering, *IB.* If the piece is half-back style, the *IB* includes the cushions attached to it. If it's a half-back sofa with three cushions, the cushions are *left, right* and *center—LC, RC, CC.*

To save you the trouble of counting, there are fifteen pieces of upholstery fabric in the average full-upholstered chair or sofa, plus the number required to cover the cushions, at the rate of three pieces per cushion, plus the cambric, which technically isn't a piece of the upholstery. If wings and skirt are omitted you can subtract the pieces that would go into them.

What makes this itemization and identification of each piece of fabric important are two of the procedures which make reupholstering by this method easier than any other you can use. The first procedure really goes into each step of the job; you remove each piece of the old fabric in the order just listed, and replace each piece in reverse order, with a minor exception which we'll get to a bit later. The identification is important because as you remove each piece of the old fabric, you write its initials on it to identify the new piece you'll cut using the old one as a pattern.

Complicated as all this preliminary explanation may seem, the actual work of removing the old fabric, cutting new fabric and putting it in place is neither as difficult nor as tedious as you might be thinking right now. You'll realize this when the job is finished.

Before we start doing anything to the chair or sofa you're going to reupholster, there's one piece of equipment that isn't exactly essential but will make your work more pleasant and help you work faster. This is a platform of some kind. If you plan to do only one or two reupholstering jobs, just put a half-sheet of plywood or hardboard across a pair of sawhorses. If you intend to reupholster everything in the house, it'll pay you to make a low platform, which can be nothing more elaborate than a 3- or 4-foot square of plywood or hardboard fitted with legs that will bring its top 14 to 16 inches above floor level. Casters will help, if you add them, for they'll enable you to rotate the work and save steps.

If you happen to have a Black & Decker Workmate, you'll find the dual-height model set low makes a good platform. You can top it off with a square of $^1/_2$- or $^3/_4$-inch plywood or hardboard that has a cleat nailed along the center and clamp the cleat in the Workmate's adjustable jaws, as shown. Your work will go faster and you'll be saved a lot of tugging and hauling, bending and stooping, by using such a platform.

STRIPPING THE FABRIC

Now, we're ready to begin stripping and replacing. Start with the cambric. Use a tack and staple puller, as shown in the photos, to remove the fastenings. Lay the cambric aside whether it's in reusable condition or is going to be replaced with a new piece; if it's to be replaced, the old piece will serve as your pattern.

Take a piece of chalk or a felt marker or a piece of soapstone at this point and mark each piece of upholstery fabric with its initials. Use abbreviations: *OB* for outside back, *ROW* and *LOW* for right and left outside wings, and so on until you've marked each piece. You're going to discard the old upholstery fabric anyhow, so marking up the sections this way won't deprive you of anything usable. If you're going to salvage some of the old material, use chalk or soapstone, which can be washed off.

Start removing the old fabric with the first piece on the list, the outside back. If will be tacked or stapled to the bottom frame. Work from the bottom to the top. The sides of the fabric may have been blind-stitched to the outside wings and outside arms as well as having been stapled or blind-tacked. Straight fabric lines at the corners of upholstered pieces are obtained by using a thin strip of cardboard in the fold of the fabric; a blind-tacking strip is first studded with tacks, the tacks are pushed through the narrow inside turn of the fold and the tacks driven from outside, through the upholstery fabric.

Lay the outside back fabric aside and remove the skirt, then go on to the outside wings, if the chair or sofa has wings. Pull out the tacks or staples that hold the skirt and outside wing fabric and lay these pieces aside. Lay them on your growing stack of fabric that's come off the chair or sofa, and remove the outside arm pieces. Take off the front panel, and finally, the inside arms.

That's as far as we go at the moment, and for a very good reason. When you begin to put on the new upholstery fabric, you're going to have to do a lot of tucking of edges between the inside arms and deck. If these pieces are taken off at this stage, you'll find your fingers getting caught in the padding when you begin squeezing your hands into the crevices between the deck and the inside arms.

More and more often, the once-traditional muslin that covered the padding is being omitted on upholstered pieces. It's now generally used only on those chairs and sofas that are to be covered with thin, delicate fabrics that lack the tensile strength to hold the padding firmly in place, or which are so thin that the padding would be visible through the fabric. And, if the piece you're working on lacks a muslin layer in the underlay, you'll run into problems when you begin putting on the inside back fabric. If the underlay is foam material, it will cling to your hands and make the tucking job more difficult. So, leave the inside wing, inside arm, and deck fabric in place for the moment.

INSTALLING NEW FABRIC

Now, spread out the new upholstery fabric on the biggest flat working surface you have. This will probably be the floor. Put newspapers down before unrolling or unfolding the new material. Spread enough material to allow you to cut the pieces of fabric you've taken off—the outside back (*OB*), outside wings (*LOW* and *ROW*), the outside arms (*LOA* and *ROA*), and the new front panel (*FP*).

Smooth out the old pieces on the new fabric and pin them in place. Be sure the folds and creases in the old fabric have been straightened and flattened out so they'll be included in your new pieces when they're cut. You'll find various slits and U-shaped or triangular cuts in the old fabric pieces; don't try to duplicate them at this stage of cutting. If you encounter

STRIPPING A CHAIR

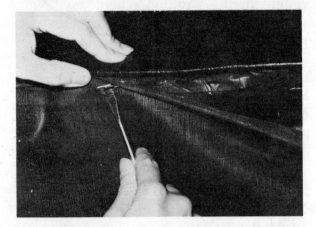

1   Remove old pieces of fabric in a well-defined sequence. First, upend the piece and remove the cambric.

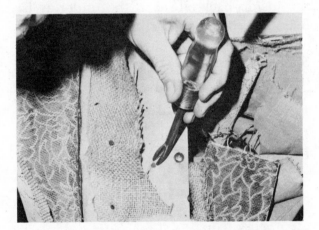

2   Next remove the outside back. Follow by removing the outside wings, outside arms, and apron or skirt.

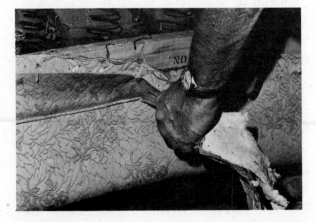

3   Rip off welting, but save each length and use it to measure the new welting.

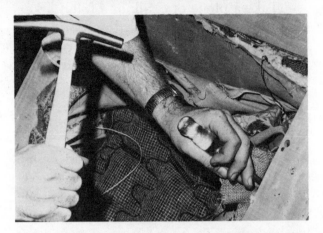

4   Smaller pieces of fabric can be ripped away and the old tacks or staples removed later.

5   Remove inside arm and back pieces. Tacks or staples holding these pieces to the frames should be removed.

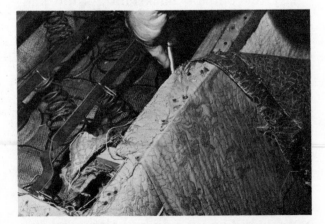

6   Upend the piece and remove the tacks or staples that hold the inside arm and back to the inner sides of the frame, under the seat.

any welting on the old pieces being used as patterns, remove it and cut separate pieces for those it joined. Save the old welting for the moment so you'll be sure to include its length when you're making new welting later on, but don't waste time in making new welting at this stage.

If your new upholstery fabric has a stripe or check or any kind of pronounced design, keep in mind the need for matching this design where the pieces will join when they're on the chair or sofa. Lay out the old pieces—your patterns—to achieve this result. You'll have to do a bit of shuffling in placing the old fabric patterns on the new fabric, in order to match the stripes or checks or whatever kind of design it has, but this will be time well spent.

When you've done the necessary matching and have cut pieces from the new fabric corresponding to those taken off the furniture, lay them aside without removing the pins that join them. It's time now to go back to the chair or sofa.

Your first job is laborious, but necessary. With your tack puller, screwdriver, awl, pliers, and hammer attack all the old tacks and staples left in the exposed sections of the frame. *All* means just that, even if it means removing tacks that hold to the frame the old upholstery that you haven't yet removed. You're doing this in self-defense. You've now reached the point where within the next few steps you're going to be slipping your hands into the old upholstery covering the inside arms and deck, and the head of a tack, the small sharp end of a broken staple, can give your hand a very ugly cut when you're putting the new fabric in place. If you're inclined to shrug this off, remember that new fabric. You don't want to drip blood all over it, do you?

This is also the stage in your work when you'll be handling the frame and tacking strips, and stray unpulled tacks or bits of staple ends can stab you while you're doing this. You have virtually all the frame members exposed at this time, as well as the springs. Check the wood frame sections for cracks or splits and mend any that you discover, using the methods outlined in Chapter 8. Also take a look at the springs, and finally, the burlap.

Helical springs, also called Z-springs or easy springs, should be pulled back into alignment if they've slipped, and secured with lengths of wire, on the assumption that if they've slipped before, they'll probably slip again. The best wire you can use for this purpose is an old coathanger. You don't have to do any fancy wrapping, just a simple hook bend at each end that can be passed over the spring at the necessary places and the ends crimped shut. If any of the clips that hold the spring need to be fixed, gaps can be squeezed together with pliers, the clips can be pounded into the frame with a hammer. Actually, these clips very seldom need any attention.

Coil springs may have slid out of alignment, or the cord ties that hold them spaced out may have broken. Use hog rings to hold them in place after you've straightened them up. Today, coil springs are generally attached with these rings instead of the old-style cord tie.

Also, check the burlap at this stage. You can tell whether it needs attention by inspecting it from the back and bottom. If it does show rips or badly frayed spots, you'll have to wait to replace it until you've taken off the old fabric from the deck and inside back, and naturally the padding will have to be removed and replaced. Nine times out of ten, you'll be able to use the old padding, though. Generally, all the burlap will need is a bit of retacking.

Now, you're ready to go to the inside fabric sections. Begin with the inside wings, right and left. As you take these

Coil springs may be held in a frame by metal supports, as here or by interwoven webbing.

Helical springs, also known as zigzag springs and Z-springs, are attached to the frame by special clips.

pieces off, clear the frame or tacking strips of old tacks and staples. Take off the old fabric from the inside arms next. Use the old pieces from wings and arms as patterns to cut the new fabric. As before, ignore any cuts into the old upholstery; just cut the outlines, leaving the usual $1/4$-inch extra margin. There's a reason for bypassing those slits which you'll see in the wing and arm pieces. They're relief cuts, places where the fabric must go around frame members. No two pieces of upholstery fabric have the same amount of stretch or give, and the cuts in the old fabric might not be the same length as the ones that you'll cut later in the new.

Take the new fabric for the inside wings and arms back to the piece you're working on and install them. Attach the arms by tacking or stapling the front edges of the fabric into position along the front and top sides of the frame. Now, tuck the bottom and back edges of the inside arm fabric into the crevices between the deck fabric and that of the inside back. This is why you haven't taken off the old fabric of these pieces. The crevice is a tight fit, and as you push the new fabric into place, you'd run the risk of pulling out the padding if it's cotton. If it's foam, the padding

would grab your skin and make the tucking more difficult.

When you begin smoothing the new fabric down by tugging at its bottom edge and by pulling at the back, gathers or folds will form around the places where there are frame members. It's time now to make those relief cuts you didn't make when you were cutting the new fabric. With the fabric of the inside arm stretched smoothly, slide your hand between the new fabric and that of the seat or deck at the front corner. Locate the corner of the frame with your fingers. This is a job you'll have to do by feel, but it's not as hard to do as you might imagine.

Make a fold just above the corner of the frame and hold the fold when you pull the fabric out. Cut the relief channel as shown in the diagram, at a very slight angle toward the center. Then, remove the strip with a cross-cut that leaves a small vee-shaped tab, as shown. This tab is turned under when you retuck the fabric into position, which is what you're going to do before you go to the back of the seat and cut a relief strip for the back frame.

Stretch the inside arm fabric smooth, pulling first at the bottom, then at the back. You may notice low spots in the pad-

INSTALLING NEW FABRIC

1 Pin the old pieces of fabric to the new material and use them as patterns. Duplicate each piece *in general outline,* cutting about $^3/_4$ to 1 inch larger.

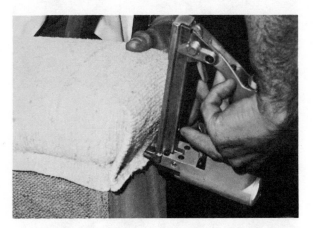

2 You can either sew the armrest cover to the inside arm fabric before installing it, or you can staple on the armrest cover (as here) and then staple on the panel. Stapling is generally faster than sewing.

3 Simple tucks at the end are the easiest finish. If the armrest pieces are sewed to the inside arm panels, they must be fitted at the corners. This method takes half as much time.

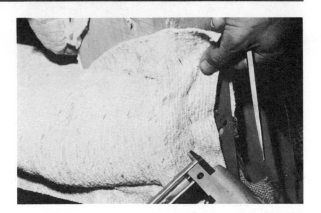

4 Bring the armrest pieces around the outside of the frame, pull them tight and staple. No wrinkles should be left in the fabric.

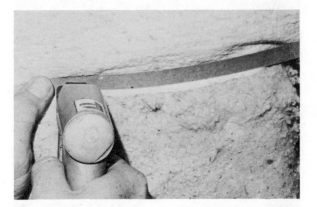

5 Attach the inside arm panels, beginning at the front of the arm frame. Use a strip of cardboard as shown here to establish a straight line under the armrest fabric.

6 Staple the inside arm panel to the frame, underside out, and then pull the fabric down. You may not need to carry the cardboard strip along here.

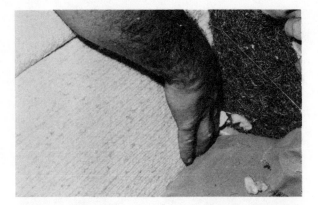

7   Tuck the fabric on the inside arm panel between the inside back and the deck. Fabric must be pushed all the way through so it can be tightened two ways.

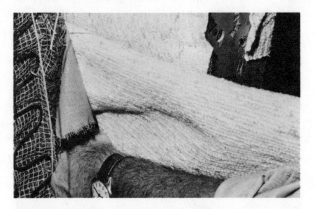

8   Go around to the back of the chair and pull the fabric tight and smooth.

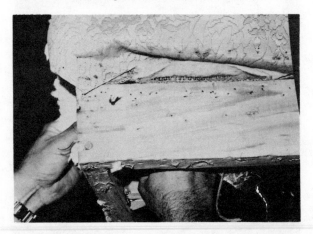

9   Upend the piece and pull the front edge of the fabric tight and smooth. Do not staple yet; you must first make relief cuts.

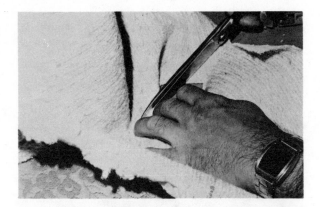

10   Slide your fingers down along the frame until you feel the fold where the fabric meets the frame. Grab this fold, pull out the fabric, and make relief cuts as previously shown.

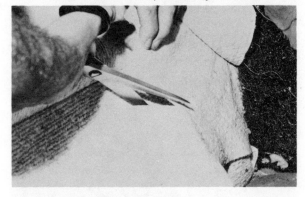

11   At the back of the panel, locate the ends in the same way, and make a similar relief cut for the back frame member. Do not staple the fabric yet.

12   Now, with both inside arm panels and armrests installed, your job should look like this. Remember, you did not strip all the old fabric from the chair.

ding when you do this, so put in thin strips of fresh cotton or foam to fill them out. Don't tack or staple the fabric into place even when you're satisfied with the way it fits unless the piece has both upper and lower tacking strip running from front to

13 Now remove the deck fabric. Separate its component pieces and use them as patterns to sew a new deck from the new fabric.

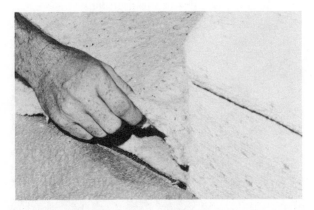

14 If a new layer of padding is needed under the deck, now is the time to spread a fresh layer of cotton batting over the old padding.

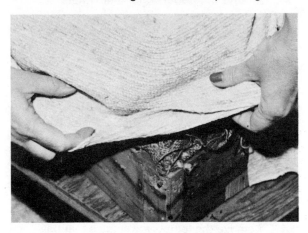

15 Fit the new deck fabric at the front corners. You may need to put in more padding to fill out the corners so the fabric will be tight.

16 Tuck the deck fabric in along the sides and back and smooth it into place. Again, the fabric must pass through the gaps and emerge below.

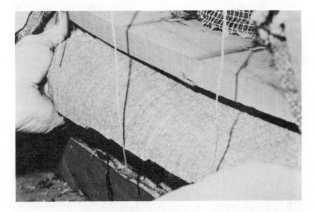

17 Pull the deck fabric tightly over the back and side frames, wherever it was attached before and staple it in place.

18 Remember, you haven't yet stapled down the bottoms of the inside arm panels. Do this now, stapling them over the deck fabric.

back. If it does have these two pieces, tack or staple the inside arm fabric in place on the upper strip.

When both right and left inside arm fabrics have been installed, put the new fabric on the inside wings. Attach it along the

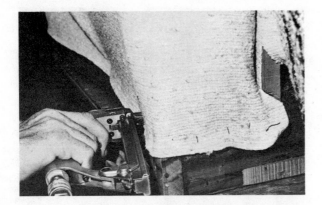

19 Pull the front panel of the deck fabric tight and smooth and staple it to the frame. The result can be seen in the next photo.

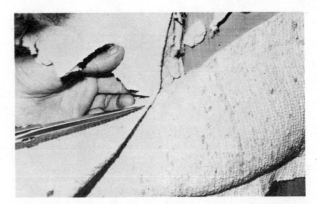

22 Make relief cuts at each side where the inside back fabric overlaps the armrest fabric. The cuts should be made to leave an edge of about 1¼ inches to fold under.

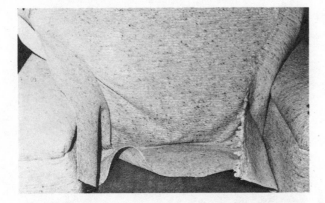

20 Cut a new inside back ¾ to 1 inch larger than the old one. Drape the fabric loosely over the back, and tack it in place temporarily with staples at the center and each corner.

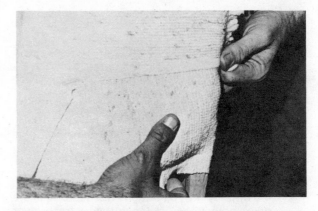

23 Pull the inside back fabric taut and smooth around the upper frame and staple.

21 Tuck the inside back fabric at the bottom between the back padding and the deck fabric. Tack it temporarily to the back frame.

24 Remove the temporary staples that have held the inside back fabric to the top frame, fold the corners as shown and staple the fabric along the frame.

front edge first, then the back. A relief strip may or may not be needed where the frame of the arm joins the back frame.

To backtrack briefly, you may have encountered welting for the first time on the front edges of the inside wing pieces.

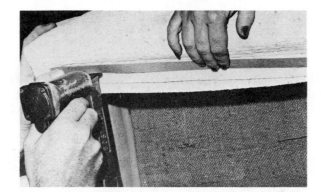

25 Install the outside arm fabric on each side, using cardboard strips to get straight lines where the fabric overlaps the inside arms.

26 Pull the outside arm fabric around the back of the frame and staple. Then staple the fabric along the back and bottom frames. Smooth it

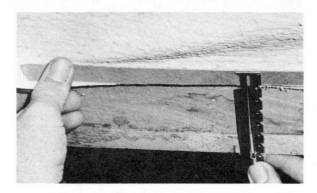

27 Install the apron next. Measure from the bottom of the frame and use a cardboard strip to get a straight line. Lay the piece on its back and staple the apron fabric to the underside of the frame.

28 Establish the top line of the outside back with a cardboard strip and staple the top edge. Then staple one side of the outside back from top to bottom, folding the raw edge under.

29 Blind-stitch the open edge of the outside back to the fabric already in place along the vertical edge of the frame. See the diagram of blind-stitching.

Generally, a welt is installed along lines of strain or fabric overlap. The purpose of welting is to reinforce areas of greatest wear and to provide a straight line along a frame edge.

Making welting is not a big job. The

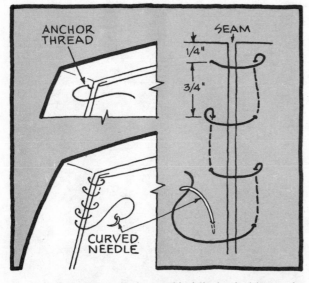

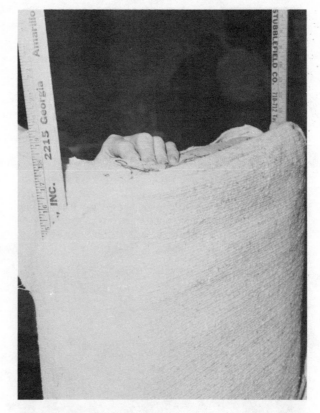

A curved needle is used in blind-stitching so it can be passed under the fabric and across the seam. Start by tacking in the thread on one side of the fabric about $^1/_4$ inch from the seam. Bring the thread across the seam at right angles, insert the needle point under the fabric and carry it about $^3/_4$ inch along the seam. Bring the needle out and pull the thread across the seam at right angles. Insert the needle point behind the thread and carry it along the seam for about $^3/_4$ inch, bring the point out, and cross the seam again. After taking four or five stitches, pull the thread tight. It will bury itself in the fabric and become invisible.

31 Inserting a solid foam pad in a tailored cover is made easier by using two yardsticks along which the pad can slide.

30 When the blindstitching has been completed, the chair back will look like this. The only job left is to cover the seat cushion.

32 With the seat cushion in place, the chair is finished.

easy way to handle it is to make all the welting you're going to need in one sewing operation. Measure all the welting you've taken off the piece, as well as all that remains on it. Don't overlook the welting that will be needed for the cushions. A typical chair will require 30 to 35 feet, and a sofa will need 55 to 60 feet. It sounds like a lot of welting, and it is, but by sewing all you will require at one sitting the job goes fast.

Cut strips of upholstery fabric 1 inch wide, enough to total the length of the amount of welting you'll require. Allow $1/2$ to 1 inch on each strip for seams. The easy way to cut welting is shown in the photo, using a yardstick as a width gauge. Mark the strips with chalk or soapstone and cut them all at the same time. Sew the ends together to form one long continuous strip of fabric.

Pile your long strip of fabric on the left side of the sewing machine, the welting cord on the right. With the cording foot on the machine, start the seam that will enclose the welting cord (see the sketch for details). Now, feed the fabric strip and the welting cord into the machine with your left hand while you guide it under the foot of the machine with your right. After a few false starts, you'll find this isn't at all hard to do.

Sew the welting on the fabric of the wings and inside arms as required before installing these pieces on the chair or sofa.

Back now to the installation. You're ready to remove the deck or seat fabric at this point. Use it, as usual, as a pattern for the new pieces. If the seat has a center insert of muslin or light canvas, reuse it if it's in good condition, replace it if it can't be reused. Sew the deck piece together. It may need a strip of welting at the bottom edge, though the welting here may just as well be sewn on the fabric of the new front panel.

Install the deck piece by tucking it into the side crevices between the fabric of the inside arms, cutting relief strips as needed, and tack or staple it in place.

Go finally to the inside back piece. Remove it, and cut a new piece. If the furniture has been upholstered half-back style, you must also make the cushion (cushions, if the piece is a sofa) and sew them to the material of the inside back. The cushions must be stuffed at this point, too. Install the inside back fabric by tacking or stapling it along the outside edge of the top frame. You may need to fill low spots in the padding at this stage, and you will probably want to use thin strips of cardboard along the top edge to give the back a smooth line.

From here on, it's all downhill. Install the front panel, then the inside arm wings and the outside arm wings. There may be welting needed on some of these pieces. The chances are overwhelming that the front panel will be welted. Usually, the welting will hold the piece of material in a straight line after it's been tacked or stapled in place, but if it doesn't, use a narrow strip of cardboard tacked on under the welt line. Use this technique when tacking on the top line of the outside arm and wing pieces as well, if the welting doesn't do the job. If the piece has a skirt, put it on next; again, cardboard strips might be needed to give it a clean straight border.

You're now left with only one piece to install, the piece you took off first, the outside back. If you've been keeping track of the procedure up to this point, you'll notice that each piece of the new fabric has been put on in the precise reverse of the sequence in which the old fabric was removed. This is why following the routine set earlier in the chapter is so important. Each piece you put on hides the raw edges of the piece put on before it.

Drape the outside back piece over the

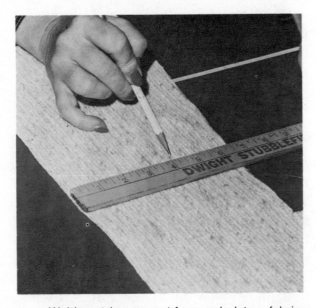

Welting strips are cut from upholstery fabric. They should be measured carefully to insure uniform width.

Equal care should be taken in cutting. This will make sewing the welting much easier.

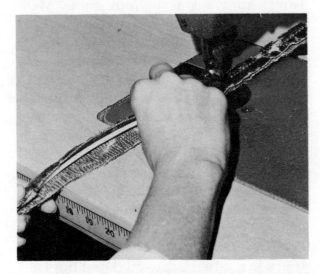

If done properly, sewing welting is a very fast operation. Sew all fabric strips together, end to end, and pile them loosely on the floor. Also lay the welting cord on the floor. Gather the cord into the fabric strip with the left hand while feeding the strip into the sewing machine with the right hand.

top of the chair or sofa with its face down on the inside. If the back frame is straight, use a cardboard strip to true up the line of the top, tacking the strip over the edge of the fabric. Leave enough margin at each end to make an inside fold. If the top is curved, use short lengths of cardboard instead of a single strip.

Fold one side of the back in and staple or tack to the frame. Use cardboard if necessary. This strip may or may not be welted, usually, though, it isn't. Fold the edge of the opposite side of the fabric under itself and align it with the side of the frame. Put in a staple at the center to hold the fabric temporarily. Stretch the fabric at the bottom in the center of the back and staple to the bottom of the frame. Staple alternately left and right, stretching the fabric for each staple.

You're ready now for the final step: blind-stitching the open side that remains along the outside back. If you're not familiar with the technique of blind-stitching, it's really not hard to learn. The illustrations show how to do it.

RECOVERING CUSHIONS

Although the body work is now complete, you still have the cushions to recover. This is a straightforward job of ripping up the old covering to provide patterns from which the new fabric is cut. There are two things to keep in mind. First, if you're working on a sofa, mark each cushion as it's taken off. There may be hidden differences between two cushions that look identical. Second, when you cut the new fabric, be sure to match the design the upholstery material has so that stripes or checks will run unbroken from the top of the back of the chair or sofa on down across the cushion and the front panel, and from the inside arms across the cushion or cushions.

As a general rule, cushions of upholstered furniture have welted seams, so you should have remembered to measure them at the time you were making welting for the body of the piece. When you sew the cushion covers, leave a side or end open so the padding can be replaced. In nine cases out of ten, the old padding can be reused. Solid pads of foam rubber can be cured of dents and sags by applying thin layers of the same material, trimmed to fit the low spot, and attaching them to the old pad with contact cement. Stuffing these formed pads into a new covering is easier if you slip a yardstick into each side of the new cover. Or, wrap the pad with any slick plastic, which you can slide out after the pad's in place. The last step in reupholstering the cushions is, of course, to close the open end with blind-stitching.

VARIATIONS

Certainly the two or three step-by-step jobs described and pictured haven't covered all the fine points of reupholstering. As was mentioned early in this chapter, no two upholsterers follow exactly the same methods. And, there are a few variants to the norm chosen to illustrate the basic upholstery procedures. We'd better look at them now.

First, there are the half-back pieces, in which the burlap forms the back of the cushion or cushions. In the deck piece, the edges of the seat cushion—or cushions, if it's a sofa—are sewed to the fabric of the deck, and the inset muslin forms the bottom of the cushion. The back cushion or cushions are sewed to the burlap, with strips of upholstery fabric between them. Usually, the cushions are stuffed with shredded foam or other loose-type padding before the unit is tacked to the frame. And, when a sofa with a three-cushion back is being reupholstered, the center cushion is always put together first.

Another upholstery variation is the channelback style, sometimes called "piped" because the back is formed of tubes or "pipes" of upholstery fabric, each one stuffed individually with padding. Be warned in advance that reupholstering a channelback chair or sofa is a painstaking job. A great deal of care must be taken to follow the old fabric exactly when the pipes are sewed, to get the seams straight, the end tapers of the pipes correct, and the stuffing uniform. The pipes are filled with shredded foam or cotton batting before the inside back is sewed to the burlap.

There are several patterns of pleat-folding which produce a buttoned inside back piece of small squares or diamonds. Transfer such a pattern to the new fabric by flattening out the old fabric and tracing the folds with a wheel, then dusting the old fabric with powdered chalk to reproduce it on the new fabric. The chalk can be removed with a vacuum cleaner after the back piece has been installed. In this case, the buttons which hold the pattern in place are put on as the folding progresses rather than after the inside back has been stapled in place.

Usually, buttons are put on after the inside back fabric has been stapled on the frame. The buttons are made on a button press, and are placed in position by threading them on a special stout button

Channelback upholstery is formed in channels, called "pipes"; each pipe is stuffed separately before the inside back is attached to the frame.

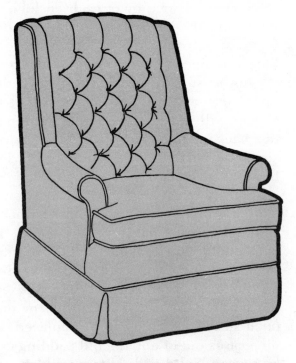

Pleatfold upholstery is usually seen on half-back pieces. The pleats are folded and the buttons attached after the inside back piece is attached to the frame, but allowance must be made for the pleats when the fabric is cut.

twine, which is then threaded into a button needle. The needle is pushed through the inside back, the button pulled into place, and tied with a self-locking slipknot around a wad of cotton which keeps the thread from being pulled back through the burlap. The photos show these procedures.

Ornamental end pieces of wood, called plaques, are often found on the arms of chairs and sofas. These are blind-nailed into place. When the inside and outside arm fabric is put on, it is stapled or tacked to the frame with enough selvage to cover only the margins of the area where the plaque will be set. After the fabric has been put on both the inside and outside arms, the plaques, which have nails preset in their backs, are tapped on with a mallet or padded hammer.

Sometimes a piece will be completely reupholstered before some hump or low

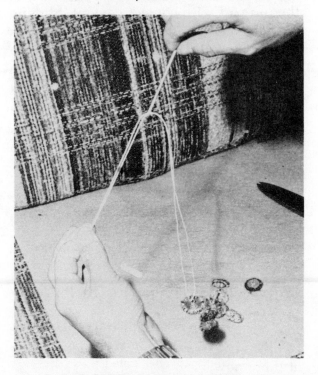

A doubled strand of button thread carrying a button is placed in the buttoning needle and the needle pushed through the cushion.

spot in the padding is noticed. Humps or bulges can be cured by stabbing a "regulator" through the fabric and redistributing the padding to remove the hump. Often, a low spot can be filled with a regulator by shifting some of the padding around it to fill the low spot. However, if a low spot doesn't yield to this persuasion, one of the seams that gives nearest access to the low spot must be opened, additional padding inserted with the regulator, and the seam reclosed, usually by blind-stitching. After you've done this a few times, you'll take great pains to insure that the padding is smoothly distributed before the fabric over it is stapled in place.

A regulator, by the way, isn't a vital tool. A buttoning needle serves very well as a regulator, and if the spot that needs attention isn't too big, an awl can be used, or an icepick.

Because there are so many upholstery styles as well as so many furniture styles,

this chapter has necessarily been confined to giving you the basic procedures that can be used in reupholstering all styles of upholstered pieces. And, you'll find that by mixing these procedures with a bit of ingenuity of your own, you can handle just about any kind of reupholstering job you care to tackle. Just remember to follow the routine given in removing the old fabric, use these pieces you've taken off as patterns to cut new fabric, replace the fabric pieces in reverse order from that followed in removing them, and you'll be home free.

Ornamental wooden end pieces on sofas and chairs are pried off before the old upholstery is removed. When reupholstering, fabric on the front of the arm that the end piece covers is tucked and stapled.

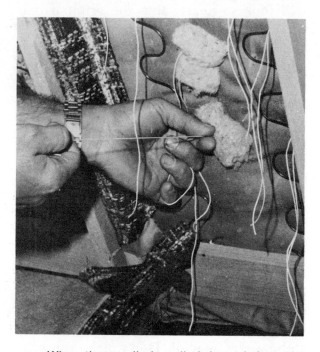

When the needle is pulled through from the back, the thread is separated, a wad of cotton is pushed against the burlap between the strands, and the ends tied off with a self-locking slip knot.

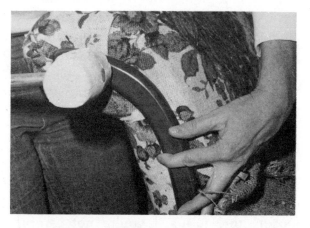

A mallet or padded hammer is used to replace the end piece over the tucked fabric.

12

Refinishing Furniture

Let's begin by distinguishing between the three kinds of refinishing you'll encounter. Complete refinishing is just that; you begin by stripping the piece of furniture down to the bare wood, prepare the wood to receive its fresh finish, and then go on to apply that finish. Partial refinishing stops short of stripping; generally, you'll remove old varnish or shellac and buff the surface, but leave the old stain alone except for minor touch-ups. Spot refinishing is the kind of job you do when you blend a repaired or patched area into the surrounding wood, matching the existing finish.

In spite of the extra time and work involved, complete refinishing is by far the easiest, especially for the newcomer to such work. All you have to do is stain and varnish or apply lacquer. You don't have the sometimes ticklish task of matching what somebody else has done, possibly in a factory that's equipped for such work.

When you get into partial refinishing, things can go wrong. You can get too enthusiastic with your elbow grease and varnish remover, and take off the stain or create patchy spots in it. You can also loosen glue joints if you're not careful. This isn't a problem when you're doing a complete refinishing job, because you'll have bare wood to work with.

Most difficult of the three kinds of refinishing jobs is spot refinishing. You must get an exact match in staining, and must use finishing materials that are either identical with those used in the piece when it was first finished, or materials that will look so nearly like the original that there will be no mismatch noticeable.

Regardless of the category into which your refinishing jobs fall, you'll need roughly the same kinds of materials and tools. We've already encountered some of each of these requirements in earlier chapters, and any repetition here is made purposely in order to set them apart from the tools and supplies required for repairing or touch-up jobs.

TOOLS FOR REFINISHING

Refinishing tools, aside from a good sander, are very simple. You'll need scrapers, not only for flat surfaces, but for crevices and corners as well. Don't make the mistake of using glass for scraping. Glass edges are never totally smooth, unless the glass has been smoothed on the special emery-belt machine used by glass shops, and if it's passed through this process it's useless for scraping. Do use good steel scrapers. One of the best investments you can make is the dollar or so you'll spend for a tool reserved for opening cans of varnish, stain, and paint. Yes, you can use a screwdriver or a wrecking bar or a beer-can opener, but the use of such makeshifts mars the interlocking rims of these cans, and allows their contents to be ruined. You'll lose many times the cost of a special opening tool in spoiled materials.

In the beginning of a refinishing operation—stripping—using a big scraper with jagged edges can make a lot of work for you. If you'll drop in at any neighborhood variety store you'll probable find a selection of wooden kitchen utensils that will include a pot scraper with a smooth tapered edge. Until these things came on the market, I made my own wet scraper from widths of 3-inch lath, but these factory-made scrapers are so inexpensive that I can't afford to make my own any more. One such scraper will last through three or four refinishing jobs, and its edge won't scratch the surface of wood softened by paint and varnish remover.

For getting into corners, Constantine has a little tool they call a "groove and cranny nooker" that gets into tight spots, and another scraper with interchangeable blades that has inside and outside curves as well as points to get into very fine carved areas. Both these are inexpensive, and you'll save a lot of time using one or the other. You can make wooden groove scrapers from dowels sawed and filed to the exact shape you need, and these work very well indeed, but they take a bit of time to make up. They're nice to use for a final clean-up, because they won't mar wood surfaces if you let one of them skid or use too much pressure.

There are a number of good commercial sanding blocks made of metal, but you're just as well off using a scrap piece of 1 x 3 lumber. In fact, you're probably better off, because you won't be tempted to use sandpaper after it should have been discarded, just because of the time involved in changing the paper in a metal sanding block. However, for grooves and edges and other odd spots, X-Acto makes a set of shaped sanders that you'll find not only handy, but very easy to use. Putting fresh paper in these is such a fast job that you won't mind doing it.

For such jobs as chair legs and table legs and contoured surfaces, the Merit Sand-O-Flex is a time and energy saver. Don't

Constantine's nooker gets into hard-to-reach spots when stripping old paint or stain from a piece of furniture.

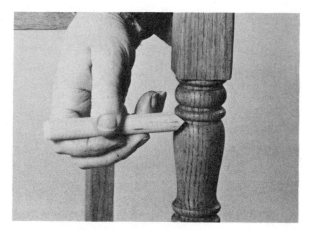

A dowel worked to a chisel edge or a point will give you an equally quick clean-up.

With a Sand-O-Flex, you can reach almost all nooks and corners, including round stretchers and splats, with different abrasives.

Equipped with its accessory steel brush wheel, a MotoTool will get into the very finest crannies.

compare this drill-operated sander with those that advertise having "tiny metal fingers." Those tiny metal fingers will cut grooves into a wood surface. The Sand-O-Flex is available in standard and small models. It uses thin strips of sandpaper, and has brushes to keep your work area cleaned. It will do a good job on any irregular surface, even small carvings or similar decorations.

Another tool that is handy for removing the last vestiges of old paint or varnish from carved or grooved surfaces is the Dremel MotoTool fitted with its accessory brushes and buffing pads. The tiny steel-bristled brushes can get into small creases that other brushes won't touch. And, if you have a really inaccessible spot to clean, you can use one of the carving or routing points in the MotoTool to strip it of old finish almost instantly.

Also included on the tool list are brushes. Your choice here is one of quality, not quantity. Many skilled refinishers use only one brush, a 2-inch varnish brush, which they keep scrupulously

clean. Others prefer to keep a brush for staining and another for varnishing and shellacking, but they also observe cleaning procedures very rigidly. Whether you go the one-brush or two-brush route, buy the best quality brush you can get, one with a chisel tip of natural black bristles set in rubber. Keep it clean by washing it with mineral spirits or turpentine after each job. Keep it in a closed container, suspended, if possible, as shown in the illustration, and wash it well just before you use it as well as after the job is completed.

It may seem odd to you to find a tack cloth listed as a tool, but this often over-looked necessity is as important as a scraper with a smooth edge or a good brush. A good tack cloth will last as long as a brush. Tack cloths, as you may know but have forgotten, are used to clean a raw wood surface before staining, a stained surface before varnishing, and a partly finished surface between varnish coats. You can buy them ready-made, or make your own. Start with an 18- to 20-inch square of cotton or wool cloth—no synthetics, please—that has been washed enough times to take out all lint and loose

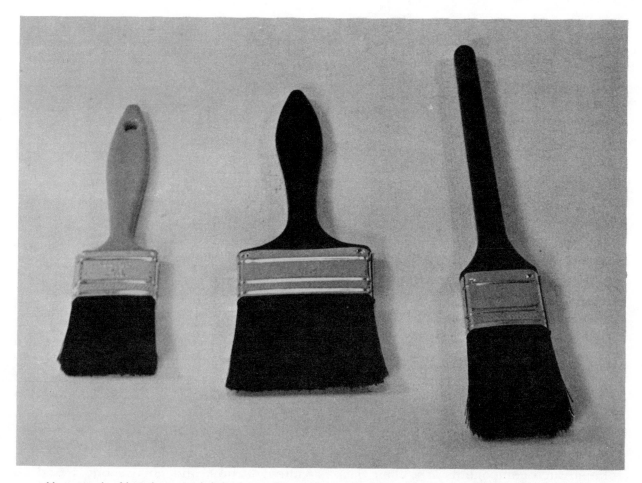

Your stock of brushes needn't be large; these three will serve all your requirements for any refinishing job. Many professional refinishers use only the 2-inch varnish brush at right for all their work.

fuzz. Moisten the cloth with turpentine, then dribble a few drops of clear varnish on it, just enough to make the fabric very slightly sticky. Squeeze the cloth to wring out excess liquid. Store it in an old fruit jar with a tight cover when you're not using it. And do use it!

That's the end of the tools list. The list of supplies and materials will be somewhat longer, because preparing a surface for refinishing is a lot less complicated than doing the refinishing itself. By the way, you'll notice there aren't any paint-removing devices that use heat listed among the tools. These are fine to use on woodwork, where large painted areas must be cleared, and mars will be hidden

Taking care of good brushes is one secret of good work. After cleaning, store them suspended in a covered container. This home-made storage system calls for a gallon can, a piece of plywood, and a few nails.

when the surfaces are repainted, but avoid them when refinishing furniture. No matter how carefully you use these heat-stripping tools, you're going to char some spots. Then, you'll spend extra time sanding and bleaching, trying to undo the damage.

We'll go first to supplies, the expendable items that you'll use in preparing the surface, as distinguished from the materials that will be used in the refinishing itself.

PAINT/VARNISH REMOVERS

Although you'll more than likely use a paint and varnish remover only on pieces that are undergoing a complete refinishing, there may be times when you'll want to use a remover to strip just part of a piece, such as a table leg or the back of a chair. Disassembly often makes it easier to refinish such components as a chair back as a unit, since the disassembly will have marred the finish of the other components.

There are many good paint and varnish removers on the market, and all of them are slightly different. Some are hazardous to use unless you take precautions with respect to ventilation and fire hazards. None of them really "removes" a finish, but all of them will soften the finish for you to remove with a pretty fair expenditure of elbow grease and a moderate stock of patience.

In today's consumer-oriented, safety-conscious climate, laws have been passed that require itemized labeling of most products, including paint and varnish removers. Caution labels are also required on products that are flammable or toxic or produce toxic fumes. In the category of flammable paint-remover ingredients, benzol is high on the list of substances

that are both highly flammable and emit toxic vapors. Propylene dichloride ranks next in toxicity but is low in flammability. Methanol, toluol, xylol or xylene, methyl ethyl ketone—these are in the mid-range of both toxicity and flammability. Isopropyl alcohol is freer from toxicity and flammability than any of the foregoing, and the lowest rating in both indexes goes to methylene chloride.

If you use a remover that has either a high flammability or a high toxicity rating, use it only outdoors and avoid breathing its fumes as much as possible. It's a good, safe rule *never* to use any remover in a badly ventilated area or in any area at all where its vapors could be ignited by an open flame such as the pilot burner of a gas range, water heater, or furnace. Never smoke in an area where any kind of paint remover is being used; even outdoors, get a safe distance from the work when you light pipe or cigarette.

Ideally, you'll read remover labels before you buy, and choose one based on methylene chloride. It should also be free from wax or paraffin, because any remover that contains either of these must be followed by a bath with a solvent that will remove all remnants which cling to the surface or have entered the pores of the wood. A new finish will not bond to a wax- or paraffin-coated surface. Then, depending on the type of solvent you use, a water bath will be needed to get rid of all traces of the solvent itself, an extra step which won't be necessary if you select the right remover in the beginning.

Wax or paraffin are used in many of the thick or gel-like removers to give them the body which makes them so desirable to use on vertical surfaces, such as the sides of a cabinet or table or chair legs. When methyl cellulose is used as a thickening agent, no solvent bath is necessary. The remover you're looking for, then, will be

Supplies should include your favorite paint and varnish remover, mineral spirits (thinner), turpentine, shellac, linseed oil, and lacquer.

based on methylene chloride, methyl ethyl ketone, or one of the other chemicals that has both a low toxicity and a low flammability quotient. If it is a thickened or gel-type product, it will use methyl cellulose rather than wax or paraffin as its thickening agent. And you will use it outdoors if possible, or in a well-ventilated room that is far removed from an open flame.

Lye and trisodium phosphate are seldom found in commercially produced removers today, but virtually everyone who's heard of furniture being stripped has heard of these chemicals being used for this purpose. True. These are chemicals used by professionals who have the equipment to handle them and the knowledge and experience to work with them safely. Both are most efficient when used in deep tanks, and a trisodium phosphate solution must be heated. Both are tricky to use. Lye is extremely corrosive; it will eat into clothing, flesh, and anything else with which it comes into contact, and will damage some woods beyond restoration.

Bleaches and surface cleaners include standard household powders and liquids as well as professional items such as trisodium phosphate, acetic acid, and a nonscratching pad for scrubbing surfaces softened by their use.

When trisodium phosphate is mixed with potash, as is done by some professional strippers, the result is a solution as corrosive as lye.

Because I consider lye far too dangerous to be used in home stripping, no directions will be given here for its use. Trisodium phosphate used alone is safe to use for pre-cleaning, though there are others as efficient and more pleasant to work with. However, you can use a mild solution of trisodium phosphate as a wash for removing a wax or paraffin remover.

Ammonia and sal soda are often recommended for removing casein-based paints from old pieces, but ammonia fumes range from unpleasant to highly toxic depending on the strength of the solution. On the rare piece you'll encounter that has a casein paint finish—these are called "refractory paints," by the way, because they are so hard to remove—denatured alcohol or sal soda are about equally effective. The best remover to use on refractory painted finishes, however, is elbow grease, and its most important ingredient is patience.

BLEACHES
AND FILLERS

Depending on the method of stripping and the type of remover you've chosen, you may need oxalic acid to bleach spots which the remover has turned gray, or into which a stain or paint from an earlier finish has penetrated deeply. Ammonia is another bleaching agent; so are a number of powdered household cleansers such as Gold Dust and Ajax, and liquids such as Clorox or Purex. Vinegar and its base ingredient, acetic acid, are used as neutralizing agents following the use of a bleach. You may need one or more of these, or none of them, depending on the success of your stripping work and on the job at hand.

If the wood in the piece you're refinishing has an open grain, you'll need a can of filler. Fillers are used on woods such as oak, the soft mahoganies, ash, chestnut, and hickory. Other open-pore woods are elm and sycamore, which today are rarely used in making furniture. Use a thick filler for these woods. A thinned filler should be used on soft straight-grained maple, walnut, beech, and the fine-grained mahoganies. For very close-grained woods such as rock or curl-grained maple, birch, cherry, and gum, use no filler at all, or one that is just a little thicker than water. You can buy fillers that are colored to match the tone of all common furniture woods, and you can adjust the tone with pigments if you wish.

ABRASIVES

Only a few other items remain on the supplies list. These are abrasives, sandpaper and powdered, and steel wool. The sheet abrasives should include papers in grades 1, 00, 220, 400, and 600; see the chart of abrasives to help you in making your choices. Steel wool, also on the chart, should be on hand in grades 1, 00, and 0000. You'll also need masking tape and plenty of disposable rags which can come from the household ragbag.

FINISHING MATERIALS

On the materials list, we begin to run into some complications, for it will depend on the type of finish you're planning. Stains head the list. If you're absolutely sure of your ground, you may need only one stain, but if you're trying to match an existing finish in spot work or partial work, then you'll need several shades in order to blend for a perfect match.

There are several different types of stains, and it's important that you choose the type best suited for the wood of which the piece of furniture being refinished is made. Usually, this is indicated by the color of the stain: oak, maple, walnut, mahogany, though stains with these names are also used to color pale-hued woods of other kinds. Each of those named comes in several tones from light to dark.

Stain bases are also important. Oil stains are the easiest to use and the easiest to blend. Water stains are more difficult. Both these types are available in liquid or powder form; the powders are mixed with the base or vehicle. Spirit stains have an alcohol base and are very tricky to use. Varnish stains perform the double function of staining and providing a finish coat in one application. Lacquer stains also incorporate stain and finish coating. Penetrating wood sealer stains should be your choice only if you're absolutely sure that the stain, when dry, will be the precise shade you're looking for.

Surface finishes most often used are varnish, with shellac next and lacquer third.

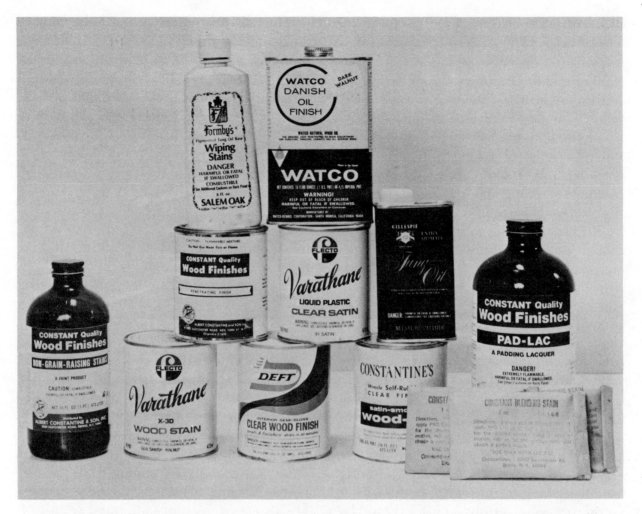

Materials you'll need include both powder and liquid stains, and your choice of varnishes: conventional, tung, or polyurethane.

Professionals use lacquer very widely, but they spray it on in a controlled working area of filtered, dust-free air. You can't match this at home, and the risk of a botched finish is greater than the fast drying which is the chief advantage of a lacquer finish. There are lacquer-type finishes that can be rubbed on, and while they dry more slowly than commercial finishing lacquer, they take a bit of getting used to.

Linseed oil finishes were once very popular, in a day when time was unimportant. They're just about obsolete, because even the best of them gets tacky or sticky in humid climates, and they take an interminable time to apply. The procedures will be given later, but I don't advise their use unless you're prepared to take several weeks in completing a refinishing job.

Varnishes vary from the traditional turpentine-thinned variety through tung-oil to the new alkyd and polyurethane-based products. The last are my personal preference, because they're so much easier to use and result in a superior finish. Varnishes are commonly divided into two groups, glossy and satin finish. It's your personal choice which one you use in your own work. Again, my preference is for the satin-finish kind, which gives wood surfaces the look of a hand-rubbed finish that normally takes a long time to apply.

Shellac, once favored as a finish material, is just about outmoded now. It does give a beautiful surface, but one that's brittle and inclined to chip if a heavy object falls on it, and one that is also affected by humid weather, when it tends to become sticky. But shellac is invaluable as a sealer coat that is applied to stop a stain from bleeding.

If the piece you're refinishing is to be painted or enameled, your choice of types is about as wide as is the case with clear finishes. Alkyd and latex paints and enamels dominate the market today, and these are as satisfactory as the old oil-based products. They're also much easier to use, as most of the after-painting cleanup can

be done with soap and water. If you do paint or enamel a piece of furniture, don't omit the undercoat. It's important when painting; even more important when using enamel. An undercoat that has been sanded with fine wet-or-dry abrasive paper and wiped with a tack cloth is a guarantee of a flawless surface finish on a painted or enameled piece.

Some open-grained woods, such as oak, require a filler that is brushed on heavily and then rubbed well to remove the excess left after the wood pores are filled. Some walnut pieces also require filling, and many veneered surfaces will benefit by the use of one, especially the inexpensive and increasingly popular "luan mahogany," which has very big pores and is almost imposible to finish to satin smoothness with varnish alone. The more

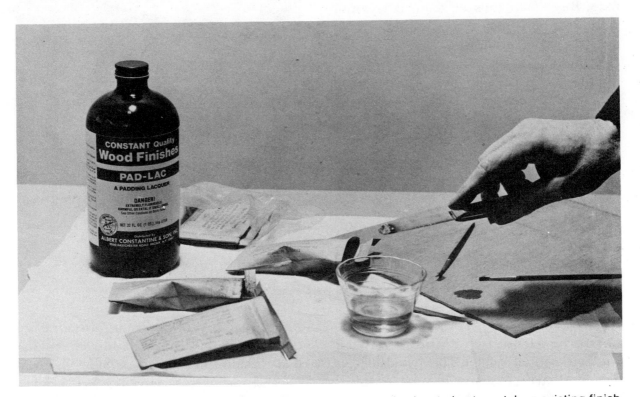

Professionals say it's easier to mix your own stain from scratch when trying to match an existing finish. Use powdered stain and a mixing vehicle such as Constantine's PadLac. Start with the lightest shade, making a very light-toned base, then bit by bit add darker tones to adjust the shade and color depth. Test as you mix, using a small paintbrush on a scrap of wood, and compare the test splotches with the finish you're trying to match.

impervious woods such as maple and cherry don't require fillers.

From all the foregoing, you can see that you'll need to do some planning and experimenting before you begin shopping for materials. Tools and supplies are pretty much standard for all jobs, but materials should be purchased for the specific job you have on hand, and then only in quantities large enough for that particular job. Don't be afraid to buy pints or half-pints of shellac and quarter-pints of stain. Shellac deteriorates rapidly in storage, and once it goes over the hill there's no return; it simply refuses to dry and must be tossed out. Stains don't deteriorate, if the cans are well-sealed, but if you have dibs and dabs left hanging around the temptation to mix in search of a new hue is often overpowering—and equally often the results of indiscriminate mixing are unfortunate. Buy small cans of stain; if you run short you can quickly get another small can.

Again, plan and test in advance to determine what you're going to need for each job before you buy a quantity of materials. This doesn't apply to such universal needs as turpentine, mineral spirits, and so on. You can safely keep a supply on hand if you store them in a proper place. I've found the best ready-made storage for such volatile materials is an old refrigerator shell, which you can usually find at a used appliance store for a couple of dollars, or perhaps you'll find such a store with a surplus of trade-ins that will be glad to give you a shell just for hauling it away.

These shells are fireproof and airtight, and can be left outside or inside your work area with equal safety. They're also well insulated, which saves loss of supplies and materials as a result of freezing if your work area isn't always kept heated in winter, or if you use a shell for outside storage. But do put a padlock on it if it's

An old refrigerator shell makes a good storage cabinet for refinishing supplies. It will keep them from freezing in winter and boiling in summer. If you keep it outdoors, equip it with a hasp lock and remove its latch.

kept outside, to keep youngsters from harming themselves by investigating your materials.

FIRST AID FOR OLD FINISHES

Before we get down to the nittygritty of techniques, let's look at a few tricks that on occasion can save you a lot of time and effort. Some of these have been covered in earlier chapters, but others haven't been mentioned because they fall into the gaps between the three chief types of refinishing.

Quite often a piece of furniture that has simply been neglected or has been in storage and unused will take on a drab, unattractive look that seems to indicate a need for refinishing. Or, if the piece has spent a long time in a damp, humid atmosphere it may have acquired light-colored streaks. If it's been in an extremely hot, dry atmosphere, or exposed to heat from a nearby stove or fireplace, or even to direct sunlight, the finish may have checked to give the pebbled effect that professional refinishers call "alligatoring." The surface of a table or desk may have suffered from ink stains or may have a white ring where a vase of flowers or hot coffee mugs or cold moisture-beaded beverage glasses have rested.

Sometimes these conditions can be cured quickly and easily without either spot or partial refinishing. If the quick cure doesn't work, you'll have to go the longer route, but give the fast cures a try first.

A neglected piece that's just accumulated several layers of dust and grime can sometimes be revived just by a good washing. Use a soft rag and warm water in which a teaspoon of shavings from a mild bar soap has been dissolved. Don't use a detergent; use a plain, uncolored, unscented toilet soap such as Ivory or Lux. Dip the rag in the soapy water, wring it lightly, just enough to keep it from dripping. Wash the piece with gentle pressure, and dry at once. You may need to rewash to remove all the dirt. Then, apply fresh wax and rub well.

If the piece has deeply imbedded layers of dirt, combined with unidentifiable stains, substitute medicinal soft soap, USP XVI, for the toilet soap. This medicinal soap is usually called "green soap." It's what doctors use when scrubbing for an operation, and most drugstores have it in stock. Soak a soft, lintless, clean cloth in lukewarm water, wring it gently, and fold it once. Put a teaspoonful of the soap on the cloth and fold it into a hand-sized pad. Wash the furniture with a rotating motion until it's covered with lather, then take a clean cloth, dip into warm water, and wring gently, wash off the lather, then dry with a fresh cloth. Apply fresh wax or polish and rub well, working with the grain of the wood.

If neither of the soap treatments brings results, heat a quart of water in an old double boiler. The water must be quite hot, but not boiling. Add a tablespoon of turpentine and two tablespoons of linseed oil to the water and stir well. Don't put the pan containing this mixture over direct heat; if you don't have a double boiler, use an old saucepan in a larger pan filled to within 2 inches of the brim with water. Dip a clean cloth into the lukewarm mixture and wring almost dry. Wash with the grain of the wood, and dry at once by rubbing with a clean, dry, lintless rag. Finally, rub with wax or polish.

If you're using any of the foregoing methods on a veneered piece, use lukewarm water *only*, and wring the washing cloth almost dry. Too much moisture and heat may cause veneer to lift. Work very fast in removing the wash water.

In Chapter 3 the method of determining what finish has been used on a piece of furniture was given. It's important that you follow the routine described there. Mineral spirits will not soften either lacquer or shellac, but lacquer thinner will dissolve either lacquer or shellac, and denatured alcohol will not dissolve lacquer. If you don't follow the routine step by step, the process of eliminating one or another finish is destroyed.

Finishes of every kind may fade with age, or become cloudy or milky in streaks or spots. You can frequently revive them. On a shellac finish, use 1 part white shellac and 2 parts mineral spirits. Rub the entire surface with a clean cloth dipped in this mixture. A badly clouded finish may have to be rubbed lightly in problem areas with a pad of 0000 steel wool dipped in the mixture. Wipe dry with a clean cloth and brush on a fresh topcoat of shellac.

On varnished surfaces, use raw linseed oil and turpentine in equal parts and rub on with cloth or a pad of 0000 steel wool, then apply a coat of thinned varnish after wiping the surface dry.

A fogged lacquer surface can sometimes be cured by rubbing with a cloth dipped in a mixture made by adding 2 tablespoons of white vinegar to a quart of water. Wipe dry and apply a fresh coat of thinned lacquer.

There are several mixtures which can be used to remove white rings or spots. All of them will work some of the time, none of them will work all the time. You'll just have to start with the mildest treatment and work up to the toughest, hoping that somewhere along the way from mild to tough you'll find an in-between solution that will remove the spots.

Begin with a teaspoonful of butter and a tablespoon of cigar or cigarette ashes—never pipe ashes, which contain coarse dottle. Mix the butter and ashes together and rub the mixture over the spot or ring with a soft cloth. Rub with the grain of the wood, not round and round the ring. Tobacco ashes are an abrasive even milder than rottenstone, and the butter is a better lubricant for them than oil or wax.

If the butter/ashes mixture fails, move up the abrasives scale to rottenstone lubricated with a light oil—sewing-machine oil or automotive break-in oil are both very good. Again, don't follow the pattern of the stain or ring when you rub; work with the grain of the wood.

Third on the toughness scale is a paste of FFF-grade pumice stone and raw lin-

seed oil. Follow the same rubbing style described for the earlier abrasive mixtures. Using this paste, you can't keep track of the progress you're making unless you clean the surface periodically to inspect it. For cleaning, wipe away the paste with a cloth dampened with a few drops of turpentine.

If none of these mixtures does the job, you'll have to strip the surface and refinish. Should any of the three be successful, clean the refreshed surface with a turpentine-dampened rag, follow up by wiping with a dry rag, and repolish.

White marks on varnished surfaces will sometimes yield to a rag moistened with lemon oil or spirits of camphor. After the spot has vanished, wipe with a soapy cloth, then a cloth moistened with plain tepid water, and follow with a dry cloth before repolishing.

Stains such as those caused by ink spills, "magic markers," and similar dye-loaded liquids are not always removable. There are so many new dye formulas in use today in commonly encountered household liquids that the art of removing them hasn't caught up with the technology that created them. Some of today's dyes strike through the finish and into the wood, and the only way to get rid of them is to strip, bleach, and refinish. You might try a surface bleaching job, using a cloth wet with household-strength ammonia or a strong solution of oxalic acid, but be prepared to strip if neither of these brings results.

Alligatored areas, even entire surfaces that have gotten pebble-rough through aging or exposure to heat, may also require stripping and refinishing. You might be able to cure this condition by wiping over it very slowly—again, following the grain of the wood—with a cloth saturated with acetone or methyl alcohol into which a bit of linseed oil or tung oil has been stirred. Wipe gently, following the wood grain. Let the surface dry naturally, and when it's dried completely wipe with a soapy cloth followed by a cloth dampened in clear water, then rub dry before flowing on a thin coat of varnish. If this doesn't remove the alligatoring, stripping and refinishing is the only answer.

STRIPPING THE WOOD

All the short-cuts fall into the category of first aid. Sooner or later, you're going to find a problem that won't yield to any of them, and then you'll be faced with the job of stripping and refinishing. When that day comes, grin and bear it. Take the piece outdoors, or open all the windows, doors, or other ventilators in your workroom, spread a drop cloth or a thick layer of old newspapers on the floor, and get ready for two or three days of work.

Plan in advance the sequence in which you'll strip the different surfaces of the piece. Try to arrange your work setup so that you can turn the piece you're working on to apply the remover to horizontal surfaces. You should finish using the remover on one surface before turning the piece to deal with the next, and it's a good idea to protect already-bared surfaces with a few sheets of newspaper held in place with masking tape, for if remover trickles or splashes onto bare wood it can cause stains.

You'll probably have to do the legs of chairs and tables with the work in a vertical position. If the rounds have turned areas in them, work on these first, and use paper held with masking tape to protect the areas below your working spot from trickles and dribbles. Remover unevenly applied can create problem areas when you get into general stripping.

Using one of the sponge-rubber

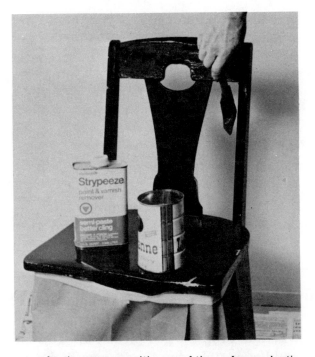

Apply remover with one of those foam plastic paddles that cost so little they can be discarded after having been used two or three times. Then there's no chance of ruining a can of varnish by dipping into it a remover-contaminated brush.

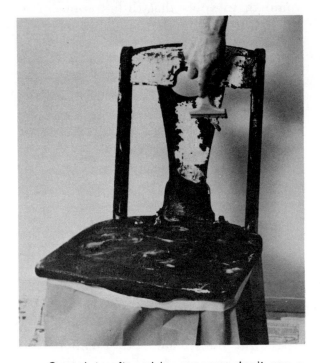

On paint softened by remover, don't use a metal scraper or you may score the wood. Instead, use a wooden scraper such as those pictured earlier, or a plastic windshield scraper like the one shown here.

spreaders mentioned in the tools list, spread an even coat of remover on the surface. Let it stand. Don't try to scrape as soon as you've finished spreading, for most removers need at least ten minutes to penetrate and lift the old finish and some need two or three times that long. Watch the spread surface, and if you see spots beginning to dry out, apply a bit of fresh remover over them.

When the old finish begins to break up and swell, bubbling up like mud in a swamp, start scraping with your wooden paddle. Use it as you would a small shovel, making a long pass over the surface and lifting off the sludge the remover has formed. Have an empty can handy in which to drop the goo picked up. Tap the paddle on its edge when you dump its load of sludge, and wipe the edge clean before beginning a fresh pass. Strip each surface this way, then go back to the first surface you worked on and apply fresh remover to spots that didn't come clean the first time around. Remember, keep the remover off bare wood to avoid stains. This is usually a quick job, for the un-cleared spots will have been worked on by the remover clinging to them. They usually give way in a very few minutes. Do this with each surface.

Inevitably, there will be areas where the old finish has penetrated the wood so deeply that remover won't lift it out. If two applications of remover didn't clean these areas, it's safe to assume that three won't do it, either. These spots will have to be scraped, but before you scrape, wash all the areas where remover has been used to neutralize its action and prevent staining.

Mix a neutralizer by adding 8 ounces of trisodium phosphate—often called TSP —in 2 quarts of very hot water. Add 4 ounces of laundry detergent such as Ox-ydol, Dash, or Cheer, then cool the solution by adding 3 quarts of cold water. Do not work with this solution until it's completely cool. Warm liquids of any kind, when put on a surface that's just been gone over with a paint or varnish remover, will cause the already softened wood grain to rise and feather, and will give you real problems when you begin to smooth it for the final finish.

After rinsing with the neutralizer, rinse again. This time, use clean water applied with a cloth that is barely moist. Wipe the surface at once with a dry cloth, then go away for three or four hours to let the wood dry. After all the liquid it has absorbed, the wood is wet for a fraction of an inch below the surface, and you need a rest, anyhow. Overnight drying is really best at this stage, especially if the area you're working in doesn't have very, very good ventilation. Put behind you the temptation to speed up the drying with a heat lamp. Only time will allow wood grain to settle; you can't speed the process a bit with heat or infra-red.

Now comes the scraping. Preferably, you'll use a cabinet scraper, the tool preferred by professionals. This is a heavy tool, and its own weight will do most of the work for you. Don't try to bear down, for on hard, dry wood too much pressure will cause a cabinet scraper to skid and you'll be left with a series of small parallel scratches that are the very devil to remove. Use the scraper with the grain of the wood, never against or across the grain. Carry it in a straight line with long, smooth strokes until you've gone over the entire surface.

Your second-choice tool, behind a cabinet scraper, is a flat metal scraper, another professional refinishing tool. This is just a piece of fine steel, ground to a straight-edge and then carefully sharpened and burnished. Use it at a 90° angle to the surface, and work with light pressure in long straight lines. Remember, what you're

Professional refinishers prefer the great control that a cabinet scraper offers, but practice using it before you start scraping a valuable piece of furniture. It's a tool that takes a bit of getting used to.

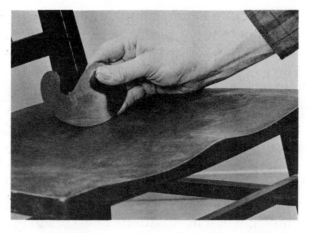

A swansneck scraper is indispensable for working on curved surfaces such as shaped chair seats.

Blade scrapers are easy to use if you keep one thing in mind. The blade must be parallel to the surface, or you'll make deep scored lines with the corner of the scraper. And use a light touch. Don't try to get to the bottom of things in a single pass.

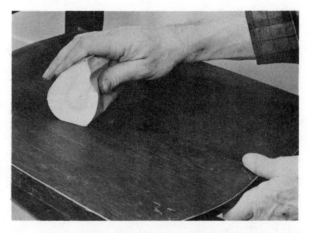

Sanding curved surfaces requires a flexible pad under your sandpaper—use a roll of foam rubber. It will conform to the surface and give you an even sanding job.

doing isn't really scraping, but shaving. Going back to that mythical microscopic examination, if you were to give the surface you're working on that kind of inspection, you'd see it was covered with patches of fuzz, like the cheeks of a youth just beginning to shave. That's what you're taking off, not wood as such.

If you should encounter long stubborn streaks, switch from a straight scraper to one with a curved edge, and if you're working on a curved surface such as the seat of a wooden chair, use a swansneck scraper to make the job go faster. By turning this kind of scraper to the right angle, you can match almost any inside curve on a piece of furniture. A shavehook, honed to a smooth edge, will also get into curves, and the pointed shavehooks will let you get into a lot of crevices otherwise hard to reach.

To get into molding lines, grooves, turn-ings, and carvings, one of the little "nookers" described earlier is invaluable. You can get into some of these quite well with the Merit Flex-O-Sand tool used in your electric drill, but I'd avoid using the tool on intricate carvings, for any sanding done on a carving is inevitably going to remove some of the surface as it gets into crannies. This sanding wheel is an ex-cellent tool for turned and grooved areas, though, when used with its finest grade of sanding strip. If you lack either a nooker or a Flex-O-Sand, use abrasive paper of the suitable grade folded in a V to reach into grooves.

As you work, wipe away the scraped-off grit occasionally, for it will contain small glass-like needle-sharp bits of old varnish or lacquer that escaped the remover and are practically invisible. However, they will put small score-lines on a surface that you might not notice until you begin ap-plying stain or varnish. Watch also for what woodworkers call "crazy grain," lit-tle natural flaws in the wood which are no-body's fault. They were put there by some accident of nature as the tree grew, and earlier finishing just didn't go deeply enough to uncover them. You may have to work down such a spot with 000 or 0000 steel wool moistened with mineral spirits, then go over it with the scraper until it vanishes.

FILLING THE WOOD

If a filler is to be used, apply it after a pre-liminary scraping. Take up a blob in a rag and rub it over the entire surface, spread-ing it with the rag or your hand and using a lot of pressure to force it into all the pores of the wood. Burlap is a good cloth to use in applying filler, its open-mesh weave will store as well as release the filler as it's rubbed across the surface.

Don't try to apply filler over too large an area at once; it will dry before you can rub it in. Fill about an 8- or 10-inch-square area, rub well, wipe with clean burlap, then move on. This will save you a lot of sanding later on. After filling, let the work stand for several hours, preferably over-night, to allow the filler to dry, then put on the sealer coat and let it dry an hour or so before beginning the final sanding. Thin white shellac with alcohol and brush it on the filled surface. The sealer will strike deep into the raw wood and minimize your need for sanding. It will also allow the surface to accept the stain more evenly.

SANDING THE WOOD

At last you have a bare wood surface ready for finish-sanding. Because of the filler and sealer, its surface will be rough under your fingertips, the grain will have raised again, and there will still be traces of filler that wiping didn't remove. If highly mag-nified, the surface would look like a moun-tain range. Sanding knocks down the peaks of the range level with the bottoms of the valleys.

If you're using an orbital power sander, it's safe to start with 120 grade paper, but if you're sanding by hand with a wooden block, use 150 grade. Always sand with the grain, never across it. After several passes, switch to 280- or 300-grade paper and go over the work again. Finally, use a 400 or finer grade of wet-or-dry paper. This final sanding must be done by hand, wetting the paper often to clear it. The technique is to dip the paper in a bucket of water before starting, shake it once or twice, put it on a block, and sand gently until the paper is almost dry. Then, rinse it and move to a new area. When you finish this final step, the surface will be as smooth as glass, even before you've wiped it with a tack cloth.

With the surface ready, the actual refinishing can start, and you'll begin to appreciate the virtues of all the preliminary preparation you've done.

STAINING THE WOOD

Begin with a stain, if you plan to use one. Stains have several functions. They hide slight imperfections in wood, emphasize grain beauty, and produce an exact tone that will match other pieces of furniture or contrast with them. Some people like uniformity in their rooms; they want all mahogany or all walnut, or whatever wood they like best. Some want a few dark-hued pieces mixed with others of a light, perhaps natural, wood finish. Some want the open feeling that comes with wood furniture that has been bleached or finished in its own naturally light shades.

There are various kinds of stains, all of them made by dissolving a coloring agent—powder, paste, or liquid—in a carrier or base that allows the hue of the stain to be adjusted from light to dark. Paste and liquid pigments are usually suspended in an oil or grease base, and must be thinned in a compatible carrier such as thinned varnish or pure turpentine or mineral spirits. Powder stains can be dissolved in either an oil- or a water-based carrier; they can be mixed in alcohol, lacquer, or water, as well as in turps or mineral spirits. Powder stains are very handy to use if you want to deepen or darken any ready-mixed stain. Ready-mixed stains may have either an oil, lacquer, alkyd resin, latex, or water base.

In addition to mixing powder stains in a carrier, and altering the tone of ready-mixed stains with these powders, you can also blend ready-mixed stains, as long as you're sure that their carrier or base is

compatible. Mix water-base with water or alkyd or latex, or combine any of these three types; mix alcohol-base with alcohol-base; oil-base with oil-base, but never mix oil with water or oil with one of the resin-based stains.

Stains with an alcohol or water base penetrate quite deeply into raw wood, while oil and alkyd or resin-based stains tend to sink into wood surfaces only marginally. Logically enough, those stains which sink deeply into wood are usually labeled "penetrating stain," to warn users of this characteristic. When applying these stains you must work carefully as well as swiftly to avoid overlaps which result in a streaked finish.

This is especially true of the group called "spirit" stains, which are alcohol- or water-based. Both strike in deeply and very quickly, and this makes brush application somewhat tricky. You can probably do a better job if you wipe these stains on with a cloth pad instead of brushing them on.

To a large extent, the type of stain you use will depend on the kind of finish you're trying to achieve. If you want the high slick appearance of a lacquer finish, you'll have to use a water-based stain to prevent the lacquer from dissolving the stain and causing it to bleed into the finish. Lacquer applied over any type other than a water-based stain will absorb some of the color that is released by bleeding, and your finish will be imperfect.

Varnish can be used over any stain, and the so-called varnish stains combine two jobs into one by giving you a stain and the topcoat of varnish in one application. Many of these stains have a tung oil base, and do a very satisfactory one-coat job.

If you want the ultimate in a fine finish, though, you'll go the three-coat route. After sanding and wiping with the tack cloth, apply a sealer coat of thinned var-

A TYPICAL REFINISHING SEQUENCE

1 Since the varnish coat is almost all gone, a power sander with #150 grade grits takes off what's left of the old finish.

2 After a wipe-down with thinners to remove all traces of sanding dust, oak filler is rubbed on, in a circular motion, with a pad of burlap. A second sanding with #180 grits follows.

3 Hand-sanding with a wooden block follows, first with #160 wet-or-dry silicon carbide paper, used dry. Then the surface is gone over with a blade scraper. Final sanding is with #400 wet-or-dry paper, used wet, on a wooden block. This is the end of the sanding.

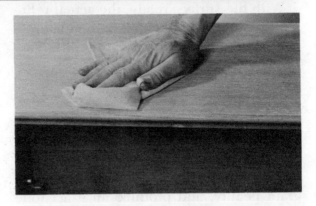

4 A thorough going-over with a tack cloth precedes the application of varnish. The tack cloth removes all traces of dust, grit, and other foreign objects.

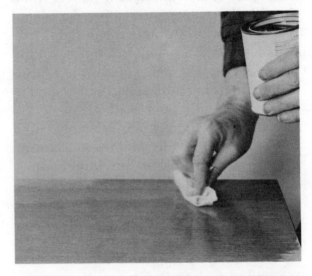

5 The surface is given a thin coat of polyurethane varnish, rubbed on with a clean, lintless cloth pad.

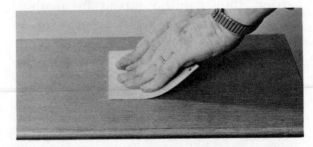

6 When the varnish is thoroughly dry, the surface is rubbed hard with a felt pad. This removes any airborne specks that have settled while the varnish was still tacky. A final rubbed-on varnish coat finishes the job.

Here is the surface before and after refinishing.

nish or shellac to keep the stain from penetrating too deeply. Mix varnish and turpentine in equal parts, or white shellac and alcohol in equal parts. This sealer dries almost instantly, fills the tiniest wood pores that the filler may have missed, and will give you a more even stain job. Apply it with a brush. Rub the sealer coat with felt, wipe with the tack cloth, apply stain, rub with felt and wipe with a tack cloth when the stain dries, then apply a coat of rubbed-on tung oil varnish. Give the work a final rubbing with felt and another going-over with the tack cloth, then rub on a last thin coat of the varnish. A lot of work, but the finished job is worth the effort.

If the stain you're using is premixed, leave the can upside down overnight and shake it vigorously before opening it. If you mix your own stain using a paste or powder, be sure there are no unmixed blobs left to haunt you. A premixed or mix-it-yourself stain in which liquid coloring agents have been used just needs a thorough stirring.

You can brush the stain on, or rub it on, unless you're using a water-based or alcohol-based stain, neither of which is recommended for the home worker. My own preference is to slip on a rubber or a disposable plastic glove and rub the stain on the wood. Apply with the grain. If you're rubbing, it's easy to avoid leaving drips or puddles; if you use a brush, pick these up at once to avoid a streak. Let the stained piece dry eight to twelve hours if an oil-based stain has been used.

You'll seldom need to apply more than one coat of stain, and if you've worked both fast and carefully in applying that coat, all that will need to be done before going to the finish coat is to rub down the surface with felt to give it a final polish. You can buy felt rubbing pads or you can cut an old hat into 4-inch squares. Remember, the key word in this operation is polishing; use the felt with a firm rather than a heavy pressure and rub with the grain until the stained surfaces glow. If you encounter bubbles, blobs, or dust grains, gently polish them out of existence with a moist scrap of 600 grade wet-or-dry silicone carbide paper, or use #0000 steel wool with the lightest possible touch and then polish the spot with felt. After the polishing, bring out the tack rag again and wipe the surfaces one more time.

BLEACHING WOOD

Now, let's backtrack a bit and look at bleached woods, which retain their popularity four decades after they left their native Scandinavia. Oxalic acid is the bleach most professionals prefer, though you can use some of the household products named earlier: Clorox, Purex, and so on,

to attain a lesser degree of bleaching. Assuming you choose to use oxalic acid, dissolve 1 ounce of powdered or 2 ounces of crystal oxalic acid in a pint of very hot water. Allow the solution to cool before applying, and wipe the bleach off before it dries on the wood. If you don't do this, the acid will form crystals which are very hard to get off. You can watch an oxalic acid bleach working, and add some of the solution to areas that look uneven, but don't let it dry. It's a good idea to wipe wood with a damp cloth after any bleaching has been done, even with the mild household products. Let the surface dry well, of course, before sanding and varnishing. Two coats of a clear varnish are usually all that you need apply to a bleached surface.

VARNISHING THE WOOD

With the advent of tung oil varnish in the 1930s and urethane-based varnishes in the 1950s, furniture refinishing became a relaxed matter. Traditionalists frown on these varnishes for the most part, but this may only be because traditionalists frown on almost everything new. Some of the chief frowners are professional refinishers, who can't logically be expected to like any product which allows an amateur to do as good a job as the professional who makes his living off his work.

The secret in using tung oil varnish is, I'm convinced, in the rubbing. Brushing doesn't result in the same thin, lustrous, impervious finish. I've used this finish on a number of different woods, over various stains, with equally satisfactory results. It's a very good shortcut to getting a varnish finish that's both beautiful and long-lasting as well as easy to apply.

The same can be said for urethane varnish. The finish produced by rubbing is very clear, two coats of rubbed-on varnish being less noticeable than a single coat applied with a brush. I still prefer two rubbed-on coats of satin urethane varnish—the glossy is quite shiny. But I've brushed on this varnish with no difficulty whatever when finishing furniture. Some of the pieces on which I've used it were finished more than fifteen years ago, and have taken cross-country trips in moving vans two or three times, and yet are still unmarred. The varnish has deepened a bit in tone with the years, but is still smooth and unbroken. The appearance of these urethane varnishes when applied with a brush differs slightly from that which is seen on a rubbed piece; the brushed coating is a bit more satiny than the rubbed coatings, which are about midway between satin and glossy.

Some refinishing experts recommend that a sealer coat be applied over the stain before varnishing. This may have been necessary in the days of uncertain paint technology, but my opinion is that it's obsolete today. In theory, a coat of drastically thinned varnish, 50% varnish to 50% turpentine, brushed on the stained surfaces, will prevent the stain from bleeding into the initial varnish coat. I stopped using sealer coats when I switched to tung oil and polyurethane varnishes, and have never had a case of bleeding stain. Perhaps I just haven't encountered a stain that tends to bleed. If you'll feel better for using a sealer, Constantine has a product called Between-Koat which will bond to all types of varnish and requires only forty-five minutes to dry. I'd use this in preference to the thinned varnish; you can't thin the urethane varnishes with turpentine anyhow.

Varnish flows better when warmed. Don't sit a can of varnish over a stove burner, though. Instead, stir it thoroughly, working the stirring paddle smoothly to avoid the formation of bubbles. If a few form, puncture them with a toothpick. Then, put the lid ring of a large-mouth glass canning jar on the bottom of a pail or can bigger than the varnish can, sit the varnish can on the lid, and fill the outer container with water to within about 2 inches of the top of the varnish can. This improvised double boiler will allow you to heat the varnish safely. Stir the varnish gently a few times while it's heating; you don't want it over-hot, just warm to the touch. Leave the varnish can in the water while you put on the final coats so it will stay warm.

If you use a brush, flow the varnish on across the grain of the wood until the entire surface is covered. Work as fast as you can, but don't sacrifice care for speed.

Varnish flows better when slightly warm, but don't put a can of varnish over direct heat. Use an old saucepan or cut-down gallon food can with a large rubber canning-jar lid in the bottom. Set the varnish can on the lid and fill the outer container about two-thirds full of water. Keep the varnish can in the warm water while using it to maintain its temperature.

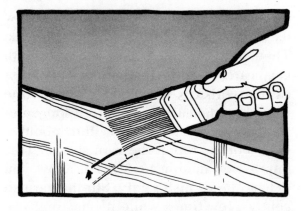

Even the best varnish brush is going to shed a bristle or two. Pick up bristles with the corner of the brush held edgewise.

Tiny bubbles often appear in brushed-on varnish. If these didn't vanish at once, burst them while the varnish is wet by pricking them with a cocktail pick or sharpened splinter of wood.

Antiquing covers a multitude of sins. This venerable chair had been wrecked by a succession of owners. Fruitless efforts to remove the refractory paint of its original finish had left its surface badly marred. It was given a smooth undercoat of soft green, and here a mahogany-brown glaze is being rubbed on.

When the surface is covered, stroke the varnish with the grain, using a well-drained brush so that any excess varnish can be picked up by the brush. Sight across the work against the light to find any bubbles or blobs or dust grains, or any stray bristles that might have been shed by the brush. Puncture bubbles with a toothpick, and use the tip of the toothpick to lift out dust or bristles. Let the varnish dry overnight before putting on a second coat. Except in the case of the urethane- and tung-oil-based finishes, which generally cover with one coat, you may want to buff the first varnish coat with a felt pad or #0000 steel wool before the second coat is applied. If you want a satin finish, buff the final coat with a felt pad or #0000 steel wool, then wax.

ENAMELING THE WOOD

Furniture made of common woods such as pine is frequently given an enamel or antiqued finish. The secret of a glass-smooth enamel job is the use of an enamel undercoater. This is a thick, creamy preparation

Because an antiqued glazed finish requires a relatively thick varnish coating, a brush is used rather than the rubbing technique.

that is flowed on over a thoroughly sanded surface, and then sanded when it dries with 400 grade wet-or-dry paper used moist and washed frequently to clear its grits. Wipe the undercoated piece with a tack rag before flowing on the enamel. Apply it with a brush in long smooth strokes and let it set overnight before using the piece.

Antiquing attained fad status in the early 1970s, and the market was suddenly flooded with kits that make the job very easy. After the customary surface preparation, a coat of semigloss paint of the desired color is brushed on and allowed to dry. A translucent glaze is brushed on over the paint and wiped down before it dries. The remaining glaze is then allowed to dry, and the piece is given a coat or two of satin varnish. Each manufacturer's products require slightly different techniques, drying times, and so on, so no precise directions are being given for antiquing. Your best bet is to buy a kit and follow the instructions that go with it. Antique finishes are easy to apply, and often can be put on over an old finish without the need for total stripping. However, follow the instructions that come with the product you select, and you'll have no trouble.

That's a pretty safe statement to make regarding any of the several refinishing processes this chapter covers. Follow the rules, no matter how tedious they seem to make the job, and you'll wind up with furniture that displays a beautiful, professional finish.

Appendix 1

This is a listing of mail-order sources for tools, repairing, refinishing, and reupholstering supplies and materials. All the firms listed have catalogs detailing their specialities and the range of products they offer. All have excellent histories of providing prompt and reliable delivery service and in maintaining good customer relationships. In addition to mail and phone order service, several of the firms listed have retail outlets at their central locations; some have more than one such outlet.

BROOKSTONE COMPANY
127 Vose Farm Road
Peterborough, NH 03458

Tools, materials, and supplies. Specializes in unusual and hard-to-find hand tools. Mail and telephone order service, accepts credit card charges.

CONSTANTINE
2050 Eastchester Road
Bronx, NY 10461

Tools, materials, and supplies. Specializes in veneers, plywoods, hardwoods, stains, varnishes, upholstery and refinishing materials, cabinet hardware. Mail and telephone order service, accepts credit card charges.

CRAFTSMAN WOOD
   SERVICE COMPANY
2727 South Mary St
Chicago, ILL 60608

Tools, materials, and supplies. Specializes in hardwoods, veneers, hand and power tools, upholstering and refinishing materials, cabinet hardware. Mail and telephone order service, accepts credit card charges.

HERTERS
Mitchell, SD 57301

Limited stock of hardwoods suitable for furniture use; limited stock of hand tools.

MINNESOTA
   WOODWORKERS
   SUPPLY COMPANY
Industrial Boulevard
Rogers, MINN 55374

Tools, materials, and supplies. Specializes in veneers, furniture trim, cabinet hardware, refinishing and upholstering materials. Mail order service, accepts credit card charges.

OLD GUILDFORD FORGE
Guilford, CONN 06437

Specializes in black iron, brass and porcelain pulls, knobs, hinges, and period or antique cabinet hardware. Mail-order service, accepts credit card charges.

PERIOD FURNITURE
   HARDWARE
123 Charles Street
Boston, MA 02104

Specializes in reproductions of all styles and periods of cabinet hardware. Will make reproductions of any type period hardware on special order.

H. L. WILD
510 East 11 Street
New York, NY 10218

Specializes in veneers, veneering, and finishing supplies.

Appendix 2

This is necessarily an incomplete listing of manufacturers of tools, finishing supplies and materials, and other items used in furniture repairing and refinishing. The firms listed do not sell direct to individuals, but all have nationwide product distribution through a variety of retail outlest.

BEHLEN COMPANY
Amsterdam, NY 12010

Maker of stains, varnishes, solvents, and related products used in finishing or refinishing. Distribution through paint and lumber dealers, chain retail outlets, homewares and housewares stores.

BLACK & DECKER
Towson, MD 21204

Manufacturer of power and hand tools for home and industrial use. Distribution through hardware, housewares, home supply variety stores and supermarkets, lumberyards and building supply stores.

BORDEN COMPANY
Columbus, OH 43215

Maker of adhesives for home and industrial use. Distribution throug lumber yards, homewares, housewares, hardware, building supply, variety stores and supermarkets.

DREMEL
4915 21st Street
Racine, WIS 53406

Manufacturer of Dremal MotoTool, MotoShop, MotoLathe and accessories for these tools, including burrs, routing bits, engraving points, saw, sanding, polishing and buffing wheels. Distribution through hardware, building supply, craft and homewares shores.

MERIT ABRASIVES COMPANY
201 West Manville Street
Compton, CA 90224

Manufacturer of Sand-O-Fles, Grind-O-Flex and Mini Grind-O-Flex drill-powered contour sanders, Power-Loc abrasive discs, and other abrasives. Distribution through hardware, building supply, craft stores and lumber yards.

MILLERS FALLS
Greenfield, MA 01301

Manufacturer of power and hand tools for home and industrial use. Distribution through lumber yards, building supply and hardware stores.

ROCKWELL INTERNATIONAL
Power Tool Division
1755 Lynfield Road
Memphis, TN 38138

Manufacturer of power tools for home and industrial use. Distribution through hardware, building supply, craft, variety homeware and houseware stores and supermarkets.

SKIL CORPORATION
4801 West Peterson Avenue
Chicago, ILL 60646

Manufacturer of power tools and accessories for home and industrial use. Distribution through hardware, building supply, housewares and homewares stores and lumber yards.

STANLEY TOOLS
New Britain, CONN 06050

Manufacturers of power and hand tools for home and industrial use. Distribution through hardware, building supply, housewares, variety stores, supermarkets and lumber yards.

X-ACTO
45-35 Van Dam Street
Long Island City, NY 11101

Manufacturer of X-Acto knives and files, saws, and other small precision hand tools for home and industrial use. Distribution through hardware, housewares, homewares, craft, graphic arts, and variety stores.

Index